CHANGE MANAGEMENT IN INFORMATION SERVICES

Change Management in Information Services

Second Edition

LYNDON PUGH
University of Wales, Aberystwyth, UK

ASHGATE

Published by
Ashgate Publishing Limited
Gower House
Croft Road
Aldershot
Hampshire GU11 3HR
England

Ashgate Publishing Company
Suite 420
101 Cherry Street
Burlington, VT 05401-4405
USA

Ashgate website: http://www.ashgate.com

British Library Cataloguing in Publication Data
Pugh, Lyndon
   Change management in information services. - 2nd ed.
   1.Information services - Management 2.Information services
   - Tecnological innovations - Management 3.Organizational
   change 4.Information resources management
   I.Title
   025.5

Library of Congress Control Number: 2006929370

ISBN: 978-0-7546-4665-5

Printed and bound in Great Britain by MPG Books Ltd, Bodmin, Cornwall.

Contents

List of Figures

Preface

In their vision statement designed to guide the organization until 2010, SCONUL (2003) set out their view of trends in information services over the coming years. Almost at the halfway point in the period spanned by the document, it is interesting to consider their predictions: personalisation, collaboration, the implications of virtual space, non-traditional activities, process-based management, 'the development or importing of alternative skills', the delivery of personal help – 'either face-to-face or via web-based services'. There is talk of communities and virtual organizations, the individuality of users and 'converged service cultures'.

In the wider world, there are proposals to meet much the same challenges through ambidextrous organizations, by which is meant structures which are both centralised and decentralised, with the advantages of being both large and small as well as local and global. What this litany means is flexibility and being able to adapt quickly. Davila (in Davila et al, 2005) offered his answer to the conundrum of how organizations could be all these things at once in the interests of effective change management. He advocated strong leadership, a culture of change, constant technological development and better ways of using the results, and 'embedded strategy'. Others have referred to the power of networks as the basic organizational unit for supporting change, while there is a school of thought which advocates the more powerful use of the technical tools of management, including better measurement, tighter processes and more robust planning. On the other hand other writers have castigated the dead hand of bureaucracy, business plans, mission statements, administration and performance assessments.

Foster and Kaplan (2006) explore the issue of continuity in contemporary organizations and argue that today's organizational environment calls for the abandonment of long-held assumptions and the adoption of a radical approach to organization development. This is part of the problem in information services: there are many conflicting elements. There is a need to combine new and traditional skills, to develop cross-boundary working while at the same time retaining old specialisations and absorbing some new ones. Libraries becoming involved in collaborative working will in some important respects still be competitors, and there will be a need to continue to work with the mixed economy of conventional and digital resources for some time to come. It could be said, against this background, that the essence of change management in information services will be found in the ability to deal with diversity, and with complexity in the sense that there are no obvious solutions and no clear courses of actions which will lead to the resolution of the issues faced by libraries.

The problem of complexity is exacerbated by the existing mental models of library organizations, and this book spends some time in outlining new organizational metaphors. Paradoxically, our own role in supporting the free flow of information increases the complexity.

The theoretical basis of change management in libraries is also shifting. Where some 10 years ago the convergence referred to in the SCONUL vision would have emphasised the creation of a common culture, we are now beginning to see the relevance of theories of organizational creativity and creative abrasion widely acknowledged in mainstream management for sixty years or more. Ideas like this should lead us to revise our views about the unity and homogeneity of organizations, about what a common culture actually means, and about the dynamics of team behaviour – still a critical feature of change management. Our conception of networked organizations, and the implications of virtual organizations will also develop in line with ideas already prevalent elsewhere. It is also profitable to consider the reworking of ideas about managerial roles, styles and behaviour – perhaps along the lines of the concept of the player-manager which exists elsewhere. All of these things will affect our view of communications, leadership, organizational structures and the position of the individuals at the heart of change management. The psychological implications of change have always been important in terms of motivation, resistance and the impact of psychological issues on the staff of organizations. This book attempts to address the priorities emerging from these issues, and tries to emphasise the interrelated nature of the key aspects of organizational life. While it emphasises the importance of the 'people issues' it acknowledges the continued importance of the planning and implementation processes in managing change.

Once again, the case studies used in some of the chapters all happened, although none of them occurred in the settings and circumstances described in the book, but have been transposed into an appropriate setting while the events are unchanged. No particular individuals or institutions formed the basis of the narratives.

Lyndon Pugh
Brecon
Powys
Mid Wales

Acknowledgements

Two of the figures used in Chapter 6 (Figure 6.2, The Formal Structure, and Figure 6.3, The Informal Structure) are derived from the author's 2005 publication *Managing 21st Century Libraries* (Lanham MD/Oxford: Scarecrow Press).

Chapter 1 is strongly influenced by earlier work by the author (2003, 2005). The work of Kurt Lewin is the foundation of the process described and analysed in Chapter 4. In Chapter 5, the ideas on alternative structures are influenced by work done over some years by David Clutterbuck. The section on network analysis in Chapter 6 is based on the work of Cross and Parker (2004). The Red Arrows case study in Chapter 7 makes use of material included in the work of Hilarie Owen (1996) as specified in the bibiliography.

Chapter 1

The Nature of Change

In the last six or seven years, change in information services has begun to assume a character which has in many ways been totally unforeseen. This may well be a facile statement of the obvious, but while most of the texts written in the late 1990s and the first few years of the 21st century – including the first edition of this one – tend to show there was little difficulty in identifying and analysing the major characteristics of change, there were few which were able to anticipate accurately the way in which the landscape changed as the technological revolution in information services gathered force. This chapter looks at the characteristics of these changes, and begins to consider ways in which managers and organizations can respond to the features described (see Figure 1.1).

Characteristics of Change

One of the most striking things about change in information services is that it has become the norm. There might even be a grain of truth in snappy but meaningless sound-bites like 'change is the only constant'. In the wider economy, change is often seen as one of the focal points of life in institutions making a whole-organization response to global developments. While these developments are often outside the control of the players, it nevertheless seems to be important to adopt a proactive and dynamic attitude to the question of change. If there is an appropriate aphorism it could be Cage's comment (2005): 'If it ain't broke, break it.'

The first edition of this book opened with some strictures on the limited impact of technological change on library services, arguing that our application of technology was too narrow, therefore sapping its strength as a force for change. It is no longer possible to scorn the power of technology as a change instrument in libraries, for the evidence of the impact of technological change is all around us. But the assertion of narrowness is even more pertinent today than it was a few years ago. To embrace Cage's exhortation is to confront and challenge the power of the technological revolution in an imaginative and creative way: yet the charge against technology in the information sector today is that it has paradoxically become a powerful support for the status quo in libraries; that is, until now.

But it is now the technologists who are beginning to change this. There are signs, particularly in the growth of the Web 2.0 and Library 2.0 initiatives, of an emerging strand of broad thinking amongst the technologists, and this is taking information services into what can be considered to be the second stage of technologically-based change. This is when the massive emphasis on the nature of the technology itself, still the norm in wide swathes of information services, begins to be replaced by what is sometimes described as a cultural view of technological change (Tebbutt, 2006). This

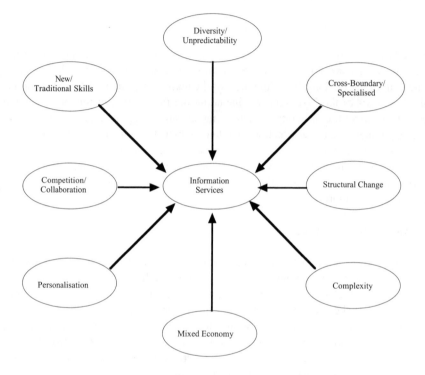

Figure 1.1 The Nature of Change in Information Services

is seen in the way in which Web 2.0 and Library 2.0 both drive the move to realise the concept of the personalised library service, and take libraries to the user in a major reworking of the idea of libraries without walls.

Most of the characteristics of change identified in that first edition referred to earlier are nevertheless still relevant in practice today. While this is correct, it is also true to say that technology, and the way it is approached and handled, is at last beginning to show its true power to enhance the change forces, rather than mitigate them or paradoxically act as a brake to change. This retarding effect occurred mainly because of the specialist nature of the early technology and the way it was handled.

It is now technology which can release the transformational power dormant in most organizations. The impact of technological change therefore runs throughout this chapter.

Diversity and Unpredictability

It may well be that some libraries are now amongst the most highly diversified organizations in the world. In terms of the spread of resources they make available, and the extensive development and variation in services which has been accompanied by significant role change, they are in many ways models of diversification in a managerial sense. This characterisation draws added piquancy from the increasingly diverse nature – again in a managerial sense – of the personnel employed in contemporary information services.

Because of new configurations which have brought libraries into relationships with other services, and encouraged in their wake an influx of staff from different disciplines, with different traditions of training and education and different perspectives, most libraries now exhibit considerable variety in their services and their staffing. These conditions have been created, at least in part, by the development of technology. It is because of technology that libraries can now be staffed by combinations of:

- Librarians
- Technologists
- Graphic designers
- Media technicians
- Other non-librarians of various types.

They can also be managed by non-librarians, and by imports from business and industry. Technology has increased the physical reach of information services, and facilitated the entry of information workers into organizations, and areas within organizations, where they would not traditionally have been found.

Technology has contributed much to the broadening of the scope of library operations. It is technology which has created a requirement for library staff who have matured in different environments and bring different viewpoints, skills and experience to the task of managing and operating in organizations. This multiplicity of perspectives is an important factor in change management, provided that it is used in the right way.

Diversity also stems from the mix of technological and political influences which have been at work on libraries since before the early days of electronic collections and digitisation. Political and economic factors led to mergers in academic institutions, and one of the prime but sometimes best-concealed motives for convergence in university libraries was the need for financial savings in the organization of information services (Pugh, 1997a). The mergers, and the demergers, are still continuing in some areas, and the ongoing financial impetus for change cannot be better illustrated than it is in Case Study 1, which is a contemporary example of the use of technology in support of ostensibly more effective information provision at a lower cost.

On the other hand, the history of the eLib programme in the UK offers good examples not only of cooperation between institutions, but also of the kind of cross-sectoral collaboration which in many cases can bring together different traditions and work cultures (Pinfield, 2001, 2004). These situations also demand a different emphasis in the overall skill of managing change, and they may well become more prevalent as time passes.

The essence of the environment in which the hybrid libraries of today will increasingly operate is unpredictability. This unpredictability comes from a number of sources. The web, an important feature of the information map, is still an unpredictable landscape. That the information on it is unstable, and not always susceptible to evaluation in the conventional way, has been well documented.

Access rights to some information sources are increasingly complicated. This complication has reached such a pitch that it has given birth to yet another professional specialisation – that of digital rights. The way in which we handle specialisation is not only another barrier in the way of exploiting diversity, but it also increases unpredictability and complexity – of which more later – through its effect on communication and other organizational features.

It is also of course true that user behaviour, and in particular the emergence of technologically-competent users capable of self-organization and with the potential to manage their own information needs, represents an even more acute source of unpredictability. This development holds out the singular, if not eccentric, prospect of the user possessed of a high degree of self-sufficiency in the search for in formation, along with the will to use it. If anything this development, the apotheosis of true librarianship, is in some respects the main reason for seeking to understand the nature of contemporary change forces in libraries. To fail in this is to leave libraries, and librarians, susceptible to the dangers described in Case Study 1, and out of work.

All this is related to the sheer pace of technological change. For how long have we actually been able to conceive of the user who can navigate the information map him- or herself, then evaluate, store, retrieve and use the resulting information without the aid of the librarian? Users can now, if they are so minded, single-handedly create and manipulate their own digital libraries. Providing and organising services for these prodigious characters represents real uncertainty and the ultimate diversity. One of the issues raised by those who evangelise on behalf of Web 2.0 and Library 2.0 is the need for a far more imaginative involvement of users in library services. This will create the opportunity for far-reaching change.

To sum up, Figure 1.2 shows the way in which technology has actually helped to create the potential for dynamic change in information services, basically through the way in which it is introducing diversity into library services, but also through its ability to break down barriers in both a physical and metaphorical sense.

We are therefore setting out to plan for further unpredictability, if that is not an oxymoron. This will impinge on the skills base, the appropriateness or otherwise of present organizational forms, the hybrid nature of information itself, and the collapse of the old professional boundaries. It will do this by allowing greater penetration by, and of, other professions. The situation will also demand partnerships and collaboration of a kind and degree we are not used to.

The uncertainty of the environment is obvious. The difficulty becomes more apparent when the attempts to deal with uncertainty in the things which surround us are based on applying some of the old certainties which stood libraries in good stead in more stable operating conditions. 'If it isn't broke, don't fix it' has not yet been replaced by 'If it ain't broke, break it' (Cage, op cit).

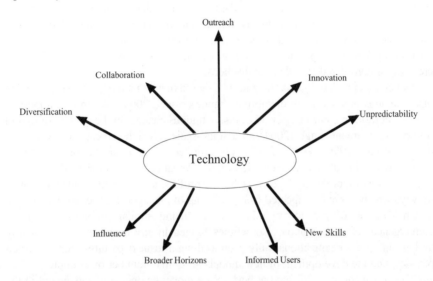

Figure 1.2 The Influence of Technology on the Characteristics of Change

The Misnomer of Discontinuous Change

It is often said that libraries are in the grip of discontinuous change. This is correct in the sense that the combination of change forces we now see is unlike anything we have seen before. It is clearly evident in the impact of technology in general. It is obvious in the more specific changes in skills requirements. It is manifest in the growth of collaboration and cooperation across organizational boundaries and between libraries inhabiting different sectors. In some senses the boundaries between the sectors are becoming refreshingly blurred.

Discontinuous change demands a distinguishable break with past practice, and requires the recognition that the former ways of doing things will not create and sustain successful organizations. This, it could be argued, is particularly so in the information sector, which now embraces a vast and diffuse area of activity. It is therefore a form of change for which there is no template in previous experience, no model of the process and consequently no new consensus about how change should be handled. The stress in the last sentence is on 'new'. One of the most comprehensive examples of discontinuous change which the traditional purist might recognise in contemporary libraries is that of converged support services in universities and colleges, and here resides another cautionary note.

When considering the impact of technology, some commentators (for example Edmondson, 2003) point to the disruptive impact of technology. They are concerned about the capacity of technology to disrupt well-established relationships. This is undoubtedly an issue to be confronted when considering the psychology of change (see Chapter 9), but it has a positive side as well. Technology also supports the formation of novel relationships which would otherwise be unlikely. The importance of this kind of relationship between opposites, or across significant differences, for organizational creativity is considered elsewhere in this book.

Developments like digitisation and ICT should mean that organizations are facing discontinuous and seriously disruptive change (Adner, 2003). Yet in one important respect, libraries are *not* in a period of discontinuous change. In the context of hybrid library management, Pugh (2004), in a small-scale research project repeating work done earlier (1990, 1997, 2002) investigated a number of organizational characteristics in public and academic libraries. What has been consistently revealed, over a period of more than 15 years, is that the profession has not responded to change in ways which might be expected from a reading of management literature, and from a consideration of practice in other sectors facing similar problems. Even the convergence referred to above, sometimes fudged in any event, and subsequently undone in some organizations, only produced significant departures from accepted practice, and the development of new models, in a small number of examples.

The above surveys indicated at best only a moderate degree of movement in the development of organizations, and even this comment would have to be heavily qualified by reference to a somewhat simplistic view of the key characteristics of innovative organizations. The successive research projects suggested that:

- There is little evidence of a coherent, methodical, and sustained approach to organizational development: one which takes into account the crucial environmental influences at work on today's libraries, and in particular the opportunities offered by technology. This usually shows up as poor structural change, and a still partial – but developing – understanding of the nature of teamwork and team structures.
- There are major problems in the development of organizational learning, and, sometimes, even in the recognition of the need for it. Organizational learning, learning from work, and self-development are part of the vital systems of any organization in any event, but particularly so in relation to change management. This has not been uniformly recognised in libraries, and as late as 2004 there were a few examples of library services where there had not been any implementation

of even rudimentary staff development programmes.

- Systems for recording and disseminating the corpus of knowledge inside library organizations are not well developed, even where explicit knowledge is concerned. How the more intractable problem of tacit knowledge is dealt with is a matter for conjecture.
- There is often little sense of the systematic and permissive dissemination of information within organizations. Too many library services appear to impose unnecessary restrictions on access to certain kinds of information, and use too few methods of internal communication.
- Risk-taking and a culture of innovation tends to be limited to technological developments, although there is some evidence of the growing questioning of conventional practice.

There is also some evidence (see, for example, Hales, 2002) that in spite of significant proselytising on behalf of organic organizations, self-management, teamwork, decentralisation and the other features of non-bureaucratic structures, the limited extent of organizational development in libraries is mirrored in their general management. Hales makes the point that while bureaucracies may be subject to a degree of modification, this is limited and so the bureaucratic structure remains an impediment to dynamic change. Innovative structures and the changes in managerial roles and styles which should accompany them are still novel experiences in many areas. Rules-based organizations and hierarchies are still more or less the norm. Responsibilities are still based on the management of discrete sub-units of organizations, and accountability is still a vertical phenomenon.

What this amounts to is the strong suspicion that most organizations, including libraries, tend to meet new challenges in the tried and trusted ways. The patient is being sustained by strong doses of bureaucracy sugared with the cautious application of some rudimentary teamwork. There is therefore little sense of a break with past practice, so the challenge of discontinuous change is answered by a traditional response. It is in this sense that it can be argued that in practice libraries do not actually reflect the characteristics of discontinuous change, although this is undoubtedly what they face.

It is possible to speculate on the innate conservatism of libraries, and to consider the certainty that libraries based on conventional approaches can continue to function and still deliver services: but to take this attitude is to dismiss the challenging opportunities for organization development largely coming from technological change.

Cross-Boundary Working

Discontinuous change is also seen in the emergence of organizations which span different cultures and modus operandi. In the wider management world, this is again a common phenomenon, and it is not new. Kanter (1997), Morgan (1997), Drucker (2002) and even earlier Heenan and Keegan (1979) trace the roots of globalisation, for example, to trading organizations working across continents in the 17th Century, and even to the international financial activities of the 15th-Century City State of Venice. There is very little which is new in management, but what is different is the way in which organizations in different sectors respond to the challenge of coping with different cultural traditions. Our organizations operate on a much smaller scale, but in some respects the challenge is the same:

● To manage what are in some ways novel organizations produced by alliances between disparate departments or services within organizations, and associations across organizational boundaries
● To do so in ways which create unity without uniformity
● To allow diversity to flourish within a common ethos and to a common end.

This can only be done through development which embraces the proper use of technology in order to promote the creativity flowing from differences and diversity.

There are examples of multinational companies which have profited from a particular approach to managing in the circumstances described above. Amongst these is BP (formerly British Petroleum), where some of the philosophy and basic techniques of knowledge management were pioneered.

The BP approach to managing across organizational and national boundaries, and retaining coordination while still making maximum use of the creative potential of the organizational setting, has been widely reported and discussed in the literature. In sum, it is based on:

● A clear and simple philosophy, founded on learning, and on creating and sharing knowledge.
● Structural change: with a large number of business units, the principles of empowerment and autonomy are married with interdependence.
● A culture of sharing, encouraging both individual attainment and collaboration. This is sustained by the use of communities of practice and an ingrained acceptance of collaborative learning. In this way, personnel learn to identify with both their immediate team, or other unit, and their peers in other parts of the larger organization.

The system of knowledge management developed by BP can also be described succinctly (Collinson and Parcell, 2001). It worked on the basis of a simple learning cycle. Any event in the life of the organization can be pivotal and the source of a learning experience. The learning cycle begins before the event, and follows a logical sequence of identifying lessons, disseminating the results, and then formalizing the learning by putting it on the intranet.

Technology, and in particular multimedia such as video streaming and multimedia imaging, is used to aid interpretation and the absorption of the lessons. In addition to this, we now have the capacity to provide extensive support for virtual learning (Genysys, 2006). This is supported by appropriate leadership styles which are not biased towards controlling the behaviour of others. There is above all an acceptance of the basic premise that the environment demands that organizations change. They cannot simply rely on old procedures and apply traditional principles in an attempt to contain situations, rather than engage in revolutionary developments in management.

If we are looking for a blueprint for managing change in the 21st century, this is a good beginning. The example of BP provides an illustration of the holistic nature of technology, organizational structures, leadership and organizational culture. It stands also as an illustration of how technology can be used positively in contemporary change management, and how discontinuous change on a vast scale can be accommodated by embracing new ideas and new ways of organizing. The proposition is that the development of a new attitude to technology, and an understanding of the positive power of technology when it comes to breaking with the past, is a key issue in change management, and if it works for BP, it will work for us.

The solution is seen in engineering a move towards new organizations – as articulated by global concerns like BP and other major players such as ABB Asea Brown Boveri, at one time said to be the apotheosis of decentralisation. Both of these organizations, and others, talked openly of bringing all the available brains and talents to bear on a problem, on learning and on communicating with each other.

In the case of BP, it appears that in some arenas the natural choice as coordinator and facilitator of this process was the librarian, but it was a librarian working under very different organizational conditions than would be found in most other libraries – relying heavily on technology, but with little hierarchy and a strong bias towards networked structures.

Engaging properly with change management means seeing the liberating power of technology as a means of supporting flexible organizations, learning, communication and networks. It is not seeing it as something which can be used to buttress hierarchies, perpetuate bureaucracies and generally maintain the specialisations and divisions inherent in much of current library practice. Beyond this, there are other, more precise organizational characteristics of contemporary libraries which should influence the approach to change management.

The Mixed Economy

What we have seen in the case of BP is evidence that how technology is handled can have a significant affect on change management. It has clearly contributed to the diversity of information services, and this is a strength which can be used in the organization development which should be the basis of change management.

The hybrid nature of libraries is an obvious sign of the emergence of diversity. One of the greatest strengths of the e-future is that in real-life information services it will be based on a mixed economy. Users already draw information from sources which can be local, regional, national, and international. This in turn is a factor which strengthens the argument that new kinds of organizations, good at working across boundaries and handling a host of cultural differences, are needed.

Acknowledging the hybridity of information services is the first step in designing appropriate organizations. Working in mixed economy organizations will call for new skills and combinations of skills: managing in them will demand a new mindset and more refined concepts of leadership, motivation, and development. Coping with change will impose the same requirements on managers and managed.

Organizational Complexity

The argument developed so far supports the idea of taking a whole-organization approach to change management. Change management starts well before the gestation period of a specific change project, or the point where a problem is identified, or a need arises. Organization development means that the first strategic concern in change management is to create a service-wide and natural capacity to take a proactive view of change. It means:

- Identifying developments in the internal and external environments which will require a response
- Organizing in such a way that talents can be brought to bear on identified problems and opportunities which arise naturally in the work environment
- Equipping everyone with the skills for working in such an organization
- Ensuring learning and development
- Sharing authority and responsibility
- Establishing robust and comprehensive communication systems
- Developing appropriate leadership
- Creating organizational structures which allow people to use all their talents
- Embedding a culture of change.

This is not simply an issue of change management, as if it is a discrete and self-contained strategy implemented through a toolkit approach. It is a question of dealing with the complexity of the organizations we work in.

Complexity should not be seen as synonymous with complication. Complication comes from routines and systems which are illogical, use resources inefficiently, are too elaborate and detailed for their purpose, or lack focus. Some information service organizations might well, therefore, be complicated in their own right, but this is another topic.

Complexity, on the other hand, comes from uncertainty, and the absence of clear answers and defined courses of actions. It could certainly be said that these features – the uncertainty and lack of clarity – are exacerbated by the negative effect of conventional structures, such as tortuous and ineffective communication systems, excessive specialisation and demarcation. The irony is that our traditional organizational structures were devised to remove uncertainty and variation, by creating standardisation. Unfortunately, technological, social and educational changes cannot any longer be constrained by bureaucracies and hierarchies.

Management ideas in themselves are amoral, and there are a number of dubious organizations in being today which actually show how an organic structure can work. While their purposes are nefarious beyond belief, they have actually created the kind of loose-coupled organization some librarians have been thinking about for over 20 years (Martell, 1983).

Complexity also comes from the perpetuation of establishment views on matters such as the separation of strategy from operations, proprietary and exclusive attitudes to management information, and fairly rigid approaches to managerial roles. Where organizations are dealing with rapid change, these issues create uncertainty because of the lack of shared information and responsibility. To counter this calls for much more sensitive and skilful management practices than will be found in the traditional bureaucracies. It is probably impossible to remove the uncertainty from technologically-driven change; it is definitely undesirable to even try to do so, because some uncertainty can be used positively. Complexity is a creative force in change management, but it has to be harnessed and used through appropriate organization development.

The Complexity of Technology, Technologists and Other Staff
Technology can mean two things. It can refer to the use of automated systems. The other, and wider meaning, describes anything and everything which is done by a library to provide its services, whether these activities are machine or paper-based, to do with people or hardware, strategy or operations. On either of these premises, it is reasonable to say that traditional library organizations have generally been routine users of technology. Procedures are repetitive, with little change from day to day. There has certainly been very little in the way of officially-sanctioned variation in how things have been done. The unofficial variations are often entertaining, and sometimes innovative and stimulating, but this is another topic which is definitely not for this book.

Readers might now be wondering why this section is headed 'Complex Technology'. Organizations based on routine technology respond well to bureaucratic management. As the technological makeup of libraries is beginning to change, the kinds of staff employed are also beginning to change. There is some evidence that technologists tend to adapt well to styles of management which are permissive, not controlling, which give people room for exercising initiative, and ultimately for self-management. Data from organizations in a range of what the literature calls knowledge-based organizations (which organizations are not?) or, maybe more appropriately, creative organizations, also suggests that flexible and devolved management systems based on teams are reasonably sound ways of running things as far as the staff are concerned. Tucker et al (2005) reported the results of a survey of workforce trends, and identified virtual working, substantial diversity, autonomy and empowerment as significant developments. Very few organizations were planning strategies to deal with these changes, and there is no reason to think that many libraries will be doing so. Key implications the authors identify are changes in leadership styles and organizational cultures, as well as changes in reward systems and the development of skills and talent. These are changes which stem from diversity and will in turn make life even more complex.

Our penchant for certainty, and the elimination of variation, has also led us to assume that in areas of routine work there is no point in considering anything other than bureaucratic control. Libraries, being predictable, are susceptible to falling into this trap. This is probably not a good thing, as Case Study 4 illustrates.

It is increasingly the case that library staff are better qualified, trained and educated than ever before. The labour market ensures that what are deemed to be routine, non-professional or para-professional posts are often filled by professionally-qualified staff. As a result, there is also a larger question of how staff with these qualifications, and those without them, can be more positively engaged in the mundane work they do. Giving staff involved in even routine work a say in how it is done will achieve a number of things. In general it is but one more step in establishing the complexity which makes for healthy and vigorous organizations. Introducing flexibility and empowering staff who can be helped to assume responsibility and exercise authority is therefore another way of developing multiple perspectives. In a loose-coupled organization this is a further boost to complexity, and creativity.

The potential of technology as a driver for change in libraries is far-reaching and double-edged. It can have a social impact in terms of organizational structures, job design, communication and learning, yet it can also isolate through specialisation; it can be liberating in terms of the potential it offers for individual growth, and restrictive in terms of its use as a tool for control. For skills, it changes the landscape because it leads to demands for more abstract thinking, better reasoning skills and flexibility (Buchanan and Huczynski, 2004), yet in other ways it deskills.

The argument about whether or not libraries are technologically-determined is a difficult one, and the answer is probably unclear and depends on who asks the question and who answers it. A pragmatic response is to say that technology itself is a two-edged weapon in change management, and it is critical that this is accepted. What counts is how an organization, or more properly how management, decides to use the technology. Here the question of the personalities of managers is a factor causing further complexity (see Chapters 5 and 9).

Technology offers options in how change is managed and how organizations develop. Deploying it involves decisions to do with skills levels, the treatment of areas of library work which can be deskilled, the status attached to the new jobs and roles created by technology, and the problem of maintaining subtle control over what is done and how it is done. These factors are precursors of the later discussion of empowerment, motivation, job satisfaction, teams, self-management, the systems approach and structural change. So while we may well agree that technology does not actually determine the approach to change management and organization development, it clearly has an all-pervasive influence and is a major factor.

The Complexity of Users

Users are also changing, as we have already noted. Their information-handling skills are increasingly sophisticated, and as they become more and more competent and comfortable with the use of ICT, so their demands will become more sophisticated and less predictable. The successful handling of change in this environment will require more than command-and-control management. We can observe a warped recognition of the growing skills of users in the emerging tendency to defoliate user services, in some academic libraries, by reducing the number of subject specialists or information officers. This is justified on the grounds that the technology now allows users to do it themselves. One riposte to this particularly robust reduction of librarianship to the level of basic accountancy appeared in no less an organ than the Johns Hopkins Gazette:

> Our library has the most effective search engines yet invented – librarians who are highly skilled at ferreting out the uniquely useful references that you need. (Brody, 2004)

In university and college libraries, users are also becoming stakeholders in a more sharp-edged way. By various routes, they are now directly paying customers. Their financial stake in their education, including the support services, is less abstract and more focused than previously. It is better to recognise this, and find ways of bringing their perspectives on the organization into mainstream strategy and execution, particularly where change is concerned. I am braced here for all the old arguments about the transient nature of the student population, but they should already be involved in the process of library development in any case, and making this input more dynamic through a new compact with users would strengthen the change process. Three years, the usual length of a UK first degree course, is actually a long time in the life of a library.

Personalisation

If there is an emerging tendency to place more faith in the power of the machine than the intellect of the professional librarian, then it goes hand in hand with the potential for the personalisation of information services. Managerial changes like the one just described, and, more importantly, the mindset behind them, tend to reinforce the growing capacity for do-it-yourself collection development. The willingness to take a gamble on the ability of technology to replace professional and subject-related expertise is actually a natural, although perhaps unintentional, outcome of the irreversible move towards access: providing material, only when it is needed, from a range of local and distributed electronic sources rather than the library's own shelves.

With the growth of distributed information sources, this area is showing real development. Except for funding, there is now no reason why academic users at least cannot 'pick and mix' to create their own library, and this leads to friction.

Decisions to reduce expert staffing by cutting personnel who act as intermediaries between users and information sources are the result of political and economic pressure, so it is not within the immediate power of librarians to alter them. It is especially piquant that the conditions for doing this have been created by our own technological advances. It may not be possible for librarians to control this process totally, but it can be influenced by putting our attitude to technology at the forefront of change management.

Kirkpatrick (2004), in a remarkably dense but nevertheless crucial piece of work on the social theory of personal computing, quotes Habermas's view of philosophy as something which should

> . . . mediate interpretively between expert knowledge and an everyday practice in need of orientation.

In a work which generally, as I interpret it, attacks the assumption that locking up the expertise of ICT is bad, Kirkpatrick asks many questions about what technology actually is, what it is for and how it should be used. On one level it can be argued that technology simply offers a superior means of operating. Users and staff sit down in front of a VDU to solve a problem in the easiest way for them. The difficulty is that the way library technology has been organized tends to disenfranchise groups outside the experts, and so restrict access to information. It becomes a political issue, and a means of exercising hegemony and control. The decision to replace subject librarians with machines is the ultimate expression of this. The question is therefore how to avoid this situation and at least temper the political use of technology in this way.

Here we will have to return again to the question of organization development (OD), and its role in change management. There are some key principles which can be built in to the expansive view of change management championed by OD and by this book:

- Closer involvement of more library staff with technology
- Opening up technology and its benefits to the whole organization
- Serious engagement with the skills issue and the question of the future role of librarians as a means of containing the power of technology and replacing the traditional view of librarians' roles
- Involving users in change and development.

In Kirkpatrick's words (op cit):

> The definitive point would be the orientation that people had to the [technology] . . . The

essence of technology should not be conceived outside of social relations.

For over 30 years, the literature has often suggested that workers' skills, their room for manouvre and the use of initiative in the way they did their jobs, would be reduced by the spread of technology. Their knowledge, and perhaps experience, would also become less important as the use of ICT increased. This was because of the control computers could exercise over what was done. There is little doubt that this is a description of the process put in train when librarians are sacked because the machine can provide more effective and economic access to information. It is what actually lies behind the 'disintermediation' described with pride in some of the literature, where the librarian is eliminated from the chain of information provision. While it is admirable to be enthusiastic and supportive of the self-sufficiency of users of all kinds, it is also necessary to stake out some territory which the librarian can occupy, and claim a distinctive place for human skills which can complement the machine.

In terms of change management, this means framing the development of organizations within certain requirements:

- Structures which eliminate divisions caused by specialisation and the retention of expertise inside boundaries, but which foster whole-organization communication
- New partnerships between staff, users and other stakeholders, with a closer involvement of users in development
- The forging of new roles as intermediaries, involving skills reappraisal
- The demystification of technology.

This latter point is of some importance. One of the straws in the wind which indicated the growing power of the technologists in libraries was the emergence of a new vocabulary which actually described old ideas and activities. Bibliographic control has been replaced by content management, metadata and Dublin Core take the place of cataloguing and classification, and the net result is more nourishment for the insidious growth of the idea that digital information is the province of the specialist. What is needed is a redefinition of the roles of librarians in a technologically-dominated environment, and an acknowledgement of the skills they can bring to the job of guiding the user through the use of a mix of digital and traditional information forms. This is where the issue of new skills becomes important.

Specialisation and New Skills

There are many writers who have investigated the skills implications of the changes in librarianship over the last 15 years. What they advocate can be summarised as

- New information management skills
- Networking, collaboration and coaching skills (Prytherch, 2002)

- Flexibility
- New roles
- Teamwork skills
- Motivational skills (Roitburg, 2001)
- Skills relevant to the use and exploitation of ICT – simply the ability to use the technology, and the mindset to engage with it
- Negotiating skills (Ashcroft, 2004)
- Powell (2002) examined the skills needs emerging from the growth of student-centred learning, and noted especially the new demands made on the design and management of the physical characteristics of the library, while Hodgkin (2003) considered this last issue to be of less importance.
- Lancaster (2003) assesses the skills which are needed to ensure the integrity and availability of tacit knowledge in an organization, particularly that of former employees. Knowledge harvesting is the issue here, and it is connected to the view already expressed, that many library systems pay little or no attention to this issue.

Our systems are very good at recording formal knowledge, at communicating it, and at restricting its dissemination amongst a carefully controlled group. Our ability to record and utilise tacit knowledge is negligible (Pugh, 2004) and the skills of doing this are fundamental acquisitions for the present organizational environments.

So the nature of change is creating complex issues to do with skills, and has an obvious bearing on how we manage. There is a link between change, human flexibility, and structural flexibility (Walton and Edwards, 2001), and this leads into the last area of complexity, that of organizational structures.

Structures

The weakness of traditional structures, especially in a fast-moving world where the trends identified in this chapter really demand a new approach to the shape organizations assume, can be simply stated:

- Poor communications
- Inadequate cross-fertilisation of ideas
- Waste of expertise, when it is locked away from users.

Once more there is nothing new in this. We have seen at least 25 years of advocacy as far as the seamless approach to information is concerned, with commentators such as Gorman (1979) arguing quite early in the debate for a broad perspective and the establishment of what he called the 'multidimensional library . . . [with] loose and more complex relationships between groups and persons'. He has been followed by others who see the way in which the digital revolution demands a revolution in management principles as well, and it has been said that change management means knocking walls down both physically and metaphorically. Existing systems already lock up the knowledge and information of expert library staff behind desks, doors, walls and internal organizational boundaries. Terris (2005), argued strongly for the pre-eminent position of the indexer, who is the possessor of

> . . . superior knowledge of the collection and how one item relates to another (historically, socially, aesthetically). More importantly he or she should have a firm and instinctive understanding of the collection's users and be able to assess what researchers have asked for in the past and anticipate their future needs. They will exercise imagination and consider a range of possibilities, all to be matched against the formality of the thesaurus.

Why should all of this knowledge, imagination, insight, experience and skill be out of bounds to users? The same could be said of many other members of staff in our current, circumscribed library structures, where there are barriers to communication and to contact between many specialists, 'pre-eminent' or not, and the user.

Competition Versus Collaboration

Bureaucracies present the ideal organizational conditions for nurturing competition. Much of this chapter, by contrast, has dealt with collaboration, with teamwork, communities of interest, and communication networks which share ideas and experience. Electronic information is all-pervasive and expansive: the idea that it can be delivered on the basis of competition between rigidly compartmentalised units which own the processes they have responsibility for is anathema.

As it is, the separate parts of traditional organizations belong to a competitive system wherever political influence, resources or rewards are concerned. This is not only enfeebling, but it is the antithesis of what digital information services actually need. Developments now often depend on collaboration, alliances and external and internal partnerships, often between people and organizations with congenital differences. Many of the key skills needs arising from the nature of contemporary change are to do with these characteristics. This is already a clearly discernable trend, but how much more effective collaboration would be if it was understood in detail, and practised within organizations as well as between them, is a moot point.

Paradoxically, the need for collaboration is also fed by the threat of competition. The digitisation of information has put paid to the position where the library was the unrivalled and unbeatable provider of information. There are now commercial interests which can emulate libraries in some respects, and there is also the emancipated user, semi-detached from the apron-strings of the librarian, to worry about. Arguably, if libraries want to retain, some say recover, their pre-eminence, they can only do so by collaboration. As a sobering aside on competition, it has been said that tabloids now beat libraries for the facts that matter.

Competition in libraries today has one other undesirable effect. Because it is often based on specialisation and the ownership of territory, it hampers the cross-fertilisation and collision of opposite views which spurs true creativity and innovation.

It might not yet be clear what the future role of the librarian will be, nor what characteristics the future library will possess. What is certain is that we will not find it at all unless we create new kinds of organizations that recognise the potential changes and find ways of harnessing all the talents and energies inside our organizations.

The Implications

The nature of the change faced by libraries is a reflection of the change forces in other sectors. We can look to ideas and practices in these sectors, and begin to develop a view of change management which makes use of the characteristics considered in this chapter, rather than basing our approach on the perception of the threats posed by these characteristics. Our approach to change will be coloured by these features, and it will also acknowledge the differences which sometimes exist between most libraries and other organizations. Nevertheless there will be some common ground in that the approach to managing change in a diverse, technologically-driven environment of rapid change, will call for:

- A commitment to organization development
- An emphasis on a broad conception of learning
- Collaboration
- Teams
- Imaginative engagement with the human aspects of change
- Innovative management skills, styles and leadership
- Novel views of motivation
- The appreciation of organization theories not often applied to libraries – to do with creativity, the creative use of differences and friction in organizations, and new ways of thinking about organizations.

Case Study 1: Ambushing the Librarians

The Background

This case study is based on contemporary events which have subsequently been repeated in other academic institutions, with similar and predictable results to those analysed here. The events described demonstrate the use of technological development as a vehicle for implementing far reaching change in academic library services.

There is usually more than one reason for change in library services, and the nature of the change has to be understood from a number of standpoints in order to manage it. Over years, several factors coalesced to create a difficult situation.

A provincial university undertook a reorganization of academic support services. The impetus for change was ostensibly the technological forces which set in train the development of electronic libraries. A small number of forward-looking institutions had, of their own volition, begun to consider better ways of providing information services to users. One or two became examples of the kind of integrated service provision, based on multi-skilled teams, which has been considered in this chapter.

Haphazard Reorganization

The position at the university in question was different. The first wave of reorganisation was far from a textbook example of change management. Although it was a trend-setting development, the change was top-down, with little consideration of alternative models and an extremely tight timetable. Ostensibly it brought together the library service, the IT service and some smaller units such as reprography: in reality the unification was never more than an administrative fiction. The degree of convergence below senior management level was negligible. Where it existed it was due more to the sporadic efforts of individuals rather than coherent and measured planning. Even in this respect, any imaginative attempt at integration was likely to fail. For example, one resourceful and committed subject librarian, who also had a diploma in counselling, put forward a paper advocating the absorption of the student counselling service into information services, on the basis that the information service was the place where most students went to obtain information in any case, and that many had consequently built up a sound relationship with library staff. This may or may not have been a workable proposition, but it deserved more than the out-of-hand dismissal and ridicule it was subjected to by the Director of Information Services.

The Dangerous Precedent of Lack of Consultation

The non-consultative way in which change was introduced had a knock-on effect. Staff below senior management level were organized into teams by fiat, so the majority of staff were unable to engage with the ethos and modus operandi of the new service. Discontent swelled to a crescendo of outright opposition. Eventually, the first Director of Information Services moved on, and was replaced by an IT expert who for upwards of eight years presided over what were a number of departments unconnected below senior management level.

The Flashpoint – A Financial Crisis and Opportunism

This situation continued for some time, until mounting financial difficulties reached crisis point. An institution-wide review of expenditure meant that the university information service was required to bear its proportion of the reduction in costs.

For university management, the way in which this was to be done was clear. The existing Director of Information Services was approaching retirement age, would accept a package of benefits and would not be replaced. The bulk of the savings would be found by the redundancy of a number of professional librarians on the basis that electronic sources of information could replace them and provide a more effective, and especially more cost-effective, service.

Ironically, after a brief campaign of resistance to the proposals, all the required savings were met by the voluntary redundancy of most of the threatened staff.

The Analysis

This case study is a good example of the complicated mix of motives and causes found in most serious efforts at organizational change. Because of the cultural characteristics set out above, and the ingrained directive management process, it was virtually impossible to draw up and propose viable alternatives. Whatever happened, circumstances were unlikely to lead to a resolution which would have been satisfactory to all the parties involved.

It is also fair to say that economic power was always likely to prevail. It is likely that most of the alternative courses of action proposed by staff would have been rejected. The weight of the culture was seen in the way that the merged service had been set up and in the way the cutbacks were proposed. It is probable also that the willingness of professional staff to take redundancy packages in the end was influenced by their perceptions of what was likely to occur, given the history of the change process in this particular institution.

The Burden of History

The process of change described in outline here had in practice been underway for years, and the history associated with it is not a happy one. For the people most affected by the change, their expectations were influenced by previous events, so that when the crisis came expediency triumphed over professional issues.

Below senior management, the integration of services was superficial, and what the case demonstrates, apart from sheer bad management of change generally, is a poor understanding of the nature of the change the information service had been engaged in for a protracted period. With the service integrated at managerial level only, and with a non-participative and prescriptive management style, staff had little incentive to take a service-wide view of the implications of the cuts.

Weak Cultural Change

The basic problem was the weakness of the service culture in this divided environment where little had altered at operational level. The absence of integration lower down, and incidents like the fate meted out to the counselling service proposal, served to depress expectations, reduce the enthusiasm for integration at ground level, and virtually rule out any creative and developmental alternative proposals.

Absorbing technology into library services calls for role change on the part of librarians, who have to subscribe to the idea of technologically-driven change in order to contain it and make use of it. The constraints suggested in the previous paragraph made this unlikely.

Tijdens and Steijn (2005) also considered that technological change, in particular information and communications technology, calls for more expansive action if it is to be successful. This means that technology has to be embraced by everyone, yet the structure of information services in this case study maintained the former specialisations and discouraged cross-departmental links. Integration, if successfully achieved, would have been one way of altering the negative perceptions of the staff, modifying the culture, and improving morale.

The widespread adoption and mastery of the technology itself would have been one way of protecting the position of the so-called traditional librarians in a technologically-driven organization, and making it rather more difficult to remove virtually an entire cadre of professionals. This could create, as it were, seamlessness. The evidence of this would be present not only in the provision of information in all formats, but in the way in which the different specialisations could have been accommodated in team structures, for example, and in the less restricted roles which could have developed over time.

This is a course of action which demands very clear and articulate strategies for ICT and for all the different kinds of personnel involved. The technology also needs to be widely adopted and intensively used, so that it becomes embedded in the work of everyone. This is not just true of the housekeeping aspects of work, but also as a fundamental tactic in the approach to the provision of information by all staff. The history of organizational change in this institution, with at least two attempts to merge services followed by a reversion to the traditional structures, and the ease with which the desired cuts were achieved by voluntary redundancy, indicates that none of the desirable organizational features existed. Structurally, culturally, philosophically, and procedurally the health of the organization was poor, and organization development was minimal.

Weak Structural Change

The organization development approach to change management embraces structural change, changes in personnel management and the development of learning systems which allow staff to accumulate new skills and then crucially transfer those skills into genuinely hybrid environments. What happened on the ground was that the once separate departments continued to operate in the old way, with clear demarcation lines between technologists and librarians who had acquired little more than first-line familiarity with basic IT techniques and search protocols. Understanding the intertwined nature of traditional librarianship and digital library services was a vital step. If this had been supported by some of the other changes concomitant on the characteristics described in this chapter, the result could have been the development of multi-skilled teams with both librarians and IT specialists inextricably embedded in the fabric of information delivery to users.

Changes in Managerial Attitudes

To create an organization which would be good at managing change, it would also have been necessary for management to show more understanding of the new environment and the change forces within it. They needed to develop not only new roles, but more importantly new attitudes: to issues like shared inputs into strategy; the sophisticated personal development necessary for effective working in hybrid environments; the capacity and willingness of managers to work more closely with operational staff where they make an impact on users; the innovative use of organizational structures; sensitive and imaginative use of communication systems. Even if this had happened, it would still not have been possible to win the battle. But it would have been harder to identify a particular group of staff whose elimination could provide the financial savings. The savings could only have been made through a broader exercise resulting in a less damaging affect on the health of the organization, and less disruption to the service provided by users.

Organizational Health

The willingness of the staff to accept voluntary redundancy is linked to the question of organizational health. Poorly-managed change in the first instance and changes in senior personnel and stagnation over a period of years inevitably took their toll on morale. Motivation in modern information services is a more complicated issue than in a traditional bureaucracy, and the difficulty arises from the nature of the organization and the characteristics of the changes it is facing. Understanding the process, and appreciating the significance of its characteristics as it unfolds is the first step to managing it. This is often the only way in which the crude mix of politics and economics in change management can be moderated

This was a discontinuous change, brought about by changes in user behaviour and technology, and it was answered by a tedious application of old and gnarled ideas. A different strategy over the years could have put the library service in a position where they were seen to be in the vanguard of a new approach, and totally enmeshed with technology. Then their political position, while it would not have guaranteed total safety, would at least have made them more formidable opponents.

Chapter 2

Change Theories

Chapter 1 identified the major forces driving change in modern information services. Most of these are the consequences of digitisation and the development of electronic sources of information. It was argued that they represent an unique set of circumstances, offering an opportunity for the innovative management of library services in ways which can accommodate and harness change forces in the 21st century. The ideas which lie behind organizational change processes are examined in this chapter.

The previous chapter also quoted from Cage (op cit), and this is an appropriate place to offer another comment from the same paper:

> However, it's beginning to look like the phenomenon of change is something different. For starters, the idea of 'change' is hardly an advanced analytical concept. You don't need a degree in statistics to recognize change when you see it. What's tricky is realizing that the meaning of corporate change has been transformed completely. Whereas change used to be peripheral and occasional, it has now moved toward the center of organizational life. The meaning of change has been upended. In the past, change was the element of entrepreneurs or, within the corporation, of discrete projects aimed at producing specific innovations or solving problems . . . Change management is not the latest theory to be applied to corporate strategy: it is the unfolding response to, and increased understanding of, a complex and irreversible sea change.

The quotation above illuminates the broad development of change theories. Based on standard management theory, this journey starts with scientific management, which saw change as a spasmodic and top-down, often autocratic process, and ends with more exciting contemporary ideas. The latter have a more specific focus on supporting a change process which is the central motif of the organization. Cage's comments are the story of how the view of change as the prerogative of a few organizational figures, usually in the upper echelons, controlling and prosecuting change through prescribing discrete projects, has developed into the realisation that change can become organic, and that there is a holistic approach to organizational change and development. Another way of looking at this development of ideas is the often-quoted one of 'push-versus-pull' highlighting the contrast between the top-down, directive way of achieving change, and the consultative and inclusive approach. In the networked organization the 'pull' philosophy now extends outside organizations, and is connected with ideas about networks and communities of practice. The major advantage of this line of thinking is that it is decentralised and focuses on creating connections between a range of diverse participants. It is also connected with the ideas about organizational creativity to be examined later in this chapter.

For the better part of our history, the prevailing ideas have been to do with not changing. This is true in the sense that most information services organizations have been based on ideas about stability, standardisation, and certainty – not necessarily the best harbingers of successful change programmes. Conversely, it is also true that most library organizations *are* changing, but they are doing so on the basis of minor modifications of the same classical management theories. It should also be noted that not all the contemporary, or near-contemporary, ideas are inevitably about empowerment, workplace democracy or the development of an open culture offering a broad and influential involvement in organizational change. Business process re-engineering and resizing, and some forms of quality control, for example, are not about things like empowering staff. They reinforce ideas about control. In one example, Jones (2003) reported on a research project which identified the way in which 'broader conceptions' to do with technology transfer, embedding organizational learning, skills and knowledge improvement, and securing and improving employee commitment were ultimately subverted and compromised by other notions which led management into autocratic behaviour. This was at the hands of a management team which was reasonably open and receptive to some new ideas, and was committed to product innovation and change, but without the involvement of the staff. In other words, 'push' can still win over 'pull'.

It is also possible to envisage circumstances where a change strategy based on traditional thinking could be necessary in the short term, so there is no particular premium to be attached to the embracing of ideas because they are novel. The question is what works. In the end this cannot be answered with finality, but it is a question to which we will return.

It flies in the face of reality to deny that bureaucracies can support change under some circumstances. Library managers no longer assume that their organizations are stable, although significant change programmes are being implemented through the application of tried and trusted ideas. The general difficulty with an approach based on the modification of classical theories and traditional structures is that it probably does not develop a holistic and natural capacity for change within the organization. Nor does it focus the considerable collective talents of library staff on developing a natural appetite for organic change. There are also specific issues to do with most of the change theories, including those newer ideas which allow for the dynamic expression of individual and group talents. These will be examined later.

Change and Classical Management Theory

The exercise of control is one of the main preoccupations of classical management theory (see Figure 2.1). The literature sometimes distinguishes between classical management and scientific management, and usually on the basis that classical management was more concerned with general principles like the overall shape of an organization, while scientific management was concerned with the analysis of tasks and a form of micro-management.

For the purposes of this section the term 'classical' will be used as a generic label. If we take scientific management, bureaucratic management and administrative management as three overlapping elements in the general theory of classical management, then it is possible to identify the major characteristics of the genre and assess their relevance to the change management process. Classical management principles identified major organizational characteristics, mainly to do with the creation and control of stable organizations.

Specialisation

In classically-structured organizations, specialisation is applied to skills and responsibilities. Tasks and roles are delineated on this basis, and are then grouped with related tasks in subgroups which form sub-units, usually in a sectional, departmental or divisional structure, where the internal boundaries of the organization reflect the divisions between the specialised groups.

A basic design principle is therefore that of function. This is seen at its clearest in conventional acquisition, cataloguing, and interlibrary loan units, and lately, albeit slightly more sophisticated, in the emergence of electronic information divisions. It might also, more arguably, be seen in the emergence of posts responsible for access rights to electronic information. All of these arrangements are functional in that they are concerned with the delivery of a specialised part of a wider service.

This feature is perpetuated as layers of management are added in order to deal with the resulting specialised sections, and the end is division of labour. Lower levels of the organization naturally reflect this quite strongly, where it is possible for staff to concentrate on one aspect of a task without involvement in the complete process. In this way, functions can be well defined, and areas of responsibility clearly demarcated, with a clear and unambiguous chain of command. This tendency was seen at its best in the early days of post-Berlin Wall 'liberalisation' in Eastern Europe, when organizations introduced new services or new product lines and promptly engaged a whole battalion of managers to control them, adding more bureaucracy to already highly bureaucratic structures.

Specialisation not only applies to the way in which work is organized. Perhaps an equally damaging fissure occurs because of the separation of strategy and policy creation from implementation and operation. The centralisation of power and authority in this way can cramp the initiation and execution of change initiatives because it reinforces the monocular, management-biased view of the organization and its development.

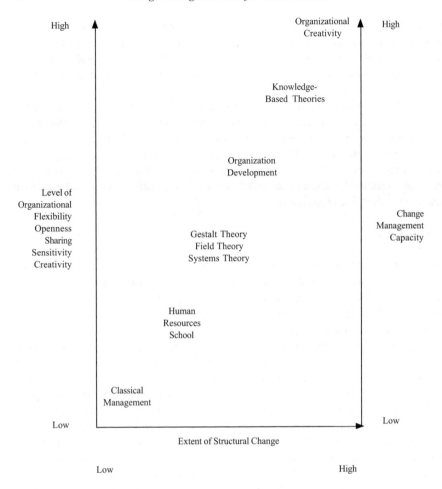

Figure 2.1 Change Theories and the Capacity of Organizations to Manage Change

Formal Communication

Communication patterns tend to follow the organizational structure, being primarily vertical. There will be some concessions to cross-boundary communication via special projects, managerial posts with integrative responsibilities and other devices. Of particular interest, traditionally-organized institutions do not make deliberate use of the informal networks which exist, and which are critical in change management. From the change management point of view, all this underlines the general weakness of the classical theories of organization, in that the resulting structures do little to make it easy for information, skills and knowledge to be shared and applied across the organizational boundaries. In rapidly-changing environments this is a serious disadvantage in dealing with multi-faceted change.

Formal Control, Hierarchical Structures and Standardisation

Classical organizations are rules-based, relying on the use of legal power and formal authority. The shape of the organization is based on a conventional pyramid, and control is centralised. The effect of the formal organizational aspects is to create a compliant workforce, where obedience is a key characteristic. Looking back over a period working in a bureaucracy, managing a bureaucracy, and many years spent in trying to engineer and consolidate a move away from bureaucratic organizations, I am in no doubt of the strength of this particular characteristic. Without any empirical evidence to support this statement, I can think of no significant instance in well over thirty years when the management perspective did not eventually carry the day. Perhaps it was charismatic leadership.

This needs to be qualified by the observation that one strand of classical management – administrative management (Fayol, 1948) – actually acknowledged the problems of communication across the rigid internal boundaries of classical organizations, and also showed an appreciation of the need for more inclusive use of discussion and debate in problem-solving. This was likely to ameliorate the effects of the division between strategists and policy-makers on the one hand and the implementers on the other. Even so, change management in a bureaucracy still runs the danger of top-down, management-initiated change.

The same might well be true in non-bureaucratic organizations, but in the latter it is possible to harness inputs from areas outside management, and create managerial processes which reflect organizational diversity and the interests of all the parties involved in the organization.

Skills and Training

Skills and training are emphasised in bureaucracies, as part of the need to develop professionalism and in the interests of efficiency. Yet they are prosecuted within the same prescriptive framework which controls the other activities of the organization.

This means that the skills and expertise of individuals are actually used to buttress the structure of what are traditional organizations already based on the grouping together of specialisations. Mintzberg (1983) labelled this the professional organization, where groups within the organization are built around shared knowledge and skills. This categorisation could well be applied to libraries.

On the other hand, more diffuse and subtle policies to do with self-learning are less evident in the training and development mix of most libraries (Pugh, 2004).

The Problems of Managing Change in Classical Organizations

Organizations designed on the basis of classical management theory can be effective vehicles for certain kinds of change. Libraries operating in the way described in this chapter so far can certainly implement effective change. In stable conditions, when change is prosecuted through the management of specific projects, traditional organizations can contribute much to a change project:

- They can bring considerable expertise to bear on a problem.
- They allow people to operate effectively in steady-state conditions where there is a degree of certainty derived from working in a rules-based organization.
- There is clarity in terms of the delineation of responsibilities, communication, and the allocation of roles.
- Classical management produces organizations and staff possessing administrative competence, and good planning skills. There is still evidence of the high failure rate of change initiatives, particularly those which embrace more than a single change project. Figures as high as 80 per cent are frequently quoted, with the implementation process pinpointed as the major area where problems arise.
- It is quite likely that in an emergency situation, or where a change has to be implemented with tight timescales, a bureaucracy will be effective.

It is therefore a reasonable assumption that change management based on classical principles can occur effectively – but usually when the organization and the environment is not subject to turbulence. It is also possible to envisage a situation where even the most decentralised, loose-coupled organization can, of necessity, revert to a bureaucratic type when faced with the need for rapid change in an emergency.

Instability

The disadvantages of attempting to manage change today with the structures and ideas of yesterday can also be easily stated. The first of these is that libraries no longer operate in a stable environment. At this moment, they face unique circumstances.

For the first time, they are encountering serious competition in the provision of information. This competition comes from non-traditional providers of information and from the increasing confidence of users who are competent in their ability to bypass libraries and meet their own information needs.

Technological change is massively unpredictable and uncertain. This is not so much because of the technology per se, as Griffin (in Raitt, ed. 1997) tentatively suggested:

The technological issues may well prove to be the most tractable.

This statement may well be true – as long as technology is regarded simply as technical mastery. In the broader context of the organizational implications of the technological change associated with digitisation, and its human impact (see Chapter 9), we are no nearer to dealing with the issues raised by technology than we were in 1997, or even earlier.

In a review of Raitt's book, and this is point-scoring, as well as manifestly unfair and underhand, Pugh (1997b) drew attention to Batt's view on change in public libraries:

> There is a good mix of practical projects, conceptual papers and some admirable but risky crystal ball gazing: 'It seems to me highly likely that within a timescale of, say, 20 years, most public libraries will not look greatly different from today. There are many public libraries in the UK today which do not look significantly different from the 1960s or earlier!'

Never having been afraid of saying 'I told you so', it is difficult to imagine a better illustration of the perils of predicting the course of technology, or a stronger case for the use of the editor's pencil to protect the author. An increasing number of public libraries world-wide would not be recognised as the same institutions they were in 1997. Nor will they be in 2017, unless the clock is put back.

The Importance of Precedent
Batt's comment that many public libraries in 1997 looked no different than they did in the 1960s is an illustration of another problem to be encountered in trying to manage change on bureaucratic principles. The predictability of organizational life under classical management means that precedence is crucial. Planning is carried out partly on the basis of what has already happened, and what worked before. In the technological environment, this is no longer advisable.

Lack of Ownership
Another of the key difficulties is the lack of wide ownership inherent in closed change projects imposed on an organizations by senior management. If the diversity and breadth of opinion, skills and knowledge inside an organization is not taken into account and used in change projects, two main problems will arise. The project will achieve less because all the available talents and resources have not been used. As well as suffering all the consequences of using restricted problem-solving processes, the project will not be subjected to the proper level of scrutiny, and all the attendant problems of motivation will be exaggerated and will suppurate in the body of the organization. This is because people will not face a sufficient challenge if their roles and responsibilities are restricted. Nor will they be fully engaged, thus weakening motivation. These issues are made more intractable by the difficulties of communication between parts of the bureaucracy, and the possible use of motivational skills which are inappropriate for novel operating circumstances.

The General Weaknesses of the Professional Bureaucracy in Change Management

In spite of the bureaucracy's many strengths, referred to earlier, when innovation is considered, the form is still subject to the same general weaknesses:

- All bureaucracies can respond only slowly to stimuli in the external environment.
- Conflict is a permanent feature of bureaucracies: some would say that they thrive on it. Professional bureaucracies, probably representing the dominant organizational form in information services, add something else to the standard mix. They can foster conflict between the authority of the professional and the authority invested in the power structure built into the hierarchy. Many librarians, and managers, will be familiar with this both inside their services and between the library service and the parent organization. Conflict and its proper use is an essential part of change management: when it involves the power structure and a potentially unequal struggle with significant political overtones, it is destructive.
- While no organizational form can stop people collaborating informally, some tend to put up barriers against effective collaboration and sharing responsibility. Professional bureaucracies are very good at laying down each individual's responsibilities. They are good at setting out what can be done and especially how it can be done, based on a body of professional knowledge and skills, but they are not good at providing ways of sharing this knowledge and skills.

To sum up, the key issues are: that change based on classical management principles ignores the vital role to be played by individuals; it devalues or constrains leadership, motivation, and the influence of groups; it pays little heed to sharing responsibilities and the benefits of bringing to bear multiple perspectives and varying views on organizational development; vitally, if not fatally, it ignores the influence of the environment, in the sense that one of its primary purposes is to protect the organization from environmental shocks.

Alternatives to Classical Management

Classical management did not specifically consider the need for change. It did not entertain it as a necessary course of action. Viewing organizations as static entities, it embodied the view that change, if it was forced on an organization, was no different from any other exercise of management responsibility. In an organizational world based on certainties, it is perhaps no surprise that the conception and execution of change projects remained a management prerogative.

A major problem here is the failure to acknowledge the complexity of organizations. For example, all organizations possess informal structures based on a network of relationships and communication. Unseen, these networks represent a considerable organizational force, and one which is capable of exercising an influence on all organizations irrespective of their formal structures.

These relationships work across internal boundaries, and are capable of strengthening the unity of organizations. Brass et al (2004) provide an overview of the significance of networks, and Oh et al (2004) affirm the value of social relationships in terms of their role in creating social capital and therefore benefiting group and organizational effectiveness. Unfortunately, the informal networks are not, by definition, within the immediate compass of management. Another consideration is that they are of course focussed on the individual, rather than the machine. This kind of thinking led to the emergence of the human relations school.

Human Relations

The work of Elton Mayo (1949) is generally recognised as the starting point of the human relations school, which to a degree sees the bureaucracy as an obstacle to innovation. Human relations provides the antidote for concepts of formal authority which are regarded as inhibitive, bureaucratic communication channels which are too long and time-consuming, and internal organizational barriers which compartmentalise, stop the development of ideas and stunt thinking. Crucially, the human relations school offers an alternative to the slow-reacting bureaucracy.

Graham Buttrick (1997) referred to open and closed change projects. Closed change projects tend to be limited in their objectives, work on a narrow front and might be limited in their duration. They are also related to simple problem-solving. Rittel and Webber (1973), and Mackinnon (1978), explored the difference between various kinds of problems, and identified 'wicked problems'. These are akin to open change projects:

- They begin with imprecise objectives
- There is no immediate solution
- There may be only one opportunity to get things right
- It may not be possible to evaluate the solution except in the long-term.

A project to automate an information service is a closed change project based on a simple problem. A project to introduce digital/electronic information, or even e-books, into a library service is usually treated as a closed change project. It has clear objectives, a clear timescale, and it can be accurately costed. The results are measurable because of the way the objectives have been drawn up, which is to say that the services concerned will be slotted in to the existing organizational structure and conform to the rules currently in force. Within limits, the project will undoubtedly produce a successful result if a few simple project management rules area followed.

The difficulty is a cultural one. Inside a classical bureaucracy, change cannot be conceptualised in any other way. Most of our change projects, especially those which introduce ICT, have been framed in this way. They actually preserve the status quo, and often reinforce control systems. Change in information services is rapid, unpredictable and dislocational, unconnected with past practice. To look for guidance in change management from principles used to develop stable organizations designed to maintain their equilibrium and remove uncertainty, is unwise. Today's ICT-based change in particular affects all aspects of organizational life. If its impact is to be maximised, it has to be governed by ideas which will take advantage of all the skills, talents and opinions available. Change will have to be viewed as intrinsic, and the system will have to support creativity and entrepreneurism. None of these things can easily come about in an organization based on regularity, specialisation and standardisation.

Everything depends on how an organization fit for change is visualised, and this is looked at in more detail later. Here it will be sufficient to use a simple illustration of the difference between closed and open change. As indicated earlier, the introduction of digital information into libraries is almost invariably treated as a closed change project. Yet in practice it has implications for organizational structures, skills, roles and specialisations, organizational learning and development, and personal development. It is whole-organizational change, and its treatment as an open change project would produce quite startling results.

Approached as a problem-solving exercise, with the right questions asked, instead of a limited proposal to introduce a relatively uncomplicated service, the result would be the start of wide-ranging organization development. This would lead to a fitter organization, and one capable of proactively managing change through the more effective use of all the talents available to it.

Healthy organizations are based on the comprehensive exchange of good information, and the devolution of authority, among other characteristics (Neilson et al, 2005). Unfortunately, these characteristics are hard to create in a classically-defined environment. To make them come about, it is necessary to consider theories which emphasise individual roles, the capacity for decision-making, various forms of self-management, new patterns of communication, and the generation of new ideas which could come from maximising the impact of the various perspectives to be found in modern information services.

Elton Mayo's research at the Hawthorne plant of Western Electric in Chicago occurred during an eight-year period in the mid-1920s and early 1930s. Mayo joined the team in 1928, and his work yielded many ideas on the improvement of the working environment. This was not specifically in the context of change management, but by extension it had a particular relevance to motivation in times of change. It also presented alternative ideas about teams and leadership. By the 1960s, his work was being reappraised, and there have been a number of criticisms of his methodology and conclusions – not a topic for this chapter. For change management in general, Mayo and the Hawthorne experiments were important because they symbolised a break with the shibboleths of classical management, and an assertion of the role of the individual.

The human relations approach advocated the kind of organization which valued:

- The role to be played by social relationships
- The central position occupied by individuals
- The contention that the parts of the organization could interrelate with each other in ways which made it the antithesis of the machine
- A broader view of leadership
- The role of teamwork
- The ability of disparate elements to work together, foreshadowing late 20th Century ideas about creativity and abrasion in organizations.

This led, among other things, to an emphasis on flexible structures, intrinsic motivation and a change in the organizational climate. Some of these ideas are significant in the context of complex modern library organisations, although once again we need to beware: the human relations zealots were as certain that they had found the best way to manage as were the classical management school.

Developing the Human Relations Approach

Whatever criticisms were levelled at the work of Mayo (see, for example, Gillespie, 1991) the Hawthorne experiments led to a focus on issues which are particularly relevant to motivation in change management, and will be considered in detail in Chapter 9. The school of thought sometimes called ' neo-human relations' is represented by the work of Maslow (1943, 1968), Likert (1961), McGregor (1960) and Herzberg (1966). The literature here is a body of work which in sum, at least in this writer's interpretation, represents the view that the bureaucracy is inappropriate for change and innovation. The specific foundations of this argument are as previously stated: the inhibitive nature of authority, the length of the communication process, the compartmentalisation of thought and activity, and slowness in interpreting environmental changes and acting upon them.

The literature on this area also indicates a concern for the social and psychological implications of organizational life, and in general points to the need for an organization where structures, leadership, the use of power and the general approach to management recognise the potential of individuals. This moves the debate forward from a view of the organization as a machine to be controlled by management to a perspective which attached much significance to the ability of the individual to respond to alternative ways of managing. Another early member of this tendency was Argyris (1964), who stressed the concern for the psychological well-being of the individual and the need to weaken the superior-subordinate relationship in organizations.

Rensis Likert was one of a number of writers who developed the proposition that a healthy organizational culture was important, and the human resources school were by now beginning to sketch out what that culture might look like.

McGregor (op cit) also considered the idea of organizational culture, and what he saw as the need to reduce the inevitable hierarchical character of most organizations.

Although his own distinctive contribution was Theory Y, this was but one of a range of ideas he developed. They all stemmed from his concern for the role of the individual in organizations, and his belief in the relevance of organizational culture. McGregor attacked the harsh negativity of classical management theory, termed Theory X:

> The philosophy of management by direction and control, regardless of whether it is hard or soft, is inadequate to motivate because the human needs on which this approach relies are relatively unimportant motivations of behaviour in our society today. Direction and control are of limited value in motivating people whose important needs are social and egotistic.

Crucially, McGregor pinpointed the likely affect of the bureaucracy on the willingness of individuals to embrace change:

> People deprived of opportunities to satisfy at work the needs which are important to them, behave exactly as we might predict – with indulgence, passivity, unwillingness to accept responsibility, resistance to change, willingness to follow the demagogue.

This quotation has far-reaching implications for change management. Given the changes in library personnel described in Chapter 1 it is an even more telling criticism of the bureaucracy than it was over forty years ago, and it has implications for the kind of leadership which is likely to be effective in managing change in the 21st Century.

We are beginning here to see the strengthening of a movement away from the bureaucracy, however liberal and humane, and an assertion of the role of the individual. McGregor attached the label Theory Y to organizations based on these characteristics. Crucially, he felt that this theory could be applied to the professional bureaucracy.

It is instructive to look at the kind of organization libraries predominantly adopted at the time McGregor's ideas began to assume some prominence. Demone and Harshberger (1974) looked at what they called human service organizations, and identified some key characteristics:

- A strong service ethos
- An overall mission to alter behaviour
- Managed by professionals untrained in management
- Structures tending to be based on professional values
- Relative difficulty in measuring their output
- Use of technology
- Consensual ethos
- Good relationships between professionals and other groups in the organization
- Primary loyalty to the professional peer group rather than the organization
- Still hierarchical

● Dependent on clear linkages with the external environment in order to function properly.

This might almost be a description of the modern information service. During the same period other writers (Kinzes and Mico, 1979, for example) were also commenting on the overwhelming influence of the bureaucratic model on organizational theory. They criticised its use as an organizational form for human service organizations, which would include libraries.

Additionally, it can be criticised as a basis for organizational change. Control in these organizations was still imposed by the system, and the restrictive influence of this and the supporting hierarchy provides the most pointed criticism of classical management as a base theory for managing change. Theory Y saw control as emerging naturally from the combination of a number of features in the organizational culture, and in order to foster this, Kinzes and Mico (1979) argued for the development of loose-coupled systems and collegial models.

Theorists calling for more subtle forms of control could also find succour in the developing Japanese management systems. Ouchi (1981) described an organization in which control is rooted in shared objectives subscribed to by all, and stemming from the values of everyone involved in the organization, including the users of the service provided. Rather than specifying the detail of operations, activities and roles, this approach offers coordination and regulation based on a framework of values. Decisions can be taken in the context of the culture as a guiding influence, and courses of action can then be developed within the framework of cultural norms.

This idea may be seen at its most obvious in Ouchi and Price's clan theory (1978), which postulates a shared set of common values and objectives. Tied to beliefs about how to work together to achieve objectives, the clan replaces the hierarchy. Success depends on the total absorption of all members into the clan, and the problem – that everything is based on other features of the Japanese social and industrial system which cannot be reproduced – is obvious. Yet there are two strengths to the idea as far as change management is concerned:

● The force it attributes to organizational culture
● The significance of users.

The latter point was taken up by a ground-breaking study (Martell, 1983). In his argument for the client-centred library, Martell added a socio-cultural view of the organization – the library as an open system involved in interpreting and interacting with the larger system of which it is a part. This demolishes the classic bureaucratic structure, which admits to little interchange with the environment, and allows little capacity for change except in the most prescribed circumstances. The client-centred library is an open system, emphasising the significance of:

. . . groups operating on its boundary, or the points at which the library interacts with its user groups.

Martell's organization embraces:

- A highly developed communication system
- A structure of groups
- Decentralisation leading to a flat structure
- A powerful culture
- The force of organizational culture
- Distributed technology: by this Martell meant the systems which keep the library running, such as acquisitions, cataloguing and classification.

A coherent philosophy which could support change management in a way which classical management theory cannot is now beginning to emerge. Perhaps surprisingly in view of what has gone before, I would stress that it takes something from classical management. This is the emphasis on good administration and project management. But from the human relations school, it takes its other main characteristics:

- Organizational decentralisation
- Unity and control through cultural norms
- All-embracing communications systems
- The ability to interact with the environment
- People-centred organizations
- Client-centred organizations
- Values-based
- Strong motivational impulses
- A concern for the psychological implications of change
- Good administration.

The Common Thread: Gestalt Theory, Field Theory and Systems

The human relations approach reappraises the role of the individual in organizational change. It changes the circumstances in which people engage with change, from discharging clearly-delineated roles, to broader and more flexible participation. This also changes other requirements. Where people have to accept a circumscribed and limited set of responsibilities in general, or a strictly defined part in a change process, they tend not to be party to a wide spectrum of information about the change, nor do they inevitably enjoy a more general understanding of the nature of the change and the surrounding organizational circumstances. If their involvement becomes wider and less predictable, their information needs increase, as does the requirement of an awareness of the bigger picture of the organizational environment.

Kurt Lewin (1951) set out the need for this understanding of the organization in its environment. He argued that any single event was the result of multiple factors, and these were interdependent. An organization and its environment makes up a field. Events on the boundary of the field, as well as within the field, are crucial and linked factors. The internal events can be sparked off by individuals, groups, sociological, political, governmental, technological, economic or educational developments, and conflicts. The forces of change are therefore external and internal. Field theory states that phenomena should be examined in their entirety. Innovation is seen as the result of the action of a number of forces within the organization's systems, and calls for an understanding of the organization as a whole. Lewin also propounded some ideas of value in any consideration of the change process and models, and these are dealt with in Chapters 5 and 6.

Gestalt philosophy also offers something to our understanding of the theory behind change management. Wertheimer (1959), an early protagonist of the theory, had much to say about problem-solving. This technique is itself part of change management, and his problem-solving process is a good general guide to change management procedures. By developing a holistic view, Wertheimer argued that:

A new, deeper structural view of the situation develops . . . Directed by what is required by the structure of a situation for a crucial region, one is led to a reasonable prediction, which like the other parts of the structure, calls for verification, direct or indirect. Two directions are involved: getting a whole consistent picture, and seeing what the structure of the whole requires for the parts.

Gestalt theory advocates:

- Adopting a problem-solving approach to change
- Identifying the real issues beneath the surface
- Working to develop insights
- Establishing new ways of thinking about change, and about specific problems
- Treating change management as a learning process.

This approach is related to the question of open and closed change projects discussed earlier in this chapter. The project to introduce e-books into a library was treated as a closed project. A problem-solving approach would have turned it into an open project, and asked questions about what would be the best way to deliver digital information to users. It would have raised issues which were below the surface, for example to do with the hybrid nature of libraries and consequently the best way of organizing services. To make the proposed change productive would have required a broad environmental knowledge, an awareness of related issues, and the involvement of a larger group of staff than was needed merely to implement an e-books service. In the literature this process is sometimes called framing. Ellis (1938) provides more information on the roots of gestalt philosophy.

Systems theory is similar to both field theory and gestalt theory in that it views organizations as a series of sub-systems. Wertheimer (op cit) advocated taking a view of the system as a whole, while Lewin (op cit) argued that any disturbance in an environment would lead to a reaction aimed at restoring stability. This is a fairly accurate interpretation of what happens during change in a bureaucratic organization. Burnes (2004) provides a succinct and perceptive view of open systems theory, which supports the idea that organizational subsystems are all related to each other, and that change in any one part of the organization will trigger change in other subsystems. This is in line with Lewin's view of the action-reaction response to a disturbance (or change) in the organizational environment. It also accords with gestalt theory's proposition that insights into the whole organization are essential. All these ideas reinforce the need to take an organizational view of change, whether the change is an organizational redesign or projects which are apparently one-off. It also underlines the need for organizations to be equipped for environmental monitoring in ways which classically-designed structures probably are not.

The other contribution systems theory can make to change management is to do with the related, and perhaps even more intractable, one of structures. This is further investigated in Chapter 6, where networked organizations are considered as vehicles for change. Libraries can be broken down into subsystems (from Burnes, op cit):

- Technical subsystem: skills, processes and knowledge
- Values subsystem: the aims and objectives of the service
- Psycho-social subsystem: the culture
- Managerial subsystem: the things that managers do
- Structural subsystem: the organizational framework.

Obtaining a clear understanding of the subsystems – the parts of the organization which are not necessarily reflected in an organigram or organizational chart – will raise questions about the form an organization should take. Returning to our old friend the introduction of e-books, applying field theory, gestalt theory and systems theory to the change project would have called into play accumulated knowledge, experience and intuition residing in a number of staff spread throughout the organization. It would have shown up subtle connections, and would have identified implications for the structure, and for skills needs, as well as for the way power was exercised.

Bringing it all Together: Organization Development (OD)

This is an approach to change management which has possibly already seen its high water mark, according to some commentators, but still exerts an influence on this one. There is a succinct assessment of its continued significance, and a balanced view of its strengths and weaknesses, in Buchanan and Huczynski (2004).

OD has proved to be a particularly powerful force for cultural change in organizations, and it is often seen as an extension of the human resources approach outlined earlier, and of open systems theory. Some definitions of OD interpret it as being concerned with top-down change. Certainly, earlier advocates of the OD approach to change management sometimes saw it as strengthening the management grip on the ownership of change projects. It is also true that OD practitioners have advocated the prosecution of change through teams of 'change agents' inside an organization, but this does not reflect the OD approach to change management in its entirety. Cummings and Huse (1989) defined OD as

> . . . the systematic and long-term application of behavioural science knowledge and theory as a means of improving organisation effectiveness as measured by its ability to adapt its goals, structure, culture, style, etc *in response to change*. (this author's italics)

It begins with the proposal that individuals have a complex and sophisticated reaction to change; a reaction which can be modified and nurtured through providing information and through broad and influential involvement in the work of the organization. Because of the nature of this reaction, conventional bureaucracies are not considered to be the best organizational environments for managing change, and most OD interventions are concerned with diluting the bureaucracy in one way or another.

In general, OD possesses a number of features which present a positive approach to change management. It can be summed up as the application of a number of techniques designed to increase understanding of an organization and to help the organization achieve its objectives. It pays attention to the structure of the organization, its power bases, social and political systems, the technological make- up of the organization, and the human resource implications. Practitioners seek to apply a range of these techniques to the organization in order to facilitate the achievement of its objectives. Some of what it says, if not most of it, is obvious: it calls for:

- An understanding of the organization
- A comprehensive consideration of the implications of the change
- A particular concern for the implications of change for the individuals and groups in the organization
- The need for a plan
- Systematic implementation involving the process analysed in Chapter 4
- Whole-organization change
- A problem-solving approach.

Sirkin et al (2005) set out the need for a structured approach to change, supported by the provision of information, incentives to change and empowerment. Here we have a succinct and simplified summary of OD as a change tool. In general, later adherents to the OD approach place less emphasis on the top-down or management-owned approach to change, and stress the need for a broad involvement of personnel. Participative decision-making therefore becomes a key aspect of change management. This can only occur when information is shared, where there is an culture of openness and support, and where systems for identifying environmental change forces and the concomitant planning process are strong.

Much of OD was at one time carried out through the intervention of external consultants, but the approach has merit because of the value it places on the role of the individual and for the all-embracing organizational implications for organizational cultures, the emergence of flexible structures, HR policies, job design, and learning. This has led to the entirely reasonable view that OD should be viewed as a desirable set of techniques to deploy, irrespective of its relevance to change management. What it actually offers is a win-win situation. Organizational effectiveness, job satisfaction, morale, communications and general organizational health all improve.

OD is based on ideas deriving from the study of the psychology, the sociology and politics of individuals, groups and organisations. It develops, through group and inter-group dynamics as a means of change, to a view of change as a whole-organisation phenomenon. The importance of OD is that it takes these ideas, and what are in fact a list of characteristics of organisations which will be good at managing change, and fixes them in the context of unstable external environments and internal complexity: two of the characteristics which are most influential in today's information services. There is finally a set of theories which are specifically directed at managing change in modern organizations.

OD is particularly relevant to complex modern organisations, operating in unpredictable circumstances. It is concerned with identifying the characteristics which help organizations to manage change in a satisfactory way, and to deal successfully with the vicissitudes of change. It applies selected techniques to the task of organization development, and sets out to make the best possible use of everything available, especially the human resources. OD is aligned with theories which stress the value of individuals and their ability to learn, to take responsibility and to grow, so it also means creating Theory Y organisations.

By implication OD is also an open systems idea. It indicates that intervention in one subsystem or part of the organisation will affect all the other subsystems or parts, and it is based on changing the whole organisation and the way it operates.

OD works through applying a range of methodologies. One of these is the use of team structures for learning. Allied to this are the techniques of job enrichment and job enlargement, with related ideas of empowerment, skills acquisition and self-management. Therefore structural change, new attitudes to individual development and changes in management styles and the exercise of power can also be a part of OD, although it is of course much more than simply creating a flexible structure.

In some ways the concept involves a confluence of ideas developed in the 20th Century as the attention of management theorists began to move away from the emphasis on the organization as an efficient machine, and towards ideas which began to place the individual at the centre of an organization built on a series of linked subsystems. If it is a summation of ideas embraced by McGregor, Lewin, Wertheimer and others, it also looks forward to fashionable ideas of the late 20th century and the beginning of this one. This is seen in the way in which OD also places learning at the heart of organisational activities. The learning process is moved forward through individuals and through teams. It is work-based learning. Change, experimentation and, crucially, making mistakes are seen as learning experiences. What we are observing is a growing web of theories and attitudes, because things like learning and risk-free operations in a no-blame culture also have major implications for structures, management styles, and human resource policies.

For some people, a major element in the OD approach is the belief that it can be used to create an ideal organisational form. For this writer, one important attraction of it is that it appears to be an appropriate cocoon for a number of different approaches which could be crucial for managing the diversity which is now a part of information services. In that sense it is non-prescriptive and gives people the opportunity to create an organization which suits them rather than one which fits any particular theory.

It is therefore possible to describe OD but not to prescribe it as a universal remedy for libraries. In some parts of information services it could be argued that bureaucratic forms will still be the most appropriate, and, counter to the possible impression given in a later chapter, teams are certainly not a panacea in libraries, even when they are properly implemented.

Change in libraries is long-term, systematic and systemic. Sirkin et al (op cit) also argued that long-term projects stood a greater chance of success than short-term initiatives. OD offers a way of making change management a natural and enduring part of organisational life. Utilising the values system of OD, and using features like job design and a recognition of the centrality of learning, it can produce a whole range of organisations which might have a lot in common but can still reflect different responses to change forces. So the results of OD should produce a number of different organisational forms. Its simplest practical implications are seen in team development, flatter structures, new leadership styles, new middle management roles and in putting flesh on assumptions about the human behaviour and values referred to above.

Implementing organisation development involves using a number of approaches to alter the behaviour of managers and managed. All of these approaches can be seen as increasing employee participation, sharing decision-making and widening involvement in the control and direction-setting activities of the organisation. Each of the proposals represents substantial and complex long-term development. Taken on their separate merits they do not amount to OD. They become part of OD when they are seen as elements in a coherent and integrated plan. Organization development itself is the most sophisticated form of change management because it sets out to create an organization with the power to innovate. Chapter 1 made much of the difference between change and innovation: while it may not state it implicitly, OD's overall aim is to create a constantly-evolving organization through systematic and comprehensive redesign. In other words, innovation is harnessed in the interests of long term change.

OD is about changing attitudes. It is about refocussing people's perceptions of the organization they work in. It is also about improving communication and interaction through new structures and through harnessing the informal patterns which underpin structures. As this is done, the capability to innovate grows as the organization becomes more adept at making the best of all the talents available to it. Buchanan and Huczynski (op cit) give an account of the range of techniques which can be applied in OD initiatives. The impact of the techniques is felt in:

- Structural change
- Team development
- Improvements in the technology of management – decision-making, the deployment of power, environmental scanning, problem diagnosis, analysis, communication and the flow and accessibility of information, feedback
- Improvements in people management
- The development of individuals
- General improvement in the organization's subsystems, particularly learning.

In some ways, OD can be seen as the fulcrum of change theories. It takes much from the earlier ideas discussed in this chapter, but two key factors in its successful prosecution are first the idea of organizational learning, and second the idea that OD supports a multiplicity of organizational forms. It looks forward to theories about learning and knowledge in organizations, and it refines and develops the idea that the organizational environment defines the techniques to be used and the character of the organization which will emerge. In this, it underscores the significance of contingency theories and more recent developments.

Knowledge-Based Theories

Learning is one of the major components of organizational development, and later theories refine and strengthen the application of individual, group and organizational learning in change management.

Widely supported during the 1990s, when some influential work was done by Pearn and Mulrooney (1995) and Pearn, Roderick and Mulrooney (1995), the idea of 'the learning organization' actually has its origins in the neo-human relations school described in this chapter.

The Learning Organization

Argyris (1964) laid the basis for this idea. Learning in this context refers to the ability of organizations to change and to improve their performance. To achieve this state requires certain characteristics on the part of individuals, groups and the whole organization. These themes run throughout the works of Argyris, and his collaborative work with Andrew Schön. The argument is that people working in organizations behave in a defensive way based on a desire to retain control. While this can minimise threats to the individual and the organization, the negative aspect of this behaviour is that organizations also become negative and defensive. This attitude creates a barrier to learning, and by extension to effective change and innovation. This can be changed, and people can be encouraged to think differently, and to learn, if organizations develop certain characteristics. These are:

- Open communication systems
- Empowerment
- Collaboration
- Honesty and realism in the affairs of the organization, including the ability to learn from mistakes in a culture which permits this to happen.

To achieve this state of affairs calls therefore for actions on the part of individuals, groups, and the organization in general:

- A culture of sharing must be nurtured.
- Communication between managers and managed must be more extensive, must be open and must include feedback – it is a two-way process. Ideas should also be shared.
- Structures should permit shared experiences across organizational boundaries.
- People should be encouraged to question and to challenge accepted practice and thinking.
- The environment should be blame-free and supportive.
- Creative thinking and team learning are fundamental.

To realize the learning organization means innovation in strategy, structures, motivation and management and leadership styles. The basis of the theory is the acquisition and application of knowledge, which is acquired in a particular way. G. E. Bateson (1999) developed the concept of double loop learning.

Double Loop Learning
This concept lies at the heart of the learning organization. It describes the form of learning which underpins many of the characteristics listed above. It involves scrutinising the way in which things are done currently, and questioning the accepted wisdom. It is challenging the organization, and fostering originality, risk-taking and a multidimensional view of problem-solving and development. It leads to large-scale organizational change.

Knowledge Management

The idea of embedding learning in an organization as a means of ensuring innovation and projecting an inbuilt capacity to deal with continuous change as a permanent condition, depends on many connected features. A key aspect is the way in which information is used. This chapter has described an organization which depends on the acquisition of work-based learning and personal development. It is also an organization which is decentralised, and tries to devolve decision-making to the lowest level in the organization. The rest of this book describes other characteristics of organizations which manage change well, such as the ability to identify environmental changes which stimulate change and innovation, and the need for effective teams, powerful motivation and novel management styles. All these are all reliant on an information system.

Knowledge management can mean all things to all men. In the context of change management the thesis is that its prime value is in managing information so that the activities described in the coming chapters can flourish. So this book takes a view of knowledge management as a philosophy which is concerned with:

- Identifying, collecting, organising and making available information.

This is not immediately to do with the role and influence of librarians as such, although this comes into it. Libraries are obviously part of a process which takes raw date and gradually turns it into information which is organized and retrievable. The crucial step which converts this into verifiable and usable knowledge is something which is done by others. Librarians may well claim a more dynamic role in this transformation than is strictly justified by their input, vital though it may be, in making this information accessible to other professionals and experts who add something of their own expertise to the process. In this sense, they are knowledge managers.

In the context of innovation, knowledge management provides the system which allows an organization to protect and develop its intellectual capital, and supports individuals and groups as they learn to handle empowerment, take decisions, develop their capabilities and play a full part in organizational life. Implementing knowledge management means that organizations must be based on certain principles.

Openness and the Power Structure
It was suggested earlier that our organizations tend to be based on specialisation, and specialisation depends partly on retaining control of a body of knowledge. This exclusivity is seen in several ways, and if an organization is to become truly innovative it has to redefine its view of authority. This is the same as saying that *managers* have to redefine their view of authority. They can do this in several ways: by adopting a consensual and consultative approach to managing; by implementing structural change – decentralisation; by taking a broader view of motivation; perhaps

most far-reaching, by creating an open communications system, because all power is based on information, and particularly on the retention of ownership of information by management.

Information systems are a structural feature. It is enough here to say two things: that change management calls for a comprehensive information system which protects only that minimum of information which should remain confidential for personnel reasons; and implementing this open information exchange is a cultural change, moving from a closed organization to an open one.

This is a revolutionary view of communication in many organizations, but it can be justified. The most valuable knowledge in an organization is often carried round in the heads of individuals, often in the form of lessons learned from work which can be easily lost to the organization. Even if captured and systematised, the information is only of value if it is disseminated. Once this is done, it improves every aspect of the organization, including not least the performance of individuals. To disseminate information, people must learn not only what to share, but how to communicate it. Much of the information in contemporary libraries is, if not actually jargon, part of a specialised argot belonging to the technological experts. We need to discard this attitude in the interests of open communication.

Learning Systems
Even if people are conditioned to share information, and if the organization facilitates it, there is still much to learn about how to share, and what indeed should be shared. Once these skills are mastered then more information is created and turned into knowledge.

The learning system should facilitate how to learn, what to learn, and how to transfer skills and knowledge across the organization. This again has implications for management styles and motivation. The aim should be to create an information system in which data flows around the organisation. By doing so, resource and user needs, development proposals and solutions to problems are enriched by the addition of perspectives and knowledge not only from senior management but from others. In turn the learning process is strengthened and finally, all the layers and groups in the organisation gradually acquire the knowledge base which allows an informed input into policy and strategy while still enabling managers to manage. This is how the sharing culture of a learning organisation is laid down.

A number of other theories with a loose connection with learning organizations have emerged in the literature. Open Book Management, for example, can be seen as an extension of the idea of sharing, advocating the development of a partnership between managers and managed. The theory also places some significance on the transparency suggested earlier, with widespread access to information, including strategic and policy-making information.

Long before the emergence of learning organizations and knowledge management, Burns and Stalker (1994) proposed that there was a crucial link between the environment and the internal arrangements of the organization. More recently, Child (2004) re-emphasised the requirement for new organizational forms which would improve efficiency, make life better for the staff and for those the organization serves, and provide fulfilling experiences. These writers saw the need for structures to change in response to environmental change, and Handy (1981) also emphasised the link between the organization and the environment.

It is argued that organisations which cope best with change reflect a high degree of internal differentiation, in that they are permissive enough to allow different areas to operate with different structures and different rules, while still maintaining overall integration. This view is supported by Chaos Theory, which states that organisations naturally work in a state of uncertainty which is so unpredictable that organizations should accept it as the natural state. To deal with this uncertainty calls for the maximisation of all available resources. The key points about chaos theory are that it affirms the need for environmental sensitivity, and that uncertainty represents opportunities. Modern information services, with a much greater degree of differentiation, complexity and heterogeneity than ever before, provide an excellent seed bed for change management.

All of the theories say something about the need for new ideas. This is why information sharing and broadening the contribution of individuals are important developments – because they create the circumstances in which new ideas can emerge. Uncertainty also fosters creativity, and the idea of organizational creativity is the final piece of the theoretical jigsaw.

Organizational Creativity

This concept has a long pedigree. It has been written about and talked about for over 50 years, and is seen as particularly relevant for creative industries and knowledge workers. Organizational creativity can be defined as

> . . . the development of a new kind of thinking, which is applied to solving problems, and generally dealing with working situations that are new, and perhaps not susceptible to conventional ways of thinking. Essentially, it depends on people learning and thinking, and applying the results where they work. (Pugh, 2003)

It has been memorably described as what happens in an organization when 'know-what and know-why become know-how'.

There is of course much more to it than that. It is a part of knowledge management and a characteristic of learning organizations in that it is to do with the creation and exploitation of new knowledge. It leads us once more to consider role change, structural change, and teams: it is therefore central to the theory of change and innovation.

Howard Gruber, whose lifetime study of creativity ranged from Charles Darwin to

Piaget, wrote his major study of creativity in 1974. He eventually used the term 'pluralism' to describe the collaboration, interplay between individuals, the structure of relationships between the collaborators, the problem-solving and the multiple projects which cross-fertilised each other and which amounted to creativity. To Gruber, it was the networks which were vital to creativity.

Another relevant aspect of Gruber's work is his view of the process of creativity. Other writers have also commented on the fact that there are no flashes of insight into problem-solving or innovative development. What appears to be intuition is in fact a long process of collection of data, exchange of views, analysis and the gradual elimination of alternatives until a preferred course of action or solution is left. There is much in this to illuminate our view of the process of innovation.

While creativity may date back to the middle of the last century, it may be Dorothy Leonard Barton (1999) who first coined the phrase 'creative abrasion' to describe the results of a particular development process in organizations. It explores the emergence of new thinking and new ideas through the introduction into an organization of varied and sometimes discordant views. Multiple perspectives in decision-making and development, for example, make the processes of innovation, problem-solving or functional changes more comprehensive and inclusive. The friction or abrasion which can arise from differences, and also from outright conflict, can be positive and lead to new ways of doing things. Properly handled, these forces can also lead to true collaboration. Hargreaves (2003) described educational innovation in similar terms:

> An innovative school has to create and sustain a culture of innovation. A school contains several communities of practice, such as subject departments or pastoral teams, in which often there is already a fund of social capital. Innovation opens the way to the foundation of new communities of practice that spring from a cross-disciplinary or mixed team formed to innovate in a novel area. Such teams, which pool different kinds of intellectual capital, are more likely to question taken for granted routines and to support knowledge creation needed for radical innovation. But the membership of non-natural groups needs judicious selection: only cleverly constructed combinations yield the brightest ideas through 'creative abrasion'.

Another way of looking at creativity and creative abrasion is that of Leonard and Sensiper (1998). To them, creativity comes from the social interaction which leads to the abrasion which in turn supports creativity. The process produces energy which sparks off new ideas.

What Makes for Organizational Creativity?

Contemporary information services offer the prospect of a fertile breeding ground for creative abrasion. For the first time in their history, they are bringing together staff from separate disciplines and people from outside the profession of librarianship.

Organizations are now homes to traditional librarians, information technologists, media specialists and a new breed of digital information experts working in new specialisations. The mix of attitudes, proclivities, traditions, skills, education and training, priorities and ways of working presents the ideal opportunity for harnessing creative abrasion.

Florida and Goodright (2005) set out some of the basic conditions necessary if organizations are to foster creativity:

- Jobs which challenge people
- An internal environment which is supportive
- Egalitarianism – creativity is a whole-organization function, with all staff capable of being creative.

What emerges from the literature on this issue is that heterogeneity in an organization is good for creativity, while homogeneity obviously reduces conflict. As conflict can be a positive feature of organizational life in the right circumstances, I would support heterogeneity. What is finally required to make creativity work is a set of guiding precepts.

The Principles of Innovation

There is no such thing as a template for change, but the burden of this chapter has been to set out some underlying ideas which will offer a range of possibilities for innovation. Essentially, it is a set of principles on which to base an innovative organization – equipped to work on long-term development but also good at short - term change projects. These principles could be summed up as:

- Environmentally sensitive organizations
- An open and on-going commitment to change as a whole-organization process
- An understanding that change involves a social process
- Creating common values and shared objectives
- An open systems approach
- Decentralisation
- Administrative competence in the area of project management and business planning
- Reliance on learning as a fundamental building block for change
- Questioning the status quo should be axiomatic
- Information, knowledge and learning systematically managed as open systems
- Organization design for creativity and creative abrasion.

Putting these principles into practice takes us back to organization development, and building an organization with these virtues involves major cultural change.

Chapter 3

Strategies

Setting a strategy, or strategic planning, has been described in the literature (see, for example, Bryson and Alston, 2004) as a process by which an organization arrives at decisions which will set its objectives, and generally determine how those objectives will be achieved. In an environment which is characterised by uncertainty, change and unpredictability there is an emphasis on flexibility and responsiveness. Strategy-formers must be capable of interpreting this environment and building a strategy which will contain threats, and ideally capitalise on change opportunities. Strategic planning also considers resource implications and time constraints, so it is at bottom a process which arrives at key decisions concerning the organizational future. The emphasis is on developing the innate capability to embrace and use change:

> It is one thing to instigate . . . changes; it is quite another to weave them into the well-worn corporate fabric and the DNA of its workforce. Indeed, few goals are more challenging to achieve than significant, lasting change in adult human beings. (Gardner, 2004)

There is a danger that the strategy of change management can be considered as a separate entity in itself. Although it may appear to be an unrelated point, in other places in this text there is some discussion of whether or not bureaucracies are effective structures for prosecuting change. The way an organization approaches strategy is partly dictated by its structure, which is a reflection of the managerial view on many things. In an uncertain environment, strategy benefits from a wide range of inputs and perspectives, and so structural change as such becomes an important element in a change strategy, because without it the broad perspective will be harder to achieve.

Gardner's words above, taken from a text which contains his analysis of strategic change engineered by BP over a period of years, serve as a good starting point because they indicate some vital considerations. What he was referring to is the capacity of an organization to embed a willingness to change in its culture. The first step in creating this capacity to change is to take the strategy-forming process away from its bureaucratic roots. This applies as much to the content of strategy as it does to the manner of its creation.

Most strategic plans by nature include many references to change projects. Change management, to paraphrase Gardner, tackles the problem of making permanent change a part of the organizational life force – something which is a mindset and is woven into the fabric as an inseparable and essential part of organizational existence. Achieving this requires some trimming in the process of creating strategy.

There is always a tendency to regard new projects and alterations to existing services as self-contained. Systems thinking is not an instinctive habit. Chapter 2 attempted to distinguish between managing broad-based organic change and managing short-term, finite, measurable, controllable and discrete change. The first thing strategy has to do is openly acknowledge that everything is part of a much bigger picture, and it is a picture which also reflects important organizational conditions, not least:

- Diversity and unpredictability
- The implications of the mixed economy
- Complexity
- Competition
- Collaboration.

All of these are features which point to the need to view change on a much higher plane than mere projects. The process of digitisation is the example par excellence of a string of virtuous initiatives, amenable to standard project management techniques, and producing some technically brilliant results. This is perhaps not surprising, but it is no longer adequate on its own, even where performance improvement is concerned:

> Important performance improvement trends are usually the result of a free play of related ideas that lay the right kind of social and intellectual groundwork . . . For example, reengineering's associations with other trends like socio-technical systems, process design and personal computing helped build its momentum as well. (Wilson and Harris, 2004)

Innovation is about introducing new features into an organization. Change management is about developing the big picture, and of seeing the connections. Strategy therefore begins long before a group of people sit down and start to write a strategic plan. The strategy of change management demands some thinking which makes connections, and takes into consideration the other factors in organizational life. It means creating the 'social and intellectual groundwork' in which ideas can flourish, and development can take place. This is an essential idea and it is connected with a characteristic of change management which differentiates it from project management and to a lesser extent the management of innovation. The social and intellectual groundwork is to do with people, and change management is about helping the people involved in change above all else. This point underlines the need to take an organization-wide view of the relationship between strategy and features like structures and communication.

There is a symbiosis between the nature of strategy, the question of change versus innovation, and the choice between the two. There is a similar interplay between strategic planning and structures, communication, management styles, attitudes to learning, rewards and career development, and this list does not include everything. Strategic planning in conventional, hierarchical bureaucracies, for solid practical reasons, inclines towards the identification of manageable, time-bound projects of the sort described earlier. In short, it will favour innovative projects rather than change management. It will demonstrate a tendency towards short-termism. It is a common misconception to assume similarities between project management and change management, but:

> Project management is comprised of five Project Management Process Groups – Initiating Processes, Planning Processes, Executing Processes, Monitoring and Controlling Processes, and Closing Processes – as well as nine Knowledge Areas. These nine Knowledge Areas center on management expertise in Project Integration Management, Project Scope Management, Project Time Management, Project Cost Management, Project Quality Management, Project Human Resources Management, Project Communications Management, Project Risk Management and Project Procurement Management. (PMI, 2001)

The heart of this definition is to do with techniques, and it could be argued that conventional strategy formulation suffers because it emphasises techniques and the process, and fails to attach sufficient weight to the areas of communication and human resource management. Here lies the essential challenge of change management, and it is a challenge which has to be explicit in the strategy.

These observations are equally relevant when the underrated other half of strategy is considered: its execution. Returning to the issue of bureaucracies, rigidly-constructed organizations do not find it easy to deliver change management because of the checks the system imposes on communication, on thinking and on developing a broad view of issues. This is why there has been so much tinkering with organizational forms in ways which tend to improve the capacity of the organization to innovate, but perhaps not to manage change.

As a result, organizations tend to work with the greater certainties of projects with clear boundaries. In contrast, executing a change management strategy is to do with uncertainty, and it depends on the creation of organizational characteristics which thrive on this, and which might be sometimes be missing. This is to underline several points.

Embedding Change in the Strategy

The first is the obvious one that there cannot really be a strategy of change unless change is embedded in the strategic planning of the organization, so that the connections can be made, and the intent is clear. This is to develop an all-embracing capacity to adapt as a normal feature of organizational life, rather than undertake a series of project management exercises. I am almost tempted to use the inelegant and over-used label of 'joined-up strategic thinking' but will do my best to resist it.

Broadening the Inputs

Next, however consultative the process, strategy formulation should not really be the province of a group of people sitting down in a room to craft a document. This is true of strategic plans in general, and it is even more pertinent to change management. Returning for a moment to the point made about creating the social and intellectual framework, it is an advantage if this is reflected in strategies, through actually involving the people who will run the change and be affected by it in one way or another. To succeed in managing change, an organization must possess the ability to encourage a broad spectrum of inputs into strategy.

The Content of a Change Management Strategy

To sum up, from a strategic point of view, change management demands a distinctive treatment. Strategic plans should not only refer to change, they should deal specifically with change management and reflect an all-embracing organizational approach to change. Without this context, strategic plans can amount to nothing more than a series of business plans and the outlines of specific projects for one-, two- or three- year periods. They may embrace an impeccable statement of the mission of the library, and set the premises on which the strategic plan will be based: hybridisation, preservation and accessibility, collaboration, the characteristics of the immediate organizational environment and the impact of the wider world are the usual culprits today. The core functions, for example of managing the collections, preservation and serving the needs of users, will be identified and specific projects will be attached to these. Sometimes, there are subsidiary functions. In one plan, which will remain anonymous, the staff and administrative structure, information and communications technology, partnerships and collaboration, and buildings were labelled as subsidiary.

Without focussing on change, these elements are not enough. Gardner's view, quoted at the beginning of this chapter, would lead to an acknowledgement that in fact these supporting functions are some of the keys to effective change management, and have a wide-ranging impact on the organization. The first step in setting a strategy is therefore to ensure that:

● Change management is a central component in any strategic plan, and other considerations dovetail with it.

The second prerequisite is that any strategy should reflect Gardner's other concern. That is that the important changes in organizations are not to do with concrete, specific, short-term projects, although these clearly promote innovation. They are to do with attitude change, new ways of thinking, an openness to new ideas and learning and development. Creating a change strategy is about taking risks, and generally developing a culture which is conducive to novel approaches and imaginative solutions to problems. These are the things which Gardner was perhaps referring to

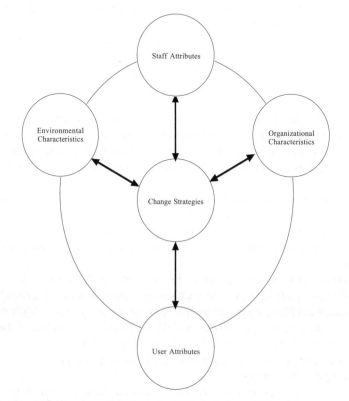

Figure 3.1 The Influences on Strategy and Their Interrelationships

when he talked about the 'significant, lasting change in adult human beings.' We can sum this up by saying that:

● Change management requires a strategy which deals with behaviour and attitude, and does not necessarily concentrate on things which are immediately measurable.

Change strategies also need to recognise a number of other things. The key elements are people, the organizational characteristics, the environment and delivery – the way the services are made available to users. To relegate any of these factors to the category of supplementary functions is to take a bureaucratic view of change. This supports the contention that many organizations are not involved in change management although they demonstrate successful innovation.

What Influences Strategy?

Figure 3.1 sets out the factors which should influence a change strategy. The characteristics of the organization – for example in terms of its structure, management style, leadership, decision-making and attitude to learning and development, will impinge on the way strategy is created. User attitudes are an increasingly powerful factor, given the increasing independence of users referred to in Chapter 1. It is obvious that the environment is a key element, as are the capabilities of the staff, so:

● Strategy should be based on the interrelationships between organizational characteristics and the organizational environment. These characteristics will include the abilities and talents of the staff and their developmental needs, the predilections of the users and the nature of the environment.

The advantage of using the management of change as the central plank of an organizational strategy is self-evident. The grand project of changing the organization rather than introducing novel elements piecemeal receives the official imprimatur. It is seen to be championed by management, and it is an early step in changing the culture.

Placing change at the heart of the process changes the focus of the organization and stimulates more sensitive and imaginative strategic thinking in general. Tushman and Anderson (2004) comment on the need for organizations to 'shift the strategy focus' because of changes in the 'underlying foundation', including the speed of change in knowledge creation and the impact of globalisation. Libraries can shift the emphasis in their own strategic planning by building the process around organic, whole-organization change.

Perhaps more important in a general sense is that the strategic management of any organization needs to proactively focus on the things which affect its survival and organizational health. The case study in Chapter 2 was an illustration of what can go wrong when misjudgements create situations which bode ill for the future of the organization. Change management is about the organizational future and well-being, so putting it at the heart of organizational strategy will strengthen strategic management overall.

At another level, change should influence all the key characteristics of the organization, and have a direct bearing on important characteristics like flexibility and adaptability. The basic reasons why organizations fail are that they are not flexible enough, not good enough at strategic change management, nor sufficiently adaptable to meet unforeseen challenges. This reduced ability to resist or, at worst, accommodate, negative external forces can be disastrous, and is at bottom a serious

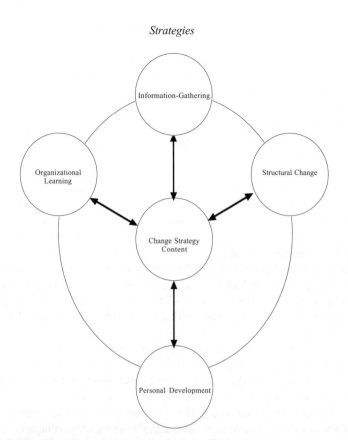

Figure 3.2 The Key Components of a Change Strategy

failure in strategic planning.

Change management is a strategic issue with a place as the key element in strategic planning at organizational level. It can be nothing else, as change itself is strategic, and as Tidd, Bessant and Pavitt said (1999), a core process of the organization. Although they use the term innovation, they quickly assert that they mean change, and view it as 'a generic activity associated with survival and growth'. Its place in strategic planning should therefore be assured.

What to Expect From A Change Strategy

Content

It follows from these strictures that a number of features characterise a genuine strategy for change. Putting change at the centre of the strategic planning process legitimises it, and fixes it as the nucleus of organizational thinking. The issue of change management then has a much greater chance of being seen to be championed by senior management, and this sends a message to the others.

In today's climate it should be a truism to say that all organizations have to change. The mission statement in the strategic plan should therefore indicate that:

- Organization development is a central, core activity
- Gathering information from the internal and external environment will form an important part of this.

This sets out in general terms exactly what the library wishes to achieve. It is an organizational state which will enable it to adapt and grow. While doing so it will make the best use of all the talents available to it, and harness these to the task of continuing to meet users' needs and provide them with the information they want in the form which suits them best.

A series of subsidiary issues can then be developed. The first of these will be structural change, whether this amounts to the modification of existing structures or a major exercise in rethinking the nature of the organization. So there is a strategic choice between trimming and putting in place the building blocks for a different way of delivering services.

There should also be a recognition of the centrality of learning and development, and the concomitant issues of communication and knowledge management, for these are strategic. Finally, a set of projects or action plans to develop the above themes, and ensure they fit with the mission statement, could be expected.

A reordering of priorities is reflected in this approach. Instead of setting out the core functions, the core processes of renewal and learning are established. A series of projects can then be framed to implement the process changes.

Framing the strategy in these terms has another advantage. From the way in which it is put together, it will have a degree of flexibility which will enable it to accommodate the unexpected developments which will surely occur. This is what Mintzberg (1994) called an 'emergent strategy.' It would not be change management if a strategy tied the library to an inflexible course of action and did not have an inbuilt capacity for adaptation. This is set out in Figure 3.2.

Inclusivity

The classical approach to strategy sees it as a top-down process, often involving what is fashionably called 'blue-skies' or 'clean-sheet' thinking. In practice it is a considerably less logical, even messy, procedure. A strategy for managing change should be inclusive in its creation, and this means that the information-gathering process should be inclusive. The breadth of the consultation and involvement is itself a change project. The literature of management does now refer to the slow erosion of the tendency of organizations to implement change through top-down, centralised, and carefully-prescribed programmes demanding predictable behaviour. This approach is being replaced by decentralised activities involving a wide range of participants, and the tendency will lead to the kind of reappraisal of organizational behaviour which should form part of strategic change management. This is not a neat and orderly task.

With change management embedded in the strategic thinking of the organization, and a series of projects identified as the means of *delivering* strategic change, rather than forming the heart of it, the second part of strategy is implementation.

The first thing to be said is that this is the area of strategy which can sometimes place almost as big an onus on the strategy-creators than devising the strategy in the first place. There is often a half-formed feeling that when the strategy is articulated the job is finished, and implementation will be taken care of by the system. This may well work for specific projects, but we are approaching change as something which pervades the whole organization, and is to do with changing minds. Implementing a change strategy across an organization means constructing an overview which embraces most facets of organizational life. If there really is a growing trend towards decentralisation, empowerment, devolved management and self-managing teams, as suggested earlier, these features will also make it necessary for those responsible for strategy to change the way they gather and organize information about how change is progressing.

Mankins and Steele (2005a) reported on a survey of commercial organizations which indicated that companies deliver no more than two-thirds of the potential benefits of their strategies. They go on to say that:

> More importantly, the causes of this 'strategy-to-performance gap' are all but invisible to top management. Not surprisingly, then, leaders often pull the wrong levers in their attempts to turn performance around – they press for better execution when what's really needed is a better strategy, or they opt to change direction when they really need to focus the organization more sharply on execution.

There is no reason to believe that public sector organizations are any different, nor that change strategies are any different, in this respect, from organizational strategies in general.

The kernel of the implementation problem is that strategy is a longer-term issue, yet it needs continuous monitoring. Skinner (2004) suggests that evaluation, as part of the change process, is rarely systematic. Instead it tends to be informal and personal. Where there is a series of separate projects which in total amount to organic change, there is a corresponding requirement for whole-organization monitoring which is actually difficult to achieve. Mankins and Steele (2005a) also offer their solution. Improvements in execution can come from the strategy formulation itself:

- Ensure that the change strategy is simply expressed and has tangible objectives.
- Do not spend a great deal of time on noble but abstract goals expressed in high-flown language.

- Establish unambiguous priorities. To this I would add that priorities, and also resources, should include skills requirements, learning and the implementation of a system to support participation.
- Attempt to answer a simple question, and indicate clearly what is to be changed.
- Attend to motivation – for this also is a strategic issue.

The same rigour should be applied to the transformation of ideas into reality:

- Continuous, formal monitoring is essential.
- Managers must change their minds in order to permanently change their behaviours. Mankin and Steele's identification of the managers' lack of knowledge of how much progress is being made on the ground implies greater involvement, which depends on role change and structural change.

Installing change management as a central feature of strategy formulation, and hence as an integral part of strategic thinking, is a vital first step. Alongside this, accepting the difference between innovation and change, and between change management and project management, is also important. Many writers, including most notably Mintzberg (op cit 1994), have offered a critical perspective on strategic management in the present organizational climate. Strategic management is seen as a rational process based on the assumption that it is possible to chart with reasonable accuracy the course an organization will take over a period of time. This may no longer be strictly accurate in a rapidly-changing environment. If inclusivity, involvement, constant reappraisal throughout the whole organization, and open-mindedness are also built into the process, there will be a better chance of planning for uncertainty. This leaves us with one final point:

- They should not be set in stone. There is nothing sacred about a strategic plan for change, and assuming that it will follow a pattern is unwise. Change management does not fit with the conventional strategic planning cycle.

Placing change at the centre of strategic planning should strengthen the growth of an organization-wide approach to change. Hammer (2005) called this 'operational innovation' and confirmed the high degree of difficulty, and the risk of failure, which lies in wait for those who attempt the practical task of changing or improving an organizational process. He uses the example of a failing organization whose first attempts at regeneration did not work, by their own analysis because their perspective was initially too narrow. Aware of the danger that broad conceptions of change can often result in the ideas remaining on the drawing board as a series of reports, investigations or recommendations that are never fully followed up, he advocates the use of an organizational framework:

The finest idea will not get implemented unless there is an organizational framework for shepherding it from concept to reality. (Hammer, 2005)

This takes the discussion forward another step, and leads into implementation strategies.

Implementation Strategies

... in the end, its about executing with excellence. But you can exhort all you want about excellent execution; you're not going to get it unless you have disciplined strategic choices, a structure that supports strategy, systems that enable large organizations to work and execute together, a winning culture, and leadership that's inspirational. If you have all that, you'll get excellent execution. (Gupta and Wendler, 2005)

We are still left with the question of how to actually move from the strategic plan to the implementation of a change programme. Implementation strategies in general fall into one of three types. The choice between strategies will again depend on how an organization is configured.

Implementation strategies, or operational strategies, are affected by the way in which power is exercised. The literature reflects a bewildering array of strategies along a continuum from authoritarian to various degrees of permissiveness. Pugh (2005) concentrated on legitimate power, expert power, and influential power as three key manifestations.

Legitimate power tends to be found in organizations which depend on rules and formal structures, and Weber (1947) saw this type as a rational and traditional approach to the exercise of power. Change strategies in organizations with these characteristics would be formulated at the top of the organization, and implemented as a top-down process.

Expert power is what it says it is. Using it places the responsibility for strategy implementation in the hands of the relevant experts, and hopefully there will be an element of this in all change implementation. But this execution can also be top- down, and carries the danger of putting implementation in the hands of an exclusive group.

Influential power, according to Pugh (op cit 2005), is the kind of power most appropriate to modern library organizations. It is a form of power which depends on collaboration and communication, and it involves a multiple exchange between leaders (or perhaps managers) and followers in a network of reciprocal relationships which do not depend on formal rules, nor reflect hierarchical position.

The Contingency Approach

Flexibility in implementing a strategy is an important consideration. There are periods in a change programme when legitimate power can arguably be used to resolve a crisis, and it can be a last resort in dealing with conflict and resistance. This is also one place where it is not necessary to look for links with organizational structures. It is perfectly possible for traditional organizations with rigid structures to implement change based on influential power, and to follow a strategy accordingly: possible, but perhaps unlikely.

Although there are many approaches to implementation set out in the literature, most of them fall into one of two groups: educative or power-coercive. The decision on how to proceed with implementation is informed by a number of issues.

This chapter set out to consider how to 'weave change into the well-worn corporate fabric' (Gardner, op cit). The intention was to offer a mechanism for embedding change in an organization, and in the psyche of the people who work in the organization. Much has also been made of the need to change minds, and to make this permanent as well. If people are to be encouraged to think differently they need to be presented with situations outside their experience, and they must be challenged and extended. They also need to be exposed to different perspectives, and to consider alternatives which might come from the wider world outside their own organizations. Finally, they have to be given the chance of testing their new ideas.

Involvement in the implementation of a change project, and sharing and collaborating in a search for valid alternatives to current practice, or for realistic and effective solutions to problems, is part of a process of development. Therefore strategies should have a clear learning component. That they do not always do this, with consequences for the staff and the organization, is demonstrated by Case Study 2. Only if there are overwhelming operational reasons, such as a potentially fatal crisis in implementation, is there any reason for not selecting a strategy on these premises. Implementation strategies need to support the ultimate organizational objectives: to:

● Introduce successful change
● Foster organization development
● Embed the capacity for long-term change
● Encourage the development of multiple perspectives
● Develop a sharing and collaborative environment
● Support individual development and learning
● Strengthen the knowledge base of the organization
● Develop a sharing and collaborative environment
● Provide experience in decision-making and the assumption of responsibility.

The change process is educative in itself, and is the best opportunity for staff development that an organization can provide. The implementation strategy must make it easier for this to be accomplished. The following categories, reflecting these needs, owe much to the work of Bennis et al (1985).

Educative/Empirical-Rational Strategies

There are a group of strategies which at the very worst assume that people are more or less rational for at least some of the time. They assume that giving people the information to arrive at judgements together, and allowing them the shared responsibility for proposing courses of action and evaluating the results, will actually produce reasonable policies and logical change implementation. They will also make a massive contribution to the development of the individuals concerned and also to the health of the organization.

Educative strategies emphasise the need to view change as something affecting the entire organization, and not merely that part where the change is actually occurring. Change is based on harnessing skills, values, attitudes and relationships throughout the organization to create a permanent modification. These strategies exhibit characteristics like a problem-solving approach using the input of the people in the system, the demonstration of the value of the innovation, an assessment of the way the change will affect the organization, and consensus as a basis for change. Educative strategies also rely on a basis of research and investigation which forms the first stage of the process.

Of equal importance, they require the active involvement of the whole organization. This can come in a number of forms. Open communication covering the entire activities of the team directly involved in implementing the change is a good start, as is the willingness of management to practise these virtues themselves from the very start of the programme. The opportunity for comment and contributions from people can be built into the process in a number of ways examined in Chapter 5. In organizations in which the parts are increasingly interrelated and interdependent, and where change is an increasingly complex phenomenon, the multiple perspectives referred to in the discussions of theory and structures are essential contributions from the start. If this strategy is adopted it will involve:

- A demonstration of the value of change and innovation to the organization
- Clear indications of the way in which the change will affect the whole organization.

These strategies fit well with organization development in the broadest sense.

Normative/Persuasive Strategies

Here the assumption is that people will be open to persuasion and will be capable of collaboration motivated and controlled by their own feelings and values. These approaches are partly derived from Lewin (1951, 1958) and are based on a recognition of the need to change:

- Attitudes

- Skills
- Values
- Relationships.

In effect this is, in Lewin's terms, to consider the whole system (see Chapter 5). It can also be seen as a problem-solving approach which makes use of the potential input of the people involved in the system. As it is consensus-based change it has attractions for non-hierarchical systems.

Power-Coercive Strategies

Power-coercive strategies rely on the legitimate power of management to push a change through. In certain circumstances this will work, and there may also be circumstances where nothing else will do. It could be necessary, at certain times in the change process, to break an impasse or remove an obstacle which cannot be removed in any other way.

Power-coercive strategies rely on a range of approaches more easily available in a bureaucratic system. Change can be brought about by the use of power in a political, legal or administrative sense, possibly by the use of sanctions and rewards, and even by the allocation or withdrawal of resources. There are then corresponding restrictions on the degree and breadth of consultation and communication, and on the ability of those further removed from the decision-making caucus to influence what is happening. There are also implications for motivation. The results are less impact on individual development and a reduced organizational capacity to make the best use of all its resources.

In a practical change situation, what would be expected is a combination of several approaches, within the general context of an educative strategy. Most managers will have a preferred strategy based on their temperaments, their education and training, their view of the organization and its people and their assessment of the change situation. One of the issues in change management is changing the manager, so that power strategies do not become an automatic response, but it is undeniable that change strategies are coloured by managers' psychological attraction to particular styles of managing and using power.

Moving from a closed to an open organization, which is another way of describing the Organization Development approach to change management, is nonsense if it is pursued through power strategies. Nevertheless it has to be admitted that it has been done in libraries, it has arguably produced some success in the short term even if the long-term future is cloudy, and it will be attempted again.

The contingency approach is relevant within the broad framework of an informed, consensual procedure. Managers can be expected to modify their styles to reflect particular situations. In a decentralised system, power can be drawn back to the centre to break a deadlock or handle a crisis, or to move a temporarily blocked process forward. Equally, it can be used to take decisions that project teams cannot, or are not prepared to, take themselves. Individuals with differing attitudes, conceptions and fears about change will be handled differently, and in particular resistance will be handled with finesse. The skill lies in managing these apparent inconsistencies.

There are inevitably points in the change process when a coercive strategy is necessary. There are also some constraints on how participatory strategies work in crisis situations. The danger is that coercion is adopted as a matter of choice, by managers with a taste for Taylorism, when the circumstances do not demand it.

What is important at this stage is the emphasis placed on change as a strategic issue, starting at the centre of strategic planning, and making the essential connections with the management of the innovative projects and service developments which form the individual components of the change process. It is at the strategic planning level that the seeds of failure can be laid down.

We can now return to Hammer's idea of the 'organizational framework' (op cit, 2005). This should be made up of:

- The involvement of senior management in a regular process of updating and reviewing innovation projects throughout the organization.
- The creation of a broader 'process council' involving senior managers and other managers with a substantial stake in the developments.
- The establishment of 'process owners' empowered to make changes across the organization. All organizations are made up of various formally-constituted groups with their own aims and objectives, work practices and sub-cultures. There are also informal groups and alliances with their own agendas, and these are capable of influencing the course of a change project. In change management, the use of individuals with the power and commitment to work through these differences is essential.
- Related to this issue of using designated figures with the power to move things forward is the need for those individuals to follow a strategic initiative through to its logical conclusions. This again means taking a general organizational view of every development. Systems theory and Lewin's field theory in Chapter 2 described the capacity of a change in one part of the organization to influence others. It is true that wider implications than those considered in the planning stages of a change project sometimes emerge, and the process owners should also be capable of dealing with this wider brief. Organizational change therefore attains a momentum of its own, and the process is another step in the creation of a self-renewing organization.
- The engagement of front-line staff:

A thousand people were exposed to the new process as it was being developed, making them feel like participants rather than victims and helping them see both the flaws in the old ways of doing things and the power of the new. (Hammer, op cit, 2005)

● A 'bias for action'. This can be taken to mean roughly that if an organization waits for everything to be perfect it will never take action. The principle adopted by the organization Hammer analysed was '70 per cent and go'. The other 30 per cent of what was desired could be accumulated later as the project developed and matured.

Figure 3.3 is the summation of Hammer's organizational framework, identifying the key inputs from management, front-line staff, the implementation process owners, and the chosen implementation strategy. The next case study turns the clock back, and looks at the antecedents of the difficulties which came to a head in Case Study 1.

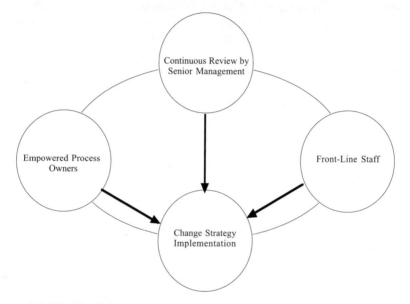

Figure 3.3 The Participants in Strategy Implementation

Case Study 2: The Drawbacks of Opportunism

The origin of the events leading to the situation described in Case Study 1, where an information service found itself forced into an unsuccessful struggle to defend the positions of a number of specialist librarians, can be traced in part to a number of strategic errors made by successive managers over a number of years. The embracing of the convergence of academic support services in university libraries has been widely recorded and analysed, lately by Hanson (2005). Contributors to this work ascribe, by implication sometimes, a number of motives to the protagonists in what could have been one of the most important organizational development issues in the history of university librarianship in the UK and elsewhere. It was usually the case that implementation procedures reflected very mixed motives.

The case study which follows charts the implementation process followed in creating the converged information service based on the library, the computing centre, media services and some smaller units. It was this process, reflecting errors of implementation, led to the consequences described in Case Study 1.

The Background

The impetus for changing the structure of support services in the university came from the director of the library service's chairmanship of the institutional teaching and learning committee.

Much influenced by the publication of two official reports which raised the question of new structural patterns for support services, by his own analysis of the increasingly close relationship between the library service, the media service and the computing service, and by the results of extensive research into the proposition, he began to craft a strategy for implementing the same pattern in his own institution.

His resolve was stiffened by the clear messages coming out of the work of the teaching and learning committee. These referred to the inadequacies of resource provision, the increasing catholicity of demands which were themselves blurring the distinctions between the three services forming the core of support, and the digitisation of the library service which was driving the library into a much closer relationship with the computing service than hitherto.

The Strategy

It would be unfair to say there was no strategic planning involved in the change outlined above. The director of library services produced an impeccably reasoned and comprehensive plan for the proposed change. It paid proper attention to the development of partnerships to support and enhance the learning process in the institution. It acknowledged the central role of academic support services in delivering institutional strategies, which would be based on the interdependence of the services providing the support. It was set in the context of the information strategy of the institution.

The Implementation

The implementation strategy was where things began to go wrong. The document prepared by the library director went straight to the senior management committee, was rapidly moved on to the deans' committee for information, and was approved subject to the appointment of a director of information services. The three heads of the formerly independent services applied for the ring-fenced position, and the director of library services emerged from the process as the first director of information services.

The implementation strategy was drawn up by the new director in close consultation with the former media services manager and director of computing services. The proposal was detailed, exhaustive, and imaginative.

The new service was to be based on a number of cross-departmental teams and was genuinely innovative. Each team was based on staff drawn from all of the former services, so another of the conditions for organizational creativity and creative abrasion was present. The plan was unveiled to the entire staff as the completed article, including staff depositions, the areas each team would be responsible for, management structures, communication, reporting lines and team membership. Costed and funded proposals for physical integration over a period of time were included.

On paper at least, integration at the basic operational user-facing level was held out as something which would genuinely be delivered. There were proposals for staff development, a skills analysis and skills audit was carried out, and some emphasis was placed on the opportunities for career development in a new and dynamic structure.

Creating this plan was time-consuming, and during this period the first cracks began to appear. Inevitably the organizational rumour mill began to operate and staff who were attempting to piece together various items of information from different sources were beginning to express their fears and doubts. The director of information services was impervious to staff reactions, and drove the proposals through.

As a result, the new structure came into being in the face of staff opposition on the grounds of lack of involvement in the process. With morale at a low ebb and a vested interest in the failure of the new arrangements, a mood of non-cooperation went from strength to strength. A frustrated director became more and more authoritative, and with progress in some areas slowing to a crawl, relations between management and staff deteriorated to the point where a packed staff meeting produced an unanimous vote of no confidence in management. With student unrest emerging, and teaching staff expressing concerns about the unavailability of resources, institutional management was finally forced to act. Two of the three senior management staff took early retirement, and the third moved sideways. A new director, with a strong and successful background in IT in business and commerce, took control.

This inevitably led to a new strategy, which was based on administrative convergence only. The team structure was replaced by a divisional structure which to all intents and purposes meant that coordination below senior management level was non-existent. The advantages of this change of direction were seen in the removal of uncertainty and doubt from the minds of staff, and this was accompanied by a more conciliatory managerial approach, with a more open communications system. On the other hand, a number of staff, while accepting the stability, were conscious of the missed opportunity to support institutional strategy by developing close collaboration, and by the fact that the fragmented nature of the service delivery was not properly responsive to developing user needs.

For several years the service continued to operate with a minimum of disruption and some solid technical development in ICT. Digitisation was increasingly embraced by the library, but without any significant exchange between the library and the computing service.

A major funding crisis was the final event which led to the situation described in Case Study 1. Faced with a serious budget deficit, institutional management disaggregated the three services and restored each one to its former independent status, reporting directly to a pro-vice chancellor. The director of information services took early retirement and was not replaced. There was a complete reversal of policy. With the library share of the budget cuts set at £300,000 a number of professional librarians who had previously worked closely with academic departments were identified as surplus to requirements on the grounds that electronic databases could provide the information more effectively and economically. In spite of the usual protestations about the significance of library services to the work of the university, the cuts were implemented.

Analysis

This chapter started by highlighting strategy as the way in which the library develops a capacity to interpret its environment and make use of change opportunities as it takes decisions about the direction the service will take. The quotation from Gardner (op cit, 2005) emphasised the need to make change part of the organizational fabric. In this context, the first thing that went wrong was that the change strategy was created and implemented in isolation. It never appeared as part of the strategic planning of the three services involved, and this isolation was heightened by the lack of involvement of staff outside the triumvirate at the top of the organization. It was also an extremely dangerous way of moving to a team organization, not only because of the obvious discord between the means and the ends, but also because the chosen approach could not support any of the long term organizational objectives.

Turning again to Hammer's criteria, senior management were never able to get beyond the initial implementation stage, and introduce the essential review process across the organization, because they were constantly battling with the uncertainty, disillusion and resistance of the staff. Linares (2005) describes a cyclical change process in which 'waves of change' were introduced at intervals, built around three or four major goals or priorities. There was little radical change from year to year, but there were significant changes in the projects which made up the 'waves'. As many levels of the organization were involved as possible, and communication was cascaded. The point is also made that however good the communication is, on its own it is not enough. Involvement is the key, and it is significant that the organization in the case study failed on both counts.

Clear and simple objectives which are easy to understand are also important in winning involvement. For Linares, the end result was a culture in which people were immersed in change, expected it, saw it as natural, and enjoyed it. Nothing of these things could be said of the university information service.

In the case study, there were also no acknowledged stakeholders outside the senior management team. There had been no consultation and no channels of communication had been opened. This contributed to the absence of any of Hammer's 'process owners'. The people who could have made a difference in dealing with doubt, resistance and non-cooperation did not exist. The subculture was able to nurture resistance to the point where it produced a shift in policy. Fron- line staff could not be engaged in a development to which they were not party, having had no input and been exposed to no more than a minimal communication process.

All of this contributed to a major weakness. This was the inability of management to follow this major strategic initiative through to its logical conclusion. While the library developed its digitisation programmes under the second director, the potential implications of this for traditional library staff in terms of skills and knowledge requirements were not considered.

It is not as if this idea came as a total surprise, because the literature of library management had been warning of the possible implications of librarians ceasing to be 'the exclusive gatekeepers to information' since at least the mid 1980s. When the decision to abandon the team structure was taken, it became even more difficult to embed technological skills and the use of technology into the work of conventional librarians. If this had happened, then a group of librarians would not have been so easily identified as an isolated phenomenon which could be picked off comparatively easily. As it was, university management embarked on a comparatively simple matter of identifying electronic information sources as a specialisation which could be preserved while more traditional approaches were dispensed with. This was a failure of systems thinking in strategy formulation – ignoring the fact that a change in one part of the organization is likely to affect other parts.

Chapter Summary

Change is a strategic issue, and as such the strategy would be expected to form a central feature of the strategic planning process. The strategy for change should embrace:

- The context in which the library operates
- The vision and mission of the library
- The goal of the process
- The values of the organization, which should be reflected in implementation
- The principles on which the strategy will be based
- The arrangements for reviewing and monitoring the plan.

The implementation strategy should be given the same weight as the initial planning process, and should reflect:

- Wide participation
- The involvement of front line staff
- The empowering of the stakeholders
- Systems thinking
- Full communication at all times.

Kaplan and Norton (2001) provided an overview of the principles of strategy formulation and implementation which is as good as any:

- Focus on the shift from strategy creation to strategy implementation.
- Make certain that the strategy matches the nature of the organization. This means ensuring a fit between strategy and structures, management styles, culture in general, the state of learning and the development of skills and capabilities, and communication patterns.
- Involve everyone in strategy.
- Ensure that the process of creating and implementing strategy is continual.

Chapter 4

Process and Models

Some of the reasons why strategies succeed or fail were considered at the end of the previous chapter. The discussion of strategy implementation opens the way to considering the actual process of change. It is here that, according to the literature, most of the failures of change management have their roots, although strategic failures also play a part. The problem is turning thinking into action. We can begin this chapter by going back to Lewin's work previously referred to in Chapter 3. Unfreezing, Moving and Refreezing are some of the key concepts expressed by Lewin (op cit, 1951) and familiar to most people involved in change management, which ought to mean everybody working in today's libraries. Put in a different way, this offers a basis for developing a tenable process of introducing change.

The Basic Process

The three-step process of unfreezing, moving and refreezing is a pithy summary of a far-reaching and perhaps most difficult part of change management.

Unfreezing: Getting the Organization Ready for Change

The change process begins well before a specific project actually sees the light of day. Its genesis is to be seen in relationships, communications, human resource management, management styles, structures, and the way strategy is formulated. These are the organizational elements which must be in good shape if any change initiative is to stand a chance of success (see Figure 4.1).

Creating a Healthy Organization

A healthy organization is the outcome ensured by going through the unfreezing process before a change project is started. Poor relationships, poor communications, inappropriate management styles and restrictive structures will hamper the change process in a practical way, and also less obviously by affecting organizational health and the way in which people regard the organization. This is also an issue which influences motivation as well as the practical implementation of a change project.

Any change proposal is approached on the basis of what people believe the

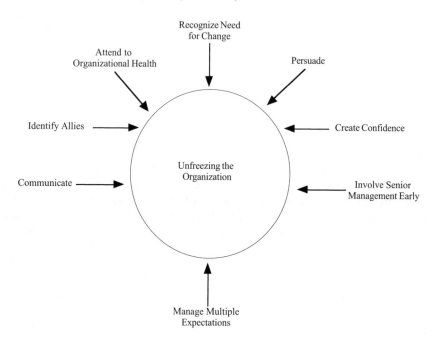

Figure 4.1　Unfreezing the Organization: Getting it Ready for Change

organization should be about, how it should meet its objectives, their interpretation of the purpose of the change, and some self-interest. If the organizational conditions are right, all four issues can usually be resolved without too much difficulty.

The general attitude to change is also coloured by recollections and assessments of previous changes, and the prevailing attitude to management. This makes attention to organizational health a permanent and long-term issue of significance in itself.

Many organizational characteristics influence organizational health. Some organizations sharply define and circumscribe the roles of their personnel. They can also display a prescriptive and perhaps narrow view of development, and offer evidence of structures which restrict the flow of information and the exchange of ideas.

The management styles deployed can be similarly unreconstructed. Hence bureaucracies can present problems in change management, but, as suggested elsewhere, ought to be good at project management. So there is a whole slew of attitudes, beliefs and behaviours which become targets for attention – in other words long-term organization development. Unfreezing is the part of the process which attempts to convince people that change is necessary. It should also ensure the organization is equipped for change. This first stage is therefore best regarded in the light of a continual process of organization development. If change is going to work properly, then the hard effort which has to go into creating an environment in which the participants accept change as a natural phenomenon is unavoidable. That people have a sense of being properly involved in change, that they can benefit from it and that it fits with their view of where the organization should go, is an essential prerequisite. This is about:

- Preparing for change as a continuous activity for managers and managed
- Genuine involvement in the process
- Communication and participation across internal boundaries
- The removal of undue restrictions on input to strategies and tactics
- The sharing of information
- Prioritising personal development and new skills acquisition.

Irrespective of organizational forms, or whether the organization is consciously involved in organization development, these characteristics are achievable and essential as the foundations of change. They are characteristics which help people to consider objectively the possibility that the organization could profit from doing things differently. This kind of positive environment can secure behavioural change, and it can contribute to achieving the far more difficult attitude change, engendering a belief in the need for change. It also underpins support for the form the change will take and the process which will deliver it.

Organizations which are generally in poor shape as far as things like communications and motivation are concerned will obviously encounter difficulties, or will demonstrate a particularly restrictive view of the implementation process, with a reliance on control and direction. The positive features listed here are to be nurtured as a natural part of management, and they come into their own in times of change. The same is true of other managerial actions in the unfreezing process, such as understanding the informal communications process, the social network and the unofficial centres of power and influence. These are all germane to the second stage – Moving.

Recognising the Need for Change

Most change projects, whether we think they represent true change or innovation, usually begin with a manager's recognition that a change is necessary. Mobilising the organization in the service of the change is a vital first step. The situation examined in Case Studies 1 and 2 may well reflect to some extent a necessary change which was a consequence of digitisation and had been a long time in coming. Nevertheless, its outcome also reflects a failure to deal with the cultural aspects of change, for want of a better phrase. What is meant by this is that management failed to win recognition that the change they proposed was necessary because of the organizational circumstances. The solution to the problem was a top-down one, there was no attempt to earn support, and no alternative courses of action were in the equation. What was also clear from the two case studies was that over a period of time organizational health had not been a priority for management. The characteristics of the organization, reflecting rigid thinking, lack of communication in depth and closed circuit decision-making among other weaknesses, simply made it harder to prepare the foundations for change. Persuasion was also noticeable by its absence.

Persuasion

Unfreezing the organization should be a matter of persuasion rather than compulsion, and ultimately of winning consent and imbuing conviction of the need for, and value of, change. There is little evidence in the literature of resistance to change in the abstract: there is substantial evidence of resistance to imposed, non-consensual change as a process in which people play an inadequate part and have no sense of influence or sharing. This is made worse if the organization itself is, in the eyes of its staff, an ailing institution. Once a project is underway, winning this consent and ensuring shared ownership is harder than if the proper effort had been expended in terms of changing minds (see Chapter 8) and creating the optimum conditions for change as part of sound management.

Catering for Multiple Expectations

This approach, which is organization development by another name, has another advantage. Within an organization, change is viewed from a number of perspectives. Managers, middle managers, and staff in operational areas (looked at in detail in Chapter 9), will want different things from a change process, and will approach it with different expectations. Involvement, communication, sharing information and participation go a long way towards creating common ground out of the various expectations, emotions, worries and objectives which swirl around change.

Creating Confidence

The other element added through this approach is self-belief. The key is again involvement, and if this is present it is more likely that staff will not only accept change as essential, but feel confident they can perform under the new circumstances. Chapters 7, 8 and 9 deal with the cultural engineering which gives rise to these conditions.

Positive Senior Management Input From the Start

Another necessity at this stage is the involvement of senior management, and the potential for error is immediately apparent. It is all to easy for managers to propose a solution to a problem as the first step in the process. The institution which featured in

Case Studies 1 and 2 demonstrated this to perfection. The problem and the solution emerged at the same time, and could be defined as a closed change project – the issue brooked no other solution than the removal of a layer of staff.

Organizational history is littered with examples of footsoldiers being informed of solutions to problems they sometimes hardly knew existed. Increasingly, these solutions are based on the departure of significant numbers of them. This is not aided by closed-circuit strategy formulation and a curia-like proprietorial attitude to management information. It all represents suspect organizational health and a failure of the process, in an organization in which change is something done to other people.

Announcing a problem with a preferred solution, then inviting consultation within the limits of a ready-made answer, is very bad news. In the two case studies already referred to, framing things differently, as a budget issue to be probed and investigated, might have avoided the instinctive and understandable resistance which occurred. The objective of change management is not to sell the solution, but to sell the problem while offering the staff a partnership in creating the answer, and only then laying some alternatives on the table.

Identifying Allies

Winning the staff over is easier if it is obvious that the issue, but not yet the solution, is vigorously sponsored by senior management. It also helps if this extends to the sponsorship of open and consensual processes. In this respect, the unfreezing process has to take account of power-brokers outside the formal structure. Managers have a responsibility at the outset for identifying the change agents and opinion-formers inside the organization.

Staff will not necessarily be discharging these roles as a result of holding a formal position. They can be part of the important informal network which influences and communicates alongside the official framework, and will represent a way into forming alliances on the ground.

The opinion-formers and popular leaders are unofficial sources, and wielders, of power. They can also pinpoint areas of resistance or blockages. Identifying these key players is a crucial move in unfreezing, as is an understanding of the informal communications process and social networks which they are a part of alongside official channels and formal structures. This underground network can often be used judiciously to go around the inevitable blockages in the formal channels. Klein (2004) refers to the Outsider-Insiders, those who through their objectivity not only bring an element of reality into the process, but can also balance this with their ability to make connections and lead opinion inside the organization. They:

> ... play a pivotal role in introducing new ideas or processes. . . . are able to see connections that pure insiders miss because they have a different way of seeing the world or explaining why things appear to happen as they do.... At the same time, they are able to leverage the existing

culture by living within the organization, another theme that is vital in the creation of true change.

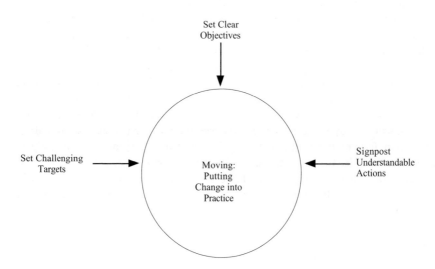

Figure 4.2 Moving: Introducing the Change

As a result, they can be key allies in formulating strategy, building alliances, communicating and generally engaging colleagues in a supportive way.

Moving: Putting Change Into Practice

Adoption is the next stage of the process. The organization is now ready to change, and people have to be persuaded. Building on what has been achieved by the successful unfreezing of the organization, change can now be implemented. At this point it is worth going back to look at some general points about strategy. There is a tendency to regard the change strategy as a finite or even self-contained part of the change process.

Compartmentalised thinking is unwise, and the point was made in the previous chapter. Strategy – the setting of objectives and the definition of broad courses of action designed to achieve these objectives – will influence all three of Lewin's stages of change. The more inclusive the strategy, the easier it is to unfreeze the organization. When it comes to the second stage, the right strategy can contribute a number of positive features, and no more so than in making things obvious, encouraging and developmental.

The aims at this stage (see Figure 4.2) should be to clarify, to persuade people that the objectives of the change can be achieved by the proposal, and that the proposal will also include an essential element of challenge which will extend the skills and knowledge of those who will be involved in the implementation of the change.

Clarity

Unambiguous objectives and intelligible courses of action improve understanding, and increase the chances that all the participants will subscribe fully to the change.

Attainability

The change process is one of the finest learning experiences an organization can offer, provided that it is participative and the objectives are within the grasp of the staff and the capacity of organizational resources. Setting attainable objectives as part of the strategy is a confidence-building measure for the unfreezing stage and clearly has a practical value in introducing the change itself.

Attainability Balanced by Challenges

From a learning and development perspective, the best change processes are those which extend the individuals concerned. Elements of role change, skills acquisition, the need for inventiveness and perhaps originality, and the requirement to take into account new perspectives can all present challenges. Problem-solving and some degree of technical difficulty are also ways in which change can be given added momentum if the right support is made available. These are factors which will contribute to motivation, and the offer of a challenge, provided it is backed up with the proper support, is good for organizational health.

Absorption into the Culture

This is Lewin's refreezing. Organizational cultures change when behaviour change becomes attitude change, and people believe in the change. Here the change becomes part of 'the well-worn corporate fabric and the DNA of its workforce' (Gardner, op cit). The mindset that welcomes involvement in change now becomes widespread alongside any procedural, technical or service delivery changes which might represent the tangible results of change. The learning, collaboration, problem-solving and communication across departments and sections becomes part of the 'way things are done around here' (Glass, 1996). The aspects of the process which ensure that the change becomes part of the organization (see Figure 4.3) are:

- Dissemination of information
- Empowerment and self-management in the change process
- Attitude change
- Structural change, which underpins these characteristics.

Organizational structures, which have a crucial influence on these processes, are a vital area for renewal, because they have a fundamental affect on cultural change.

The lessons of change can also be embedded in the culture through the

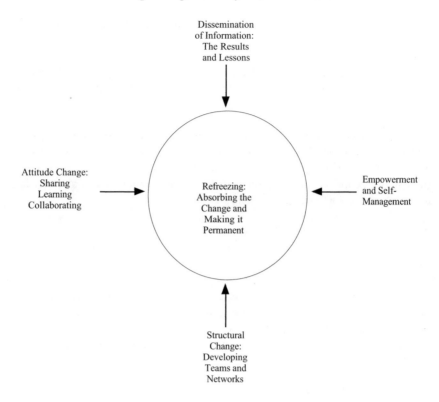

Figure 4.3 Refreezing: Making the Change Stick

dissemination of information, the steady development of empowerment and self-management, the extension and reinforcing of teams and other factors which are considered in more detail in Chapter 7.

Summary

In all organizations, there should be a change process at work on several levels. The organization development approach involves constant attention to growth at personal, group and organizational level, to refinement and modification of structures and management approaches, and improvement in communication. These are the organizational characteristics shown in the inner circle of Figure 4.4.

This is a process which should be running permanently in the background. The objective is to create the right circumstances for change to flourish, and it is cultural reengineering. It is helped along if change is a strategic issue enshrined in strategic planning, and therefore assists in creating the capacity for generic change, and lays down the cultural conditions allowing individual change projects to flourish. As

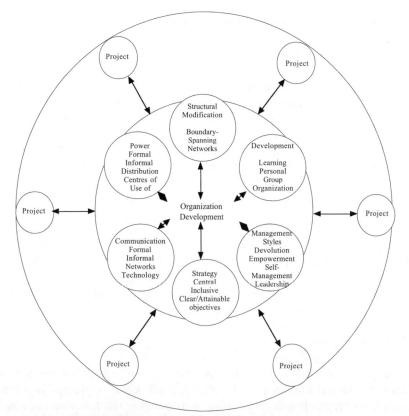

Figure 4.4 Overlapping Phases of the Change Process

suggested, it also helps to create a more unified view within the organization.

On a more practical and concrete level, there is the process of managing the specific projects shown in the outer circle of Figure 4.4. This process should reflect, and be influenced by what is happening in the inner circle – the characteristics reviewed above – and it sums up the underlying implementation process.

The elements of organization development in the centre of Figure 4.4 are the ongoing and characteristic concerns of change management. They represent continual development which creates the circumstances in which the individual change projects in the outer circle can flourish.

The affects of these in turn feed back into the organizational environment in the forms of lessons learned, experience gained, service improvement and organic growth. The capacity for managing change is constantly improved and there is a benefit for organizational health. As such, the features of the inner circle are also key elements in the development of organizational culture.

Figure 4.4 shows the relationship between the two parts of what should be an integrated approach to the implementation of change.

Change and Project Implementation

We have a model of an organizational environment in which change can flourish, and we would expect the same model to be capable of supporting a raft of smaller, more concrete, innovative projects throughout the organization. Some of the features in the inner circle of Figure 4.4 are to do with the 'soft' aspects of management. Hammer also called them the hardest, in the sense that they are the most difficult to perform well. Good implementation processes are based on these softer skills, and rely on:

- Cooperation
- Sharing
- Communication
- Flexibility
- Learning and development.

Here, there are a number of theoretical ideas with impressive pedigrees, which offer a series of practical steps.

The General Approach

Havelock et al (1969) were amongst the first proponents of the Research, Development and Diffusion model (RDD). This details a planned and orderly procedure of research, conceptualisation, demonstration and dissemination, adoption and finally institutionalisation, when the change becomes an established and accepted part of the organization. There is a reasonable fit between this and the ideas of Lewin, on which this chapter is based.

Havelock's work was refined in the Social Interaction model (SI) which places a heavy reliance on social relationships, personal contacts and group membership, and a third model was the problem-solving model.

Later, Rogers and Shoemaker (1962) broke down the change process into a series of well-defined steps, and this can again be taken as a template for the practical management of change projects.

In general, both the change process and the models are well documented in the literature of management, and in the literature of library management also. An analysis of the most widely applicable models (Burnes, 2004) shows some commonality:

- There is systematic data collection to do with the change.
- Internal and external environments are analysed.
- There is a consideration of alternative possibilities.
- Steps are taken to ensure the cooperation of the workforce.

- At some stage, the users of the service should be called in. (author's addition)

Carr et al (1996), in an exposition of Coopers & Lybrand's approach to change management, advocate a four-step process which is designed to assess the present position, decide on an appropriate change process, establish a sound theoretical framework for the change and ensure that aims are shared and personnel are involved and committed. This is achieved through the stages of:

- Assessment: justification, objectives and broad characteristics
- Planning: the entire change process is laid down
- Implementation: commitment, dissemination, training, change
- Renewal: monitoring, feedback and evaluation.

The model which emerges from these ideas charts both the process and the environmental influences, external and internal, which impinge on the process. Some of these have been described in the assessment of the strategic model of change at the start of this chapter. Before looking at this model in more detail, it is important to state an obvious caveat. All change projects are unique. The variables of organizational characteristics, leadership, environmental influences and skills and competencies, for example, all act to change the weighting given to the various steps in the process. This should therefore be regarded as one of many useful possibilities rather than a prescription for managing change, but it is still true that most of the recognisable models in the literature have a number of common features. They first of all adopt a problem-solving approach, and at some points change projects should of course use standard problem-solving techniques. What we are concerned with at the moment is a model which reflects an enquiring attitude of mind:

- A change project is usually multi-faceted, and needs to be looked at from a number of angles.
- It begins with a process of analysis in order to state the nature of the problem clearly and identify all the possible solutions. It also means identifying constraints such as time, resources, skills and obstacles. These inhibiting factors will always be balanced by positive elements which also have to be identified. This means getting under the skin of the issue and using this information as a basis for planning and execution
- It requires to be handled as a cultural, psychological, logistical and managerial issue.

Put another way, this is a process of:

- Analysis
- Goal-setting

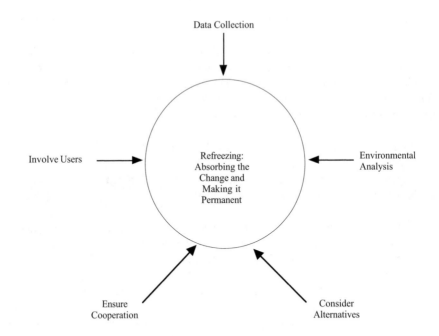

Figure 4.5 The Critical Elements in Change Planning

• Action
• Evaluation.

These steps can be expanded and modified to fit the information services environment, and are succinct and pertinent breakdowns of the stages to be followed. The common elements in planning at this level are set out in Figure 4.5.

One thing which is typical of change projects whatever their organizational context is that best practice clearly indicates the importance of breaking the process down into discrete stages. The staged approach is central to most of the literature of change models.

A step by step approach produces advantages. Provided that the proposal is not running with a pre-ordained intention to introduce the change, in other words a decision to implement has been taken at the same time as the need for change was announced, or that the solution and the problem were unveiled at the same time, as referred to earlier, an incremental development allows the entire operation to be managed so that the risk is reduced. There will be various cut-off points when a review of progress and a decision to proceed have to be taken, so that programmes can naturally be aborted if and when problems become insuperable. The worst thing that can be done with a change project is to anticipate the outcome too soon, or to assume

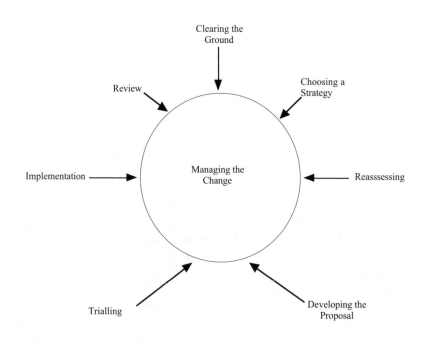

Figure 4.6 The Overall Implementation Process

a particular course of action leading to a preferred solution to a problem. We all know that the reality is often far removed from this, and that wishing something to be different does not make it so, but the fact that things are done differently in many real life change projects does not invalidate the proposition. The risks inherent in the change should be quantified and assessed in the initial stages. Moving along a controlled step by step development path allows the opportunity for reassessment, and if necessary even the option of termination at each stage. If each stage also carries a precise set of criteria to be satisfied before the next stage can be introduced, it tightens the planning and implementation.

The breakdown into clear stages should also make the change more intelligible. Apart from the advantages from the point of view of managing the implementation process, this also brings advantages in terms of morale. It is akin to the idea of breaking learning down into manageable chunks and stages which challenge learners and encourages them to extend and push themselves at the same time. Clear stages in the process can act as a spur and a safety valve.

The acknowledgement of the multi-faceted nature of a change project, and the determination to uncover and understand the ramifications of the issues involved in prosecuting a change, is a key part of this first stage of the expanded model described in Figure 4.6 and considered in detail in the next section.

The Implementation Stages

Stage 1: Clearing the Ground

The organizational climate is a significant factor in change management. Assessing that climate, and creating an environment conducive to change management, is the essential first step in implementation. This part of the process should really be grounded in a general view of the capacity of the organization to carry through the change. Can it be done? is as good a question as Who will do it? or How will it be done? For the manager, the change process begins when questions are asked about what the proposal is actually intended to do. At this stage, no one should be looking for answers to all of the questions, and the process should not commence with consideration of the change itself. It begins with a general review of the organization and where the proposal is likely to take it. In other words, and without lapsing into management-speak, does it fit with what the organization is about, how it conducts itself, and where it wants to go – mission, values and vision.

This stage is also relevant to organizational health, which is itself to do with motivation. There are organizations, whether they are libraries, schools, factories or offices, which are so riddled with demotivators that change should not be undertaken until at least some of the unfinished business has been settled. There may be general problems with communication, management attitudes, resources, working conditions and procedures. These might have nothing to do with the change, and might not actively work against it, but will colour attitudes and create a climate which is not exactly resistant to change, but is not positive. It is not impossible for rickety organizations to prosecute change, but a catalogue of problems, minor or not, will simply get in the way of the change process. This is Herzberg's theory (1966) that any discontent caused by what he termed the hygiene factors must be minimised. The time to do it is before the change process actually starts, and people are asked to consider more momentous issues. The emphasis on organization development and the establishment of a culture imbued with the idea of change as a natural phenomenon of life ensure organizational health. The question is what to do if the organization is in such a state that all of the features referred to above are in such a state that organization development becomes the change project in itself. The answer will involve a simultaneous attack on all these issues, advancing on a broad front but focussed on structural change. This is because of the all-pervasive influence of structure, and its links with almost everything else of importance which happens in an organization.

Stage 2: Choosing the Implementation Strategy

Chapter 6 considers the potential of the bureaucracy as a structure for supporting change, and arrives at some surprising conclusions. Change can indeed be imposed as a top-down process. However, once again we know that there is a far better chance of success if people are led through a consensual, open and empowering process which gives them a share in ownership and responsibility. The choice of which general principle is enacted depends on the manager's personality and the organizational characteristics. These will not only influence the approximate course to be taken, but will have a serious impact on major turning points and procedures. It is managers who mould organizations, usually in their own likenesses, and this will be reflected in the general approach to implementing change: top-down or bottom-up? Imposed and mechanistic or organic and consensual? Managerial or creative?

Once the nature of the exercise has been broadly decided, and the choice between a directive approach and a more consultative approach has been made, the other far-reaching decision to be taken is that of the communication strategy. This will follow the same general course – it will either be open and inclusive, or it will be controlled and proprietorial, depending on the organizational circumstances and managerial style in vogue at the time.

Communication is the glue which holds everything together. It is a serious influence on motivation, and without an effective communication strategy laid down at the outset there is little chance of dialogue or of effective contributions to implementation. Even in traditional hierarchical organizations, good two-way communication in a change project is possible, and will do much to narrow the gap between managers and managed. This is the point at which managers:

- Identify the Outsider-Insiders and the opinion formers: this gives them access to the informal communications network; here the key technique is network analysis
- Establish where the likely blockages will be, and decide what to do about them
- Take decisions on which communication channels and methods will be used.

However the strategy is shaped, its execution should be based on the following principles:

- Communication is an integral part of the change. This means it has to be planned with the same degree of detail and sense of urgency as the implementation programme itself. It also has to be costed, responsibilities and duties allocated, a reporting mechanism set up and an evaluation process set in train.
- Communication has to be championed in the same way as the change, and be seen to be the ultimate responsibility of a major player.
- The target audiences will be varied. Earlier in this chapter it was stated that people adopt various stances when facing change, and have different sets of expectations depending on where they are in the organization. They will also react in different ways to messages via different channels. Whatever is available as a medium should be considered: intranets, email, formal meetings, informal meetings, one-to-one, video, minutes and reports will all have their place, and will achieve their impact in different ways.

- The tactics need to be carefully considered so that specific needs and worries can be addressed without communication overload.
- Consequently, it is possible to tell people too much. In this respect, detail is perhaps not always important, but principles and consequences are. At another level there will be an obvious need for complete and detailed frankness about how a change will affect the personal position of everyone involved.
- Communication must be regular.
- Surprising people during a change initiative is unwise. The frequency and content of communication can be adjusted so that people can be told of the possibilities in an unthreatening way, and given all possible reassurances.
- Communication must break down organizational barriers, and work independently of the organizational form. This is true whether the organization is functionally based like many libraries, divisional – often reflecting the separation of digital and traditional services, a matrix form, or a more organic and team-based configuration. If the organization is bureaucratic, steps must be taken to ensure that the communication pattern does not follow the hierarchical structure or conventional line management. The communication process in change management must be distinctive, all-pervasive and separate, making use of the impact of various channels, and particularly the informal network.
- Listening is a vital part of communication, and doubly so in managing change.
- Asking questions is vital. Managers should note that clarification is also a two-way process. It is not confined to management answering questions from the rest of the organization, but is reciprocal – there are things which management also need to find out from others.
- Communication is a cultural issue. Its major purpose is to convey the sense of what is happening to everyone, and to give them an opportunity to contribute. In change management it is profitably seen as an exchange between individuals irrespective of formal position.

Stage 3: Reassessment: Stopping to Think

Having set up an implementation strategy including a communication system which will generally steer the process, the next stage should involve a pause for thought. Before the change process can be handed over to others, a period of rumination leading to a mental review of the situation is quite useful. Other questions should be asked. This is not the time for detail, but it is the time for managers, and others if they are so inclined, to sketch outlines, draw some pictures and then tell the story to their colleagues. If the project is to succeed the commitment of the staff must be ensured. How well the proposal is presented depends to a degree on how well managers can clarify it for themselves, and then how well they can convey the sense of it. They must be convinced themselves before they ask others to follow.

The credibility of the story depends on several things, as listed below.

Is There a Strategic Fit?
How does the project fit with the strategy of the organization? 'Sticking to the knitting', allegedly coined by Tom Peters, meaning to carry on doing what was already being done with at least a modicum of success, was a phrase widely used at one time when there was quite a narrow view of what libraries should be doing. Turning the clock back that far is negative, because change in information services is about managing diversity and unpredictability. But there is still a problem if the characteristics of what has to be put in place are not consistent with other organizational features.

One of the difficulties faced by information services is the tension between the changes being wrought by digitisation and the traditional values of librarianship. It is possible that digitisation projects become restricted because of an unclear articulation of their relationship to the still overwhelming traditional library environment.

What is being sought at this stage is the connection between a change project and strategy. People can be forgiven if they are unable to relate the proposal to develop digital collections to their view of the reality of a hybrid library system which still relies heavily on the expertise of traditional librarians and the human element of service.

Managers must help them make this connection, not only with the content of the proposal, but also the manner in which it will be achieved, so this stage calls for both strategic and operational congruence. However intrinsically valuable the project, simple behaviourist change theories or coercive strategies will not do for most of the change taking place in information services.

Predicting the Impact
A project is obviously conceived with a set of objectives in mind. It is also of benefit to take a broader view of the likely impact on the organization. What are the general aims? Are there any less likely scenarios which might result? Is it possible to create a mental picture of what the organization should look like when the change is implemented and is working? Does the change have any implications for structures, for management styles, for decision-making and for organization development in general? The change described later in Case Study 3 had clear implications for all of these things, because it amounted to re-engineering to create a new organization from components which were diverse in almost every way.

If funding is involved, and most change requires some, does the project represent the best use of money?

Most people approach change with some scepticism and worry. If the change is to succeed this is the stage where managers prepare the ground and dispel the worries.

Motives
Examine the motives of the prime movers. There are positive and negative reasons for introducing change. Being the first to do something, or innovation for the sake of reputation or status in the profession are bad reasons. Doing something because other people have done it can be considered in the same light. Good reasons are to do with improving the service to the users, improving efficiency and improving morale and job satisfaction. Having open and positive motives will also assist in winning acceptance.

Outcomes
What are the desired outcomes? Are they measurable? The answer here is that they must be, otherwise we will never know if the project has succeeded. If they are, how will they be measured? At the end of the change process, there will need to be an evaluation and a review.

Without setting targets at the beginning, how will the information service know the objectives have been achieved? This is one of the most troublesome parts of the process. Attaching appropriate measures to the performance of technical systems and procedures is comparatively easy; it is less easy in other aspects of the service where the less concrete evaluation and assessment are more feasible, and perhaps more important, than measurement. In areas like leadership, management styles, and the vast area of cultural change this is a problem. Yet these are the areas which are the landmarks of organizational change, and were the things Hammer was referring to when he talked about the 'hardness' of 'soft' change. Some of these questions relate to issues which should be the subjects of some thought-provoking questions by others outside management. They should be considered by all the key players in the change.

Potential Problems
What are the problems? Where are the obstacles to change likely to occur? Some of them will already have been identified through examining organizational health; others will emerge as the change process is considered in detail. Who are the likely resisters? In outline, how will they be dealt with? Whose support will it be helpful to enlist?

Alternatives
Is there an alternative way of proceeding, or another project which might represent a better use of resources? How will the budget be managed? Are there any other courses of action? The proposal might not be the only or the best way of meeting the objectives. Not making the change is always an option. What is likely to happen if it is not introduced?

Responsibilities
What is to be the role of the manager? One of the preconditions for successful change

management is sponsorship by someone as near to the top of the organization as possible, so this is one position to adopt. What will be the relationship between the manager and the group prosecuting the change? If a manager gives away responsibility for a change project to a team, giving responsibility needs to be followed by taking responsibility: for the delegation of powers; by joining and working alongside those who have been empowered; by using the skills of the coach, the leader and possibly the mentor; by offering insights into strategy and organizational politics which could only be provided by senior management. How will this role be created and put into action?

Will there be any input from users? If so, how is this going to be managed?

The Team

Who will be on the project team? Is there a need for a team? More of this in Chapter 7, but the selection needs to be done now and with great care. Once more it is not an issue for one manager acting alone. The originator of the idea (the change agent) could make a case for being there, any specialised expertise needs to be represented, there should be an administrator, someone with a development and training background, service user representation should be organized, and senior management will need to consider their relationship with the team.

There are also questions to be asked about how to achieve a membership mix which will inject creativity into the work of the team. The list can be extended considerably, but team size is a critical factor to be assessed.

Who will lead the team? It must begin work with a designated formal leader. Team dynamics will then take care of things like multiple leadership and alternative leaders.

What is the brief of the team? Answering the preliminary questions is the beginning of preparing this brief.

Stage 4: Development

Now the project team can take the brief and develop it. This is where the proposal becomes a detailed, comprehensive plan:

- Roles and responsibilities are assigned within the team
- The budgetary system is set up if needed
- Reporting mechanisms are established
- The information-gathering process begins.

The research investigates every aspect of the proposed change: the detailed characteristics of the proposal; the staffing and personnel implications; the structural implications; the financial implications; technical features and requirements; hardware and software needs; the timescale for implementation; evaluation.

Potential benefits are assessed and the perceived outcomes are compared with the existing organizational situation as objectives are set, obstacles are identified and remedies proposed. Training, or preferably learning, and development needs are established and programmes set up.

The research can be extended to cover other institutions and if possible similar concepts in ostensibly unrelated areas. The benefits of learning a little about change management in some other managerial sectors cannot be overemphasised, but particular attention should be paid to organizations which have done the same thing in similar circumstances. They might have got it wrong, there is something to be learned in any case, and their experience can be used later in the process. Any alternative courses of action are also considered.

- The work is broken down into sections
- Criteria for the successful completion of each section are agreed
- A timetable is established for each section of the work
- Regular reviews are built into the process
- Communication gathers pace.

Apart from those directly involved in the process, it is safer to spread the communication network until it covers everybody in the organization as far as possible. Users are important, and so are relevant professional and other organizations as required. The results of this communication are periodically fed into the review process, and modifications to the proposal are agreed and incorporated. The modifications are communicated:

- The team makes a recommendation.

This is going to be to proceed to trials, to alter the proposal or to abort the entire process.

Stage 5: Trialling

Information services are not good at testing innovations. There is no manager who would contemplate switching on a new computer system at 9.00 on a Monday morning without exhaustive prior testing. Yet there are many other changes which could have equally cataclysmic consequences if they go wrong, but are implemented as if they will automatically become mature parts of the operation from day one. It is possible to test most developments in information services, with a little ingenuity. Changes to housekeeping and technical systems, rules and regulations and procedures are relatively straightforward to pilot, but other changes, for example to structures and those changes involving policy and principles, and the things that librarians actually believe in, can and should be subjected to the same stringent scrutiny. Perhaps the introduction of team structures is the best example. It is rarely tested, but to do so is perfectly feasible if a small, self-contained part of the library, where any fall-out is comparatively easy to contain, is carefully chosen. Areas like this, where the necessary conditions exist for a team to operate, can be used as a test bed, if managers are prepared to wait while roles and team dynamics develop, while team learning takes place and while responsibility is accepted and extended.

This is not time wasted. Apart from allowing a judgement to be made on the appropriateness of the feature for a particular organization, it also allows other parts of the organization to see the putative benefits in terms of job satisfaction and efficiency, so it acts as an example and a motivator.

If it is impossible to create the conditions to test a proposal, it is possible to do something that might be even better and let someone else carry out the testing. In change management, as suggested earlier, there is no particular virtue, from an organizational or a management point of view, in being the first to do anything. The answer is to find someone who has already been through it and then evaluate their experience. An appropriate benchmarking exercise can be carried out at test sites identified during the research and evaluation process. There is no doubt that the guinea pigs will be willing to tell all.

During the trialling stage all of the established criteria for the project need to be matched against actual performance. There has already been a stage by stage evaluation of everything during the information-gathering stage. This has given a theoretical justification for the project and an indication that it is feasible on paper. The trialling stage has then measured the project against practical criteria, and if these are also met the first stage of the decision to implement has been taken.

This is again an opportunity to consider the practical consequences for the rest of the organization, and again answer some questions:

- Are there any unforeseen knock-on effects?
- What aspects need to be revised?

Testing the proposal would not be complete without actively involving that other group of victims — the users. Hopefully they will have been informed and consulted from a much earlier stage, but this is now the point where their input can be put to good, practical effect. This is another place where a different perspective is constructive, and where it can refresh the process.

Stage 6: Implementation

This stage should be faithful to some basic precepts:

- Breaking the implementation down into its separate parts
- Setting the criteria for the completion of each stage

- Setting the timetable
- Reviewing the budget
- Putting the personnel in place
- Identifying staff development needs at all levels
- Communicating with the entire organization
- Embedding the change into the workings of the organization
- Setting up the feedback mechanism
- Reviewing the general organizational implications
- Putting the change into operation
- Making the change permanent.

This final element, of making the change permanent, is a matter of continuing to manage the worries of staff, and dealing with the pyschological issues which will hang around while the change is becoming embedded in the culture. It helps, in the words of Kanter, to 'treat everything, including teams, organizations, procedures . . . as temporary'. Other steps which can be taken are to set more targets and to look for further developments and refinements in the completed programme. Once there is a positive response on all of these issues, the team can move into the last stage in the model, that of review and evaluation.

Stage 7: Review

Now the circle can be closed and the process of change is complete. The objectives and the criteria set out at the start of the process and revised at all stages of the model can be compared with the data coming from the feedback mechanism set up in the implementation stage, and from other data collected as the new feature operates. This data could come from management information systems, from focus groups, staff and user surveys and other techniques, from staff development and appraisal schemes, and from performance measures. Taken together, they will indicate the success or otherwise of the change. If the indications are negative, the circle of change can begin again, starting with the search for alternatives or modification, or in extreme cases the restoration of the status quo.

The review not only offers the prospect of assessing the success and impact of the change. It is possible that the process itself, being based on research, the collection and evaluation of data, communication, involvement and ownership, will reveal other opportunities unrelated to the actual change taking place. It is therefore creating a momentum for adaptability and contributing to the culture of innovation which is a precondition for managing change.

The Influences

The procedures in the model can be influenced by a number of external influences which are brought to bear on the change process: the organizational environment, which refers more to the environment of the parent organization and beyond; the service culture, which is the internal climate; staff skills and abilities; the organization structure and the preferred management style. All of these affect the nuances of strategy and the balance of elements within the change process.

The Organizational Environment

Change in many information services is sometimes imposed by a higher authority. There are instances of action being dictated by senior management against the advice of service management. It takes a very powerful, confident and supremely fireproof librarian or information service manager to hold out against pressure applied from above. Change forced upon a service is a problem. Many managers will assert that a service culture cannot but mimic the prevailing culture of the organization at large. Experience may suggest differently, but where the influence of a more autocratic culture is brought to bear, there is not a lot that a manager can do in the way of resisting the ultimate change. if the service has a more participative ethos however, there are ways in which the impact of having to bring in a forced change can be mitigated.

Given the range of individual responses to change, and the potential for resistance and conflict, it is vital that the internal sponsor of the change first presents the proposal as one they can support, in order to minimise the extra difficulties of motivation under duress. Presenting the change as one which has been imposed from above is never the answer, because of the effects on morale, the prestige of the service and the standing of service management.

It also means that there must be an even greater reliance on an open, investigatory and participatory approach, to make the process as effective as possible, and to increase the chances of modifying the scheme, however slim these might be.

Bound up with reliance on the process as a safeguard is the possibility of using it as a moderating influence in cases of forced change. Used intelligently, it can secure the best possible deal for a service obliged to make a change.

The Service Culture
Parent cultures can be all-pervasive if they are allowed to. But given the diversity of modern organizations, and with no more than a passing nod to the need for obeisance to things like financial standing orders and other bureaucratic paraphenalia, there no longer seems to be any obvious reason why a service department like an information service, run by a strong-willed manager and resilient staff, should share the culture of its parent. There are, in practice, many examples of libraries where the service culture differs from the culture that surrounds it. That some of these have arisen by accident rather than design in no way diminishes the argument. For most of the time the cultural differences need not be noticed. Allowing for the need to subscribe to common aims

and objectives, it is clear that the library could be run in a different way. There is no need for the cultures to be similar, neither is there any need for decision-making processes to match. The culture is dictated by the shared vision of the participants, and it should be able to co-exist with variants if the issue is handled properly.

The Organizational Structure

Most information services are still rudely-healthy functional bureaucracies with sturdy hierarchies. Research carried out by this writer (2002a, 2004) which confirmed trends identified in earlier work (1990, 1997a) supports this assertion. Strategy and theory allow that change can be introduced via these structures, but also indicate the cross-functional impact of change and the significance of an open process. An organization inclining towards a mechanistic approach can still use the basic features that are found in the model. It is also possible (see Chapter 6) to manipulate the operation of a bureaucracy, and reduce the impact of its inhibitory nature (Davis, 2003).

What will be absent are the benefits of diffusion. Lack of ownership is a critical factor in the failure of innovation, and ownership depends first on information, and then on involvement. Everything here hinges on the mind-set of management and the collective view of the team immediately responsible for communication. Technology now offers an answer to the difficulties of communication across organizational boundaries, and the comments made earlier in this chapter on the need to chart and use the informal networks and opinion-formers are germane. The process described in this chapter will drive organization development through releasing potential. It is not compatible with rigid structures which will have a restrictive effect on communication, but the process presents the means of overcoming this.

Management Styles and Approaches

Managing change effectively will often involve breaking with current practice, when it requires a conscious decision to put in place a change project based on a different set of principles from those which have previously applied to organizational life. Some organizations are still to some extent closed. It cannot be said that they are impervious to change, given the massive degree of innovation which is taking place. Proper change management, however, is still only breaking out in patches, and the one area where it is 'dropping slow' is the key one of organization development. There is insufficient movement on structures, team development, organizational learning and management styles. This means that unhealthy degrees of inflexible management, exclusive decision-making and functional organization still remain. Reaping the maximum benefits from change management depends on opening up the organization, building teams, encouraging natural and spontaneous change, experimenting, learning and creating involvement. It is based on a type of dual leadership which innovates while maintaining what is good in the status quo, coaches and encourages, nurtures unity and diversity, supports both structure and cross-functional working, and allows for differences. This is moving from a closed to an open culture, with organic structures and flexible management styles.

Much depends on how managers initially approach the issue. The early stages of implementation emphasised the need to take a project through a rigorous process of analysis. This involved achieving a clear understanding of the nature of the problem, and all the possible solutions. This means that good change projects start as open projects with a slightly fuzzy feel to them. The problem may be clear, but the objectives may be general and as yet unrefined, and the implementation sketchy. As the analysis and information-gathering proceeds, objectives become clearer although implementation is underdeveloped, so that they are semi-closed projects. Only in the final stages, even after trialling, should they become closed in the sense that objectives and methods are clear. The case study at the end of this chapter analyses the ultimate closed project: no development could take place because of a lack of resources. One of the first tasks of the team was to turn this reasoning on its head and begin to ask questions about how the resources could be made available. If all the options are not considered, the situation becomes rigid and affects everything that follows. Seeing the first stage of the process as stating a problem is a simple but effective reframing which immediately changes the nature of the exercise. Instead of being closed, the change is at least semi-open at the start and the change cycle looks more like an investigation of options.

Another result is a greater emphasis on the participatory features of the model. Closed change projects must be converted into open ones, by reframing the basic issue at the beginning and then using the inquisitive and exploratory elements of the change process to change the tenor of the development. As the process develops it will become more and more focussed.

Effective change processes are crucial to success. The most difficult of Lewin's three stages is the final one, that of refreezing, or 'getting the change to stick'. The important considerations which will help achieve this are listed below.

Openness

The change has to be sold on a straightfoward, honest and factual basis. The advantages, disadvantages, alternatives, degree of difficulty, areas of concern and how they will be addressed should be presented unambiguously. Equally important, there should be a realistic statement of the practical impact of the change on the operation of the service, the users and the staff. Airy-fairy appeals to concepts like self-realisation and internalisation are definitely out in this respect, although they may well have their place elsewhere.

The Soft Touch

Having said this, it is of course appropriate to remember the softer management skills. Innovation is far more likely to become a standard and accepted part of the operation if people feel that meeting their psychological and developmental needs is part of the plan.

Linkages

The general strategy and the communication strategy within this must fit with the organizational structure and the approach to managing. Genuine participation is the best way to ensure that the change becomes absorbed into operations.

Staging

From start to finish, and particularly in the implementation, a staged process will help match the pace of the activity with resources and staff capabilities, reducing stress and uncertainty, showing progress and supporting motivation.

Leading

The message given by leaders at all levels of the organization is also important. Signalling personal commitment during the change process is critical to acceptance of the new features.

The tone is set by management behaviour. Perhaps the first step in change management is for managers to change themselves.

Case Study 3: Injecting Some Realism

Background

The action took place in the educational television and media unit of an integrated information service in a university. This unit was charged with providing a comprehensive television, photographic and audiovisual facility for the university, but in practice was heavily biased towards the first of these functions. The events described here were played out during the preparation of a strategic plan and a budget, and immediately afterwards.

The university information service was a post-convergence department which had previously been made up of a number of autonomous units, reflecting varied traditions and ways of working. Each one had handled its own budget, and the exercise described here was the first attempt to introduce a coordinated approach while still vesting authority and responsibility with the teams. The director of information services was committed to participative management and devolved authority.

The information service was based on an embryo team organization which was following a consensual and carefully-researched and designed organization development project in which responsibility was being devolved to teams which had already been given control over their own budgets and staff appointments. A senior management team comprising team leaders and other personnel below management level had been created and was beginning to coordinate and oversee the redefinition of the service ethos and modus operandi, on the basis of a move towards self-management and participation. This group was also working on the restructuring of the service around a series of multi-skilled teams providing conventional library services, electronic information services, media and information technology services to support the academic programme. The objective was to provide all the necessary support services from single points on each campus. As part of this, the integration of academic computing, still a separate service, was in the early planning stages. The preoccupation with the development of an adaptable, sensitive, comprehensive and constantly improving user-centred information service was enshrined in the strategic plan, which also identified a number of specific projects to improve communications, recast the service structure as one which would be more responsive to user and staff needs, support the development of human resources, build collaboration and underpin the move to self-management.

The Problem

One of the first tasks devolved to the teams was to take responsibility for preparing their own budgets as a participative activity and a consultative exercise involving the other teams, the senior management team and user groups who met regularly with information services staff. At this early stage, the media unit threatened to derail the entire project. Their business plan contained a number of important developments designed to make the service more responsive to user needs and to update the technology in use. Unfortunately their bid exceeded the amount of money allocated to the entire information service during the previous budgetary round.

This left the director of information services with a dilemma. The media unit was a reluctant partner in a service which was engaged in a process of far-reaching cultural change. The process had been running for about a year and signs of progress were becoming clear. The director of information services was hesitant about backtracking on a carefully-wrought change project at the first sign of difficulty. After some consideration he allowed the media unit's financial proposal and business plan to go to the service management committee. It was eventually incorporated into the service's proposals, to be summarily dismissed by the university senior management group. The director of information services was required to work within an imposed budgetary limit.

In response to a request to prepare a revised programme and produce a positioning paper indicating possible ways of implementing the projects included in the business plan, the media unit director indicated that he could continue to provide the service as it stood, but that no development could take place because of inadequate funding.

The Actions of the Director of Information Services

The criticisms levelled at the media unit by university management concerned the historical lack of development in the service, the absence of accountability and the concentration on educational television at the expense of more widely-relevant media support. At bottom was the related perception that maintaining a skilled and specialised television crew, with an apparent lack of activity during downtimes between projects or while other essential preparation for shooting was taking place, was inefficient. Ironically, the budget bid was designed to make progress on all these fronts.

None of this was new to the director of information services. He was unwilling to take responsibility away from the team at this stage, but conscious of the fact that all the teams would be restructured and empowered as a result of the organization development under consideration. He therefore gave the media unit responsibility for preparing a business plan based on a modest increase in resources.

At the same time, he identified a technician with a breadth of interests and skills. He began to use this member of staff as a sounding board for ideas, as a conduit to the rest of the team and as the source of an objective perspective on the work of the unit.

Over a period, the director of information services gradually spent more time working with the media unit team, and acting as a member of that team on the same basis as everyone else. A new view of the role and functions of the media unit began to emerge. In particular, the team identified several key factors.

The Possibility of Multi-Skilling

The unit possessed several expert photographers. It was a short leap of imagination to set about equipping them to work as cameramen. At the same time, the television crew collectively possessed wide expertise and experience in the maintenance and repair of most of the equipment held by the unit. The updating and extension of these skills also became part of the staff development portfolio. A similar exercise was carried out with graphic designers, general media technicians and producer/directors. The latter, as it transpired, also possessed skills and expertise which fitted them for more expansive roles in a more innovative and flexible working environment.

A Change of Direction

Most of the work of the unit was naturally concerned with supporting teaching and learning, particularly to do with activities like the filming of routines and experiments, drama productions, student work and audiovisual equipment and support services. Practical workshops were also run.

The workload was examined in detail. Most of the technical staff had backgrounds in public service broadcasting and newspaper production. Given the role flexibility introduced through the development of multi-skilling, it was decided that there was room to develop small-scale commercial activities. In partnership with the Business School and the School of Food Science, the unit began to produce training material and publicity material for local companies. This was a commercial and technical success, working with local schools in collaboration with the School of Education.

The reprographics section underwent a similar analysis. The conclusion here was that the introduction of new printing technology would create a further opportunity for small-scale income generation without requiring a staffing increase. This proved to be the case as the unit took on the production aspects of a modest publishing venture. The activity was linked to the commercial activities of the television service, and again involved collaboration with the School of Education and external contracts for the publishing of teaching material for schools. A profitable subcontracting relationship with a local printer also developed.

Do it Yourself

Much of the television work which the unit had given priority to was static, in that use was made of no more than one or two cameras to film student activity in studios or teaching areas. The information service also possessed an observation studio which had fallen into disuse. This was refurbished and brought back into action with two fixed cameras and therefore a reduced manning requirement which further increased flexibility. This facility proved increasingly popular across the teaching programmes of the university, and led to an increase in the use of educational television.

Downsizing

The media unit's pride and joy was a mobile broadcasting unit equipped for location work involving sound and television. It was expensive in terms of equipment, running costs, other overheads and staff time. Two technicians working together, and taking advantage of the availability of compact digital equipment, redesigned the entire setup to fit into two custom-made boxes which themselves fitted neatly into an estate car drawn from the university's transport pool. The location work was then staffed by a single technician who could work across the board. The mobile unit was scrapped and further savings were made without any loss of effectiveness.

Changes in Working Patterns

One of the least tractable issues proved to be the traditional working pattern of the technical staff. With an understanding that no significant leave would be taken during the teaching year, a number of senior staff who had accrued long service leave in addition to their basic allowance were able to take leave in a single block which effectively denuded the service of its technical staff for most of the long summer vacation. This imposed a strain on the provision of the service and led to difficulties with younger staff who felt they were being taken advantage of. It took many months of patient negotiation involving the Director of Personnel and the trade unions before a fair and workable system was arrived at. For the first time, it also allowed the unit to introduce a planned maintenance service during less pressured vacation time.

Implementation

The initial work amounted to the drawing up of a strategy for change in the media unit. This process was owned by the staff of the unit, but also depended on the participation of the other parts of the information service, and the users. Linked to the strategic planning of the information service, its implementation then depended on a series of projects which were all connected, and which would have to run in the context of the bigger picture of structural change as the service moved towards multi-skilled teams enjoying a significant measure of responsibility. The implementation strategy had to reflect this. Chapters 6 and 7 consider structures in detail, so it is only necessary here to point to the issue in general.

Who does the work of implementation? is a basic question. Organization development and innovation take place as the daily routine of any service continues. The literature often advocates, as for example do O'Reilly and Tushman (2002), the creation of a special team to run an innovation project. This may well be a realistic, if arguable, proposition in the wider world, and no doubt for some big information services. In most cases it is simply not an option. Innovation has to occur alongside the continued provision of the service. The director of information services in this case had no choice, but in any event saw it as beneficial to run the projects alongside the normal staff responsibilities. This strengthened ownership, and helped in the diffusion of ideas as it strengthened the communication process. There were no barriers between the innovations and the wider service. This also called for a particular set of leadership characteristics, which are examined in Chapter 8.

Analysis

This case study provides a simple illustration of a number of the principles of managing change at both the strategic level and at the level of the change project. Of immediate interest, it illuminates implementation strategies and the initial stages of the process.

Reframing the Project

The intervention of the director of information services led to a complete reappraisal of the situation. The director of the media unit identified the problem in a very simplistic way as the inability of the institution to provide an appropriate level of funding. This immediately put his development plans into a straitjacket.

The director of information services saw it as a multi-faceted issue involving working practices, the ethos of the unit, the skills issue, priorities and the deployment of staff. All of these were interrelated and ultimately changing the skills mix had an impact on everything else. Not only was the director of information services capable of looking underneath the surface, he was also willing to involve others and lead the way in a rigorous analysis of the problem. By asking a simple question – How could the operation of the media unit be modified to create the opportunity for development? – he changed the nature of the exercise, removed the negativity of the media unit director and transformed the project from one which was closed to an open one which had many characteristics which helped him sell it to the staff.

Investigation

The early stages of change implementation were therefore marked by an exhaustive investigation which involved a number of individuals. The choice of implementation strategy was also sound. It was educative and participative, with the director joining the media unit team on the same basis as everyone else and without the need for recourse to formal authority.

Fitting the Project With the Strategic Plan

The director, one of the change agents, was aided by the fact that everything proposed was in line with the accepted strategy of the service. The clear link with strategy meant that it was easier for people to see that the proposals were central to the work of the service. The strategic plan had enshrined the central issue of progressive change in the interests of providing a better and more responsive service to users. The director of information services' involvement in the detail of the investigation and the implementation of the new ideas meant that high-level sponsorship was also obvious. Attention was also paid to communication at all times.

The Outsider-Insider

The initial action of the director of information services in enlisting the support of a member of the technical staff who was able to take a broad view of the situation was also important. This was the famous 'Outsider-Insider' – the detatched, objective and realistic expert who carried weight and brought a high degree of understanding to the process.

Conclusions

The difficulty arose primarily because of a failure of analysis. The problem was not the lack of funding but inflexible working procedures, poor deployment of staff resources, too much reliance on external services for repair and maintenance and entrenched views of entitlements. It was exacerbated by a managerial attitude on the part of the director of the unit, whose hands-off approach failed to deliver the necessary leadership and systematic approach to the organization of work in what was after all a diverse sector. A secondary factor was the perception of the unit as an unbalanced service which fell short of providing the all-inclusive support the teaching and learning programme required.

The implementation strategy of the director of information services was entirely consistent with the service ethos. It was clearly linked to a vision of what the service would look like. It was designed to be a shared process working without hindrance across internal boundaries. Crucially, it was a learning process in which all the staff were invited to join whether or not they were directly involved. It turned out to be a unifying process.

Chapter 5

Metaphors for Organizations

One of the problems associated with change management is our history. We have a tradition of the successful management of information services traceable as far back as the Alexandrine Library (Bevan, 1927). This trend-setter of an organization had an acquisitions policy which spanned the whole of the Greek world, buying and borrowing for copying – allegedly on occasions the copies were returned instead of the originals – and its librarians were also editors and publishers, assisted by poets and antiquarians and sometimes educating the crown princes. This was a peerless academic reference library and repository. So for good reasons the vast majority of libraries which followed it embraced the tenets of the bureaucracy:

- Objectives were fairly clear and relatively unsophisticated
- The library and its environment were reasonably stable and there was general agreement over:
  - What was done
  - How it was done
- The models which existed at the time were similar to those of the organization of the army of Ancient Rome and the Holy Roman Church.

A Brief Alternative History of Change Management

For most of the history of library management there has been little pressing need for much revision of basic principles, with our organizations continuing to be influenced by the development of military management. This is even reflected in the fascination with the word 'strategy' which was originally endowed with the precise meaning of a doctrine or set of beliefs for the avoidance of military activity, and, when that failed, for winning a war. The detail of management may have been refined to some extent, perhaps, by Frederick the Great of Prussia, but what we have today in all its glory remains something which is reasonably faithful in essence to most of the the ancient concepts outlined here.

This has not necessarily been a bad thing for libraries, representing an effective and efficient way of organizing enterprises which operated in stable conditions, dealt primarily with standardised and malleable material – the book – and served patrons who were reasonably restrained in their habits and accepted the relatively limited objectives of the service. Internally, libraries were simple organizations dealing with the same kind of certainty evidenced in their external environments. Complexity, in the strict managerial sense of operating under circumstances where there are a number of uncertain factors and no overwhelmingly obvious way of dealing with things, did not seriously become an issue until centuries later, with the growth of what was initially called audiovisual material, and later changes in user behaviour and expectations.

Digitisation, emphasising these attendant changes in attitudes, may well prove to be the telling strike against uniformity. In this respect it is instructive to note that the growth of non-book material, a missed opportunity for change in library management, was marked by a classic paradox. Strenuous efforts to make the formats conform physically by fitting them into book-like packages were accompanied by a mindless determination to treat them as special collections.

This is not to say that there were not other options. G. Morgan (op cit, 1997) offers some, and it seems that a revisionist history of the development of management ideas could look something like the following (with apologies and credit to Morgan).

15th-Century Venice – Global Finance

With global management a developing discipline today it is a sobering thought that the city state of Venice in the 1400s was already involved in the provision of global finance, and presumably developed their own way of dealing with the distributed organizations for which they provided funds.

16th-Century Multinationals – The East India Company and the Hudson's Bay Company

We can surmise that the international trading companies of this period were somewhat constrained in their command and control methods, being limited in their communications by the best speed which could be made by a square-rigged sailing ship. By the time instructions arrived on some distant shore it is reasonable to assume that the local manager had already taken a few decisions and that devolved management and perhaps the 16th-century equivalent of virtual teams werein operation.

The18th-Century – Bartholomew Roberts – The Pirate Captain and Modified Bureaucracies

The short but impressive career of the Welsh freebooter Bartholomew Roberts was another paradox. Rigid discipline backed up by an iron code was ameliorated by a relaxed and egalitarian system in other ways. This included, it is rumoured, the sharing of the favours of female admirers. Was this was one of the early precursors of late 20th – and early 21st – century efforts to make bureaucracies softer and more responsive?

The 1840s – Player-Managers

American baseball teams of the mid-19th century appear to have been the first to specifically use the term player-manager, although all primitive or simple organizations throughout the history of management inevitably demonstrated the strengths and weaknesses of the idea. This attempt to redefine the concept of managerial activity and managerial styles has latterly been taken up on a wider front and is investigated later in this book.

The 1940s – RAF Bomber Command – Elite/Self-Managing Teams

Our highly selective approach to taking management principles from other organizations is well illustrated by our readiness to adopt ideas from conventional military management while purposefully ignoring approaches which dispense with command and control principles. RAF Bomber Command during World War II was a highly sophisticated system of interlocking teams incorporating both specialisation and all-round abilities, decision-making at the lowest possible level in the organization, multiple leadership and an absence of hierarchy and red tape (Pugh, 2002a). There was a massive concentration on learning in the shape of incessant training and the sharing of information and expertise, an all-powerful culture and a system of interlocking cross-functional teams. These ideas are now commonly deployed in elite military units throughout the world, including present-day aerobatics teams like the RAF Red Arrows (see Case Study 5).

The point about this litany of alternative management is simply to assist in developing a new perspective on management: one which is more sympathetic to the priorities of managing change in today's environment. The first step in moving away from the predominant view of the organization of library services is to begin to think of organizations in different ways, and from different perspectives.

The contemporary managerial mindset is inevitably based on a top-down view. This is sometimes fixated on the idea of control, to the extent that it was possible for an anonymous information services manager taking part in one research project to say that in his organization they were trying to give people more flexibility and freedom by strengthening the structure, presumably to help staff understand what they could and could not do (Pugh, 2004).

There is a relationship, in theory at least, between increasing degrees of uncertainty and the development of devolved management. The initial stage of this is a process of rethinking the basic approach to organizations, and viewing them as something which is different from the machine form which has sustained us so far. Fortunately, the current literature is speckled with ideas about the new organizational forms necessary to achieve this. Figure 5.1 shows the basic development of alternative ideas, and is derived from other work by this author in 2005.

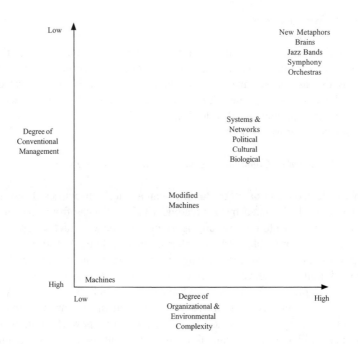

Figure 5.1 The Development of Management Ideas

Looking at Organizations in Different Ways

Our theoretical view of organizations has developed from the machine-based organization through the various forms of bureaucracies, embracing ways in which bureaucracies could be modified, to more innovative views of organizations as open systems and different forms of networks. Along the way organizations have been seen as political systems, cultural systems and as biological systems with a life cycle. The lesson of this last idea is that without modification our present organizations could come to the end of their useful life. The trick is to adapt in ways which ensure survival.

There have been a number of attempts to portray the organization as something which is less mechanistic, with references to organizations as jazz bands, symphony orchestras, choirs, operatic productions and brains among others. Some writers have seen organizational shapes as bullseyes, others have used star shapes, while others have seen ideal organizations for the modern world in terms of amoeba-like 'boundaryless organizations'.

The Bullseye

The bullseye (Figure 5.2) is a possible way forward. Here, the crucial staff layer is the one nearest to users, at the centre of the bullseye. Technical staff, administrators and managers are progressively removed from the centre as their direct influence on users diminishes. The organisational form is constructed around the needs of the user, with all the organisational roles predicated on their value to the user.

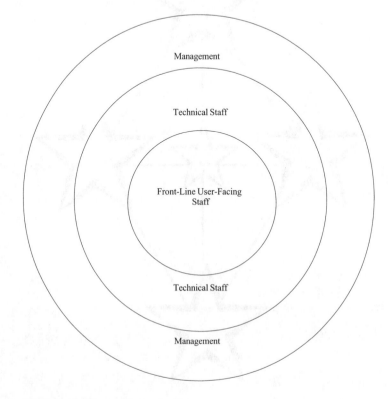

Figure 5.2 The Bull's eye Organization

Stars

Stars are also promising ways of looking at organizations (see Figure 5.3). Radiating outwards from the managerial centre, which is very much reduced in size, a group of user teams develop close relationships with users. The teams are self-managing if not fully autonomous, and they build services around user needs.

The influence of the managerial centre is exercised through the more subtle management skills. In some cases the organizational centre is almost non-existent and most of the technical services are also absorbed into the teams operating on the points of the star.

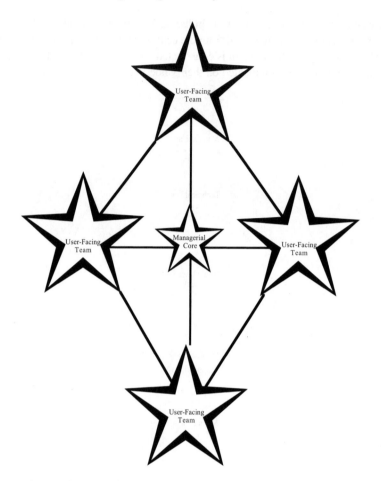

Figure 5.3 The Star Organization

Boundaryless Organizations

Boundaryless organizations are by their very nature difficult to conceptualise. This is perhaps the organisational form for the library of the future, and it has already been attempted in a crude shape. Some academic libraries, including at least one in the 1960s, took the idea of the subject specialist and transplanted it into teaching departments, so that professional staff worked on the territory of the user. At least one other, 25 years later, set out to develop the responsibilities of staff providing services to specific schools and faculties to the point where they were regarded by the recipients as their own staff rather than library staff. We may also find its characteristics in some of the small and highly specialised information services in industry or commerce. However, the concept actually has a much longer pedigree than that. What were G. Morgan's speculations (op cit, 1997) of the nature of management in the 15th-century city state of Venice, or the Hudson's Bay Company's operating procedures, if they were not conceptions of the boundaryless or virtual organizations spoken of today? Pugh (2005) also referred to distributed information services which were in existence long before digitisation, and commented on the

> . . . emergence of information systems and architecture that has revolutionised the scope and reach of distributed organisations . . . based upon a refinement and extension of traditional concepts of organization design and development.

Electronic and digital libraries, virtual universities and the like are not only challenging us to think differently about organisational structures, they are also pointing to solutions. Looking at the vast array of electronic developments in libraries, the boundaryless organisation is not only a potential structure. It also embodies a neat illustration of the link between strategy and structure covered in an earlier chapter. A simple example of strategies changing because of the link with the phenomenon of the electronic library is the development of collection management from a traditional approach through to the delivery of information to the desktop. This is described in the often-repeated phrase 'just in case, just in time, just for you', reflecting the change from that golden age – which never actually existed – when libraries sought to build broad-based resource collections to one of the core ideas of networked information. The delivery, to the point of use, of tailor-made information packages put together for a specific individual, sometimes with that individual playing the major role in identifying and organizing the information, implies the development of boundaryless organisations of some form or other.

Moving towards an organic structure is the beginning of drawing a new map of the organisation. As information and knowledge are the keys, that map is based on the flow of information around the new shape.

Organic structures all have the same weakness: while they are strong on flexibility they are at the same time intrinsically weak on control. There is a danger that their capacity to adapt to change quickly will exceed their ability to stay on the rails. The solution is not to look at control from a bureaucratic, hierarchical or structural standpoint, but as something which can be in itself organic and contribute to the flexibility of the organisation. Ideas about jazz bands, brains and the like simply help us to think differently about organizational structures, and start our search for more appropriate organizational forms from a different position. The relevant characteristics of jazz bands, for example, are that they are places where:

- Skills are learned, refined and practised by the members of the band.
- Compared with symphony orchestras, as I understand the situation, jazz bands are

relatively unthreatening and supportive units. They are environments where people can express themselves within a safe framework. They are also places where individualism in the shape of the ability to contribute variations goes hand in hand with collaboration to achieve the overall effect and ultimately play the same composition.

● Offer people freedom and responsibility in their work.
● Members are strangely uncompetitive, providing mutual support in a creative environment.

The view of the organization as brain provides yet another perspective. Here we encounter some difficulty. Management theorists who use this metaphor for organizations usually affirm that the brain has multiple centres of control and decision-making, the parts are both interlocking and independent, and information is distributed, so that there is a sharing of power and attributes. Steven Rose has demolished this approach (2005) with some aplomb.

We have to accept this view, but the metaphor is still a useful one if it conveys the sense of an organization which operates in a different way from conventional configurations, is specialised and generalist, has a network of connections which transfer information and instructions around the organization, and can understand, learn and grow. If these motifs can help us to visualise or think about organizations which are:

● Supportive: allowing people to develop and use their strengths while making up for their weaknesses
● Ensure that everyone has all the skills, knowledge, information and power to do their jobs, while continuing to learn and apply new ideas and skills
● Sensitive to environmental conditions and capable of quickly mobilising to deal with changes.

we are then going some way towards creating an idea of an organization which is fit to manage change.

The general idea of the networked basis of organizations is now an important consideration in change management. Even more important, it is a way of understanding the reality of the practical structures which lie underneath organization charts, formal communication processes and relationships. This is considered in depth in Chapter 6, but it should still form part of a new way of looking at organizational life, and a major influence on the strategy of change management.

The Implications for Managing Change

The most important contribution is that thinking of organizations differently helps break the mould. This can then be worked through into new structures, new ways of controlling an organization, more relaxed management styles, improved communication systems and the better use of human resources. Organization development is given a new dynamic because of the increased breadth and variety of the potential contributions.

While all these factors improve the technical management of change because they improve management per se, they also contribute less tangible benefits. Once the thinking – about organization structures and the way organizations actually operate – changes, then there are advantages for less tangible but equally critical issues such as motivation, and in particular the psychological issues surrounding change. Examined in more detail in Chapter 9, these are primarily to do with the enhanced stress created in organizations attempting to deal with change.

Developing new metaphors may be a symbolic first step, but it signals the development of new ideas about responsibility, autonomy, individual control over their own working environments, commitment and more interesting jobs. All of these are important factors in dealing with workplace stress, and they also affect the efficiency of the management process. All these elements are tied in with the consideration of structures and in particular with the development of teams. Above all, they foster and apply the talent needed to achieve successful change management.

Chapter 6

Structures

The conventional approach to structures is to say that before considering structure an organization first needs to define its strategy: structure is something which is dictated by strategy and comes further down the line. There is now an emerging school of thought (Kibble and Kissel, 2005) which argues that organization design, involving structure, *is* strategy. Because structure can have such an affect on strategy it should come first in the causal chain. This may well be an arid argument, but at the very least it suggests that there is a powerful connection between change strategy, the organization design or development approach to change management, and structures. This chapter will show that structures clearly have a widespread influence on organizational characteristics, and will therefore be a factor determining the nature and content of the change strategy, and its implementation. Structures will certainly exert influence on the tactical or operational strategy. So strategy and structure are inseparably linked in a more complex way than a linear relationship can suggest.

The Significance of Structure

Structure and Managerial Personalities

To take a slightly oblique approach, a very important influence on how a manager approaches the task of managing change, or indeed of managing anything, is his or her own personality. The personality of the manager is central to the nature of the organization. Most organizations, if the manager is given a free hand, will surely end up to some extent as the apotheosis of the manager's character in all its glory.

As well as a manager's style and personality, organizations are also influenced by their operating circumstances and by other factors such as their history, but overall the structure represents tangible evidence of what the manager considers to be the best way of achieving organizational objectives. It is also an indicator of how a manager thinks power should be exercised.

Structure and Power

Structure embodies a view of how much power people should be given, what motivational forces are likely to work for them, and how control should be exercised.

The kind of structure an organization operates with is therefore a pointer to how the organization treats key themes in change management, like decentralisation, motivation, responsibility, monitoring the environment, communicating and simply creating the best circumstances in which people can work.

Apart from the organizational framework, easily identifiable as structure by most people, and the communication patterns and specialisations, structure is also made up of other elements: the culture – which can be used to exercise control – and the learning system as well as the other subsystems considered earlier in this book. All of these will show the influence of the manager's favourite assumptions and predilections. It is often said that to manage change managers must first change themselves. Looking at the structure, the concrete representation of how a manager thinks the organization should be run, will provide some clues to where a start should be made.

Why are Structures Important in Change Management?

It should therefore be emphasised that structures are concrete evidence of the nature of power, of authority and control in an organization. They dictate the way resources are used and, in the context of change, the nature of the process from start to finish.

Power and Authority

If an organization operates within a bureaucratic structure, the limits of responsibility will be clear at all levels, reporting mechanisms will be obvious and procedures will be carefully laid down. Power and decision-making centres will also be clear. These factors will dictate the strategy and the implementation. They will also define roles, communication and the degree of participation. Most change projects will then take on a similarly orchestrated, managed and controlled character.

Change in organizations operates on at least two levels. Organic or generic change affects the entire organization, as seen in the 'big picture' approach. This involves the development of far-reaching and inclusive initiatives, where results might not always lend themselves to precise measurement. Usually, this amounts to long-term organization development.

At another level, smaller, discrete change projects can be much more akin to project management. They have clearly defined objectives, depend for success on the achievement of clear targets, and can be based on well-defined roles and responsibilities. Rigid hierarchical structures and the solid virtues of the bureaucratic approach can offer ideal circumstances for project management, ensuring attention to detail, the collection of data about the change, the systematic management of the implementation process, emphasis on a logical progression and the measurement of improvements in performance are some examples.

This is not to say that these attributes are not desirable where more intangible, generic or organization-wide change is concerned. It is simply to observe that bureaucratic approaches to change are appropriate for well-defined and predictable change projects which will benefit from a reasonably standardised approach. The obvious example of this is the introduction of a new library management system, which I would say is predictable and an ideal candidate for bureaucratic management. This does not mean that bureaucracies are the best way to manage such projects, but the fact that they can be comfortably accomplished within rigid structures is noted.

Conversely, the development of organizational learning, or radical structural change itself, both contain much which is uncertain, complex and negotiable. These are projects better carried out by some means other than the bureaucratic approach, and may be more easily accomplished inside a flexible structure.

It is worth repeating that it is also easy to fall into the trap of saying that bureaucracies cannot manage change because they are centralised. Decentralisation can in fact occur in bureaucracies, and bureaucracies do not automatically mean that all power is concentrated at the top. A number of writers have exposed the fallacy of this, but what cannot be denied is that bureaucratic structures thrive on standardisation and lead inevitably to a concentration on detail, on working to set procedures and following a system. This means that while they can certainly exert a positive influence on change management they tend to suffer from a number of weaknesses. Change implemented within a bureaucratic structure will be based on:

- Control by formal authority, with formal communication taking precedence
- Specialisation
- Close supervision
- Strategy formulated by management, with no real input from other parts of the organization, and implemented by others outside the management loop
- Clear and logical organization of work, with minimum deviation.

This system will work well if the change project is concrete, manageable, and finite. If it is more expansive, the structure will have a less positive affect, hampering the exchange of ideas, the application of expertise from across the organization and the emergence of a strong learning element in the process.

Earlier consideration of theory (Chapter 2) established that bureaucracies of whatever stripe can contribute a great deal to the management of a change project:

- Specialist knowledge can be applied
- Control is exercised
- Staff involved in the change are clear on their roles and the final objectives, so there is less uncertainty and any negative psychological impact of the change is reduced to some extent.

But if this approach was the perfect solution, it would not have been necessary to invent matrix management, to quote one example. Matrix forms are nothing if they are not an attempt to reduce the worst malignities of the bureaucracy and increase its permissiveness and flexibility.

Communication

Nielsen (2004) makes some points which are familiar to many old management hands, and doubtless the message has also been understood by a few not-so-old managers:

> I have learned through much good and bad experience that genuine communication tends to occur only between peers . . . what it does assert is that all members of the organization have equal standing. It is a strategic principle guaranteeing the organization will be more successful. By denying no one the chance to make decisions about issues affecting his or her work, it will increase everyone's productivity and lower costs. Our workplaces will also improve as we gain the productivity unleashed by treating one another as peers . . . the belief [is] that everyone in the organization should have an equal privilege to speak and an equal obligation to listen regardless of their position in the organization. In general this would mean that everyone shares in information, participates in the decision-making process, and chooses to follow through persuasive means.

Nielsen goes on to identify some of the characteristics of organizations with a free flow of information and a participatory approach to decision-making and the use of power:

- Openness – based not only on the full disclosure of most information held by an organization, but also on the free flow of communication unhindered by rank, hierarchy, or other internal obstacles
- Transparency, which he defines as giving people a level of participation in the decision-making process which they can comfortably handle
- Competence – meaning continuous learning open to all as of right, and including decision-making, problem-solving, strategic thinking and active listening – all of which are crucial to full participation in the operation of the organization
- Alignment, which means: freedom from conflict; absence of complications caused by 'ownership' of parts of the organization; the understanding that self-interest is best served within the larger interests of the organization; the acceptance of common and unifying interests as the best guarantee of a healthy organization.

Bureaucratic and hierarchical structures erect internal barriers based on functions, specialisation, technological expertise and other demarcations. Structure becomes ossified. Communication channels will run on exactly the same pattern as power and authority – from north to south, or top to bottom. Hierarchically integrated and vertically divided, there will be an absence of flexibility. Communication will inevitably be circumscribed by the rigidity of the structure. Neilsen's kind of organization, reflecting some of the best principles of change management – sharing, empowerment, persuasion – cannot comfortably exist within a bureaucratic structure.

The Maximisation of Talent and Resources

Structures not only exist to enable organizations to accomplish their objectives. Their other purpose is to provide a framework of a different kind. This is one in which people can grow professionally and personally.

Change management in a complex and unstable environment depends on the best use of the skills, knowledge, and experience within an organization. Rigid structures are very good at some aspects of development:

- They encourage and support the growth of expertise and specialisation
- They create an area of certainty and clarity within which responsibility can be exercised and a degree of skills development can take place
- There can be some decentralisation of responsibility.

They are less good at capitalising on other, less obvious organizational characteristics.

Identifying and Exploiting Knowledge and Information Within the Organization

Conventional structures have a weakness which is increasingly recognised. They formalise what goes on in an organization, viewed from a management perspective. One of their primary objectives is to make an organization intelligible to managers and managed. Few managers involved in structural change would look initially at the problem from any perspective other than the view from the top. This is natural and inevitable.

We are now beginning to understand that the formal structure is becoming further and further removed from the organizational realities beneath the surface. It is recognised that formal structures actually tend to fragment and inhibit the growth of powerful and positive networks beneath the surface of organizations (Gladwell, 2000). This is true of many technical managerial procedures such as job design, the control of information and the exercise of power. All of these are characterised and constrained by structural considerations.

Successful change management depends on the ability to see the broad perspective of what is happening in an organization. This means getting under the surface and looking for the alternative structure. Cross and Parker (2004) comment on the typical managerial approach to managing what cannot be seen, which is administering various fixes designed to strengthen communication and the flow of knowledge around an organization. In other words, it is to strengthen the bureaucracy.

This misses the point. There is a hidden network, performing social, professional, communicative and developmental functions, under the surface of all organizations. Analysing this, and working with it in a targeted way to improve connectivity, is the key step in improving the transfer of ideas and the development of alternative perspectives. Improving the networks also encourages novel solutions to problems. These are factors in successful change management, and they can only be developed through taking a look at structures from a different perspective.

Another important aspect is the sharing of information. Baxter (2005) discusses the concept of 'information democracy' as a response to the modern organization's need to maximise the use of the massive amount of data, accrued in various parts of the setup, but mainly accessible only by the 'information monarchy'. This is the small group of managers at the top. Once more, the point is related to the powerful need of managers to see the overall scene mentioned earlier in this chapter. Paradoxically, this is a need often frustrated by traditional organizational shapes. Rulke and Galaskiewicz (2000) comment on the ability of the network to spread information and knowledge, and indicate the empirical connection between this function and the general performance of the organization.

Sustaining Long-Term Change Capability

A series of project management initiatives on their own will not build the organizational capacity to manage change as a natural and permanent condition of organizational life. Achieving a position where an organization has an innate capacity to manage change proactively and holistically makes demands on structures which will not be met by a conventional configuration. Creating this capability calls for some precise structural characteristics:

- Small working units close to the users
- Self-managing groups
- Flexibility
- The ability to change direction quickly
- An understanding of the social network and a willingness to use it constructively
- Structures which offer genuine partnerships in:
  - The exercise of power
  - The assumption of responsibility
  - The formulation of strategy and the execution of policy
  - Organizational learning and human resource development
  - Sharing information.

There are also some other characteristics identified by Nielsen (op cit), who advocated in particular two developments with the power to substantially alter the framework of organizations. The first is what he calls rotational leadership. This is similar, but not identical, to the idea of multiple leadership discussed later in the book in relation to the team model. It is a way of reducing the power of the hierarchy, and correspondingly extending participation and improving the information flow. It is also argued that rotational leadership helps concentrate the minds of leaders and imparts a self-renewing energy to the organization, bringing creativity and innovation in its train.

The second idea is that of peer-based councils to offer participants the chance of sharing decision-making and so developing centres of power not associated with position or individual office. This introduces flexibility outside the formal structure.

The point has often been made that in the knowledge economy it is the people who are the most powerful resource. So why not create an organizational structure which actually shifts the balance from control and uniformity to flexibility, creativity and originality? Libraries provide services in an uncertain environment alongside more and more competition from other providers of information. Innovation and change are unavoidable, and they are best managed through the proper utilisation of the intangible assets in the organization – the intelligence, skills, knowledge and experience carried around in the heads of the staff. Ultimately these are the characteristics which will make information services competitive, and effective at managing change, but an appropriate and permissive structure is essential. The truth is that most of the structures in use today do not make collaboration easy, and they do not facilitate information or knowledge exchange:

> . . . vertically oriented organizational structures, retrofitted with ad hoc and matrix overlays, nearly always make professional work more complex and inefficient. These vertical structures – relics of the industrial age – are singularly ill suited to the professional work process. Professionals cooperate horizontally with one another . . . yet vertical structures force such men and women to search across poorly connected organizational silos to find knowledge and collaborators and to gain their cooperation once they have been found. (Bryan and Joyce, 2005)

Structures for Change

When it comes to change management, the most effective structural form might well be a combination of the things bureaucracies and hierarchies do well and the more relaxed and expansive virtues of flexible structures which place human capital at their centres. There are some basic principles which will guide the search for this hybrid structure.

Design for the Future

Kibble and Kissel (2005) lay down a basic doctrine for organization design in times of change:

> . . . organize around developing the talent you need . . . Managers with unique talents . . . don't emerge by chance. They emerge because there's an organizational structure in place that allows them – and challenges them – to refine and perfect their craft.

In this quotation will be found the essence of creating structures fit for managing change. We need to work on structures which will enable everyone, not just managers, to develop the talents we need for 21st-century information services. Bureaucracies and hierarchies are based on the principle that people need to be controlled, so the organization of work reflects this. Modern organizations need to consider the attributes staff will require to deal with the challenge of discontinuous and unpredictable change.

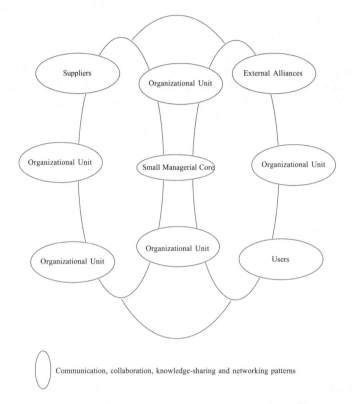

Figure 6.1 The Elements of a Relationship-Based Organizational Structure

Gulati and Kletter (2005) use the question: What kind of structure would be adopted in modern organizations if managers began with a clean sheet of paper? This is their starting point for a discussion. The answers they arrive at include a structure based on relationships – with users, suppliers, external alliances and internal networks – and they develop a model based on information-sharing and networking.

In this model the central or managerial core would be smaller, while the self-managing units on the periphery expand. Figure 6.1, developed from a proposal by Pugh in the 1980s, shows this.

Simplicity

In a well-rounded phrase, Bryan and Joyce are quoted earlier as condemning the retrofitting of 'ad hoc and matrix overlays'. These are attempts to modify the traditional line management approach, and the result is a complication of the issue. Instead, removing layers and changing roles will do more to alter the line manager's perspective and make reporting and communication mechanisms shorter.

Reporting mechanisms should also be clear, although ambiguity here, even introduced by approaches such as matrix management, can aid creativity. This introduces an interesting problem for team development, where there is a balance to be sought between clarifying responsibility and encouraging multiple leadership in the cause of the better application of expert knowledge and skills development.

Teams

Teams (see Chapter 7) are not a panacea for change management or organizational health generally. But they are the correct solution in the right circumstances. Identifying the area where teams can profitably be deployed is the first step. A detailed consideration of the role of teams will be found later in the book.

Networks

A formal attempt to develop a series of networks, which should interlock and have the express functions of developing social and professional exchanges, can unify the mix of teams and conventional departments which all healthy organizations should have. They will also provide a seedbed for innovative thinking.

Novel Forms of Supervision

In a structure like the one advocated here, conventional supervision is counterproductive. Across the broad swathe of knowledge-work organizations, there is a preference for more subtle control – not through the rule book and the over-methodical specification of routines and tasks, but through features like cultural norms, the use of motivation, the influence of the group, empowerment and novel management styles.

Working Horizontally

There is a prevalent mindset which creates a comfort zone around hierarchies, so there is often an instinctive preference for working hierarchically. The consequence is that managers intent on developing a network or teams must do so overtly, and must champion and proselytise the change from a vertical organization.

The hardest steps are engineering a different way of thinking about organizations, and developing a different visualization of their shapes. This is where the metaphors discussed in the last chapter are useful in what is a two-pronged change project. Managers must not only deal with the mechanics of new communication patterns and reporting mechanisms. They are also engaged in a project to change attitudes to the organization and the way it works, so there is a long-term organizational learning issue as well.

Further complications are caused by the existence of two kinds of networks: formal and informal. Formal networks are more visible, and being based usually on common professional or technical interests, are therefore much easier to establish and manage. Embracing people with common interests or expertise working in different parts of the organization, the mutual benefits are clear. The formal networks can be viewed as internal communities of practice in which knowledge and information can be exchanged and help and support provided. The team model in Chapter 7 demonstrates the operation of this kind of network. If the community can be extended outside the organization it can fulfil a valuable boundary-scanning function and a role as change agent.

The informal network presents a challenge for managers. It is much more elusive and time-consuming to deal with, but it is still critical. By its very nature the informal or social network is disorganised and potentially inefficient. It works indirectly, and some writers advocate that the manager should attempt the impossible and eliminate it. This attitude is damaging, for one of the informal network's key features is that it helps create the social context of work, and also of learning in organizations. It does this by bringing together individuals who might otherwise be kept apart by their jobs or positions in the organization. The profitable approach for the manager is to join the informal network, analyse it, identify the key characters and relationships, and begin to use it.

Summary

This chapter has concerned itself with the significance of structures, reflected in the way they influence:

- The exercise of power and authority
- Communication
- The optimum use of resources of all kinds
- The long-term organizational capacity for managing change and organization development.

The characteristics of a structure capable of effectively managing change were identified:

- Small, self-managing and user-focussed working groups
- Flexible and capable of changing strategy and implementation quickly
- Attuned to the networks underlying the structure

- Based on the comprehensive development of partnerships in power-sharing, responsibility, strategy formulation and execution, learning, development and information-sharing.

Finally, some principles of structural design relevant to organizations in times of change and turbulence were set out:

- Forward-looking design for future needs
- Simplicity
- Network analysis
- Team-building
- Embodying novel methods of supervision
- Replacing vertical structures with horizontal ones.

The practical implementation of these principles centres on two general options. There is an argument that organizations have faced successive waves of innovation, all of which have been predicted as heralding the death of hierarchies and bureaucracies. Nevertheless, the knowledge worker revolution, the first onslaught of IT and lately the digital revolution have all spectacularly failed to seriously dent the monolith of the hierarchy (Leavitt, 2005). If this is so, then the best option put forward by writers such as Leavitt is to attempt to modify the bureaucratic approach to make it more conducive to change and more sympathetic to the people who serve in it. The other possibility is to develop organic management structures based on the exploitation of networks and the implementation of teams.

The Trouble With Bureaucracy

The basic difficulty with bureaucracies lies in their lack of potential as long-term vehicles for change. Their characteristics are quite clear:

- They are based on specialisation and the controlled application of specialised knowledge to the work of the organisation
- They maintain service quality through the standardisation of procedures
- They rely on managerial control, with reduced room for subordinates to manoeuvre
- They reduce ambiguity for workers, but by doing so reduce the potential for development by reducing the potential for creative friction
- They run on clear and specified work processes and routines
- There is an identifiable chain of command and delineation of authority and responsibility
- They have vertical communications which inhibit whole-organization knowledge sharing

- Unity of command ensures staff report to one manager
- Centralisation concentrates power in the upper echelons, separates strategy formulation from execution and limits the responsibility of subordinates.

None of these features actually prevent bureaucracies from effectively delivering change. Yet there is less certainty surrounding their capacity to make the best use of the human resources in the organization, and to develop the skills of dealing with rapid, discontinuous change. This is best illustrated by looking at what we already know about the nature of professionals and others working in areas where there are some parallels with information services.

These are areas where broadly similar technological changes are taking place, and indeed information services today are increasingly employing more and more staff who have come from IT backgrounds and possess web design and web management skills honed in other sectors. We are also seeing the arrival of managers from entirely different traditions from that of the typical library manager. We know that areas of the creative industries, the knowledge industries, sectors where there is a heavy penetration of technology, the armed forces – all areas where there are complexities of various kinds – are working out ways to manage in times of uncertainty. They are looking at:

- Flexible structures
- The development of teams
- Decentralisation – spreading empowerment and responsibility
- Organisational learning as a key factor in development
- Communication
- New forms of leadership.

We also understand that people working in a technological environment enjoy the exercise of control over how they do the work, they prefer to take responsibility, and they prefer to collaborate and work cooperatively. As a first step towards a new structure, there are a number of ways in which the impact of the bureaucracy can be softened, to accomodate people who prefer to work more flexibly, with self-management and sharing.

Changing the Managerial Mindset

Bureaucratic management is self-perpetuating. One of the problems of library management is that we appear to have missed some of the influence of Peter Drucker. Drucker honed the idea of management as a function based on decentralisation. His enduring concern for people underpinned his view that management was about integration and its core activities were innovation and risk-taking development:

> . . . more and more of the input we need will not be from people or organizations that we control, but from people and organizations with which we have a relationship, a partnership

– people whom we cannot control . . . Increasingly, the CEO's job will be much more like the most complex job I know, which is running an opera. You have your stars and you can't give them orders; you have the supporting cast and the orchestra; you have the people who work behind the scenes; and you have your audience. Each group is completely different. But the opera conductor has a score, and everybody has the same score . . . you have to make sure all the various groups converge to produce the desired result . . . It's not about refraining from giving orders – but knowing when to give an order and when to treat someone like a partner. (Drucker, 2004)

Drucker also had his view of the organization's capacity to manage change, and in arguing that:

The most effective way to manage change is to create it. But experience has shown that grafting innovation on to a traditional enterprize does not work. The enterprize has to become a change agent. This requires the organized abandonment of things that have been shown to be unsuccessful, and the organized and continuous improvement of every product, service, and process within the enterprize . . . it requires systematic innovation. (2001)

he seems to strike a blow against the bureaucracy as an instrument of change.

One of the most noticeable things about library management is that we pay little attention to the training and education of our managers, although Drucker would argue that in any case it is impossible to do this until they have a solid body of practical experience. The obvious disadvantage we labour under is that librarians become managers because of their professional skills, not their managerial skills. Having won their spurs in a bureaucracy, and being the embodiment of the librarian's tendency to order everything in sight and impose a recognisable pattern on things, that is how they proceed as managers. The biggest influence on managerial behaviour, after personality, is the role models of other library managers. It is their behaviour which is adopted. So we assist in the process of producing managers like ourselves rather than managers fit for the challenges of the 21st-century. This is part of Drucker's 'organized abandonment of things' and it calls for a change in the mindset of managers, who should:

- Develop professional curiosity about how things are done by other people in other organizations, including the most unlikely ones which are vastly different, but only on the surface, from libraries.
- Encourage staff to challenge and question.
- Give more support to the nonconformists, the heretics and the people who are awkward and ask the difficult questions.
- Take one or two of these promising nonconformists, and put them into development programmes, if possible using an input from an irreverent, questioning and incorrigible – if not even villainous – rebel, from whom they can learn the skills of

divergent thinking and challenging the status quo, as well as the solid basis of the practice of management.

- Tie this approach into the recruitment policy, and specifically look for people who will bring a fresh perspective to the organization. There are signs that this is increasingly happening, not least as as the heinous crime of appointing non-librarians to senior posts is beginning to emerge again.

In the longer term, all these things will produce a new managerial template, and there will be a natural withering of some of the more intractable features of the bureaucracy, while its yeomanlike virtues might remain.

Modify the Structure

While it will be difficult for managers steeped in the tradition of hierarchies and bureaucratic systems to dismantle the structure, it is possible to introduce modifications without altering the basic scaffolding:

- Open up the communication system. Carry out an information/communication audit, and take some decisions on how much really needs to be kept secret. Identify all the possible channels of communication, and the potentional blocks. Remove the latter and make use of all of the former, but ensure that the result works both ways and that management communication results in feedback from all levels of the organization. Encouraging openness and honesty is perfectly feasible even in a bureaucracy. If more people know most things about the organization, and have access to information normally reserved for management, this will encourage debate, stimulate new thinking, give people the feeling they are involved, motivate them and help develop a fresh perspective on what the organization should do and how it should conduct its business.
- Alongside this changed attitude towards communication, implement a learning system. Give it strategic significance alongside more concrete systems. Nielsen (2004) argued for the systematic development of competence, meaning the skills and knowledge of the staff. Embarking on this improves efficiency and increases confidence.
- Transparency – the involvement of people in decision-making – is not dependent on flatter organizations and organic structures, desirable though these characteristics are. It can be implemented at a stroke in any organization, and is a simple exercise if there is the will to do it.
- Create some special project teams, but make certain that they fit into the communications system and the overall structure suggested above.

It should be noted that the actual structure has not been touched. With some obvious limitations, a more open communication system can be constructed. Shared decision-making and learning can be independent of structural considerations. Although without flexible structures these elements will continue to be stilted and restricted, adopting this approach will reduce the negative impact of the bureaucracy, and it will also stimulate thinking about the bureaucratic characteristics which remain. In particular, any new learning which comes out of the emphasis on competence should lead to questions about how the learning can be applied in a system which prescribes roles and positions in a hierarchy. Involvement in decision-making should provoke questions about where power resides and how authority is exercised.

Of equal importance, these changes should make managers think. The chances of realising that useful knowledge and experience, as well as varied perspectives, actually reside in all parts of the organization must surely be heightened. In the end, the prize is an organizational form which still retains enough familiar features to be unthreatening to managers and to those staff who feel more comfortable with the old

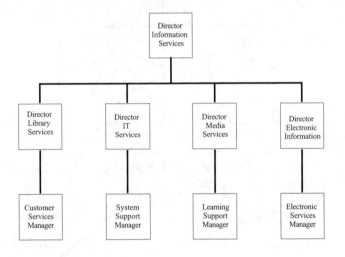

Figure 6.2 The Formal Structure

ways, but will still offer the prospect of being better able to grapple successfully with contemporary change management. This can take place in a stable and ordered universe, while others can see opportunities to make a wider and perhaps more telling contribution to the service.

Learn to Love the Hidden Structure

Most traditional organizations are teams below the surface – undeveloped but still at least embryo teams. The networks are part of the reality of life in organizations, and understanding and using them is a major step towards a more dynamic and responsive organization. It can also be the first step towards the development of genuine teams.

A typical university information service, in a simplified form, might have an organization chart something like that depicted in Figure 6.2. The chart would probably convey little of the sense of what goes on in the library except for the formal power structure and reporting lines, and as such it will have little use in aiding the understanding of what goes on under the surface of organizations. By contrast, the

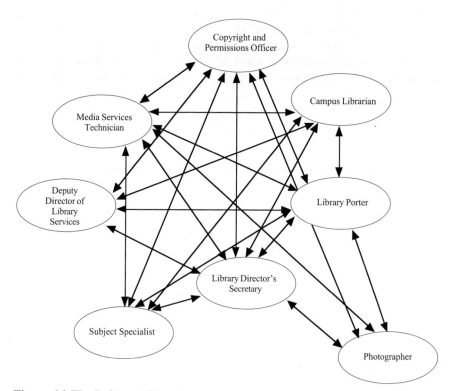

Figure 6.3 The Informal Structure

information gained from Figure 6.3 is much more useful.

The hidden organisation is made up of a network which provides a valuable social, professional, advisory and support function. Within it there will be leaders and opinion formers around whom an embryo team can coalesce, capable when necessary of acting together in the common interest and showing a degree of cohesion.

Within each working area represented in Figure 6.2, there will be an informal team developing. Inside a university information service, taking Media Services as an example, there is an influential hidden force. It is represented in Figure 6.3 by the media services technician. He interacts with a number of colleagues in different areas, so there could be a series of the relationships similar to the one analysed later in Figure 6.4. At this stage, the team will have the following characteristics:

- They are obviously not part of the formal structure. They do not have the imprimatur of management.
- They operate outside the structure and occur naturally, reflecting relationships in the workplace.
- They meet social and psychological needs as well as work-based needs.
- They can sometimes display a hierarchy, which should not be the case with well-developed teams.
- They are made up of members who cooperate with each other.
- Roles can be limited by other factors, such as pay structures or the bureaucratic structures.
- Power may be similarly limited.
- They possess cultural norms, but these are the norms of the group, not necessarily the wider organisation.
- As a consequence loyalty is to the group, not necessarily to the higher order of the organisation.
- Groups do not officially change the way in which work is carried out, although they are often innovative in practice.

The Role of Informal Networks in Changing Organisations

- They discharge a supportive function as far as work is concerned.
- They provide social and psychological support for their members.
- They can be boundary-spanning devices.
- They assist the application of skills and knowledge in areas where they are needed.
- They are capable of making use of differences between group members, and this can provide the basis for creativity and innovation.
- They can develop informal modifications to work processes, either to improve the process or make its operation easier for group members.
- Members have learning roles, which used to be called the 'sitting next to Nellie' syndrome — an aphorism for learning from each other.
- Their very informality, and the fact that they are not necessarily the prisoners of a managerial view at all times, injects a crucial dose of questioning, and fun, into organisational life.
- They are a safety net. It has sometimes been said that informal groups behave something like families, and will therefore apply their energies to resolving any work-based, and sometimes personal, problems of members.
- They are usually, in a conventional sense at least, non-hierarchical.
- They invariably appoint their own leaders, and can also display multiple leadership

whereby leading roles are taken by different players in different circumstances.

How to Manage Informal Networks

Informal groups are clearly different animals from the formal group, set up by, and overtly part of, the managerial system, and managing them calls for a different approach. Being less visible, they present problems because with informal networks managers are:

- Unaware of what is going on
- Unable to exercise control in a formal way
- Incapable of working out the impact of informal networks
- Attempting to tracking patterns of communication and exchanges which make nonsense of organizational charts.

The first step towards managing the informal network, and using it as force for change, is to understand it, and this means grasping the nature and extent of the network.

Network Analysis

Informal networks can develop inside sections and departments, they can spread into other sections and departments, and in some cases they can operate with links outside the library – library managers themselves should also be members of informal networks or groups working across parent organisations.

The conventional management view of the informal network was that it was likely to present a problem. Incongruously, most managers, while aware that the phenomenon existed, did little to harness their potential, other than attempting to contain their energies when their impact became apparent or was suspected to be risky. In some ways it could be said that informal networks are also like virtual teams, and managing them can be approached in the same way.

The Manager's Approach to Understanding and Managing Informal Networks

- Understand who is talking to whom, how frequently, and about what.
- Understand who is interacting with whom, how frequently, and in what ways.
- Identify the focal points of the network, on the basis of the number of exchanges and interactions individuals are involved in. The literature calls this Degree Centrality. People with these roles may also be opinion-formers and natural leaders. They will be vital to the management of the informal group.
- Identify the people who are involved in exchanges and interactions with others via a third party. Understand that the third party, or the intermediary, is a vital link in the chain. Without this individual, the chain will break. If management can work with these individuals, they can develop partnerships with the group. This characteristic

of informal networks is known as Betweenness Centrality.

- Identify the key positions. These are group or network members who might not interact with everybody, but are key parts in the conduit, through which most of the information passes. These members exhibit Closeness Centrality, and can be opinion-formers.
- Some people will be members of more than one group, or will have connections with groups in other parts of the organisation. These are the important Boundary Spanners, vital for change management because they can help combine different perspectives, knowledge bases, experience, and expertise.
- Peripheral Players can also exist. These are people who work on the edge of a group, with a smaller number of exchanges and interactions with other group members. Nevertheless, they may also be important, first because they can still be members of other networks or groups. Second, they can be members of networks or embryo teams managers do not yet know about. In other words, new connections can be mapped through them.
- The group will also contain important figures who might not fall into any categories.
- It is crucial to identify the key players, and how many there are of them. These are group members whose total interactions and exchanges make them significant points in the network. An informal network with only one key player is highly centralised, susceptible to manipulation and more prone to fragmentation. The greater the number of key points in the network, the stronger the network will be, and the greater the potential for development into a team. This is Network Centralisation.

Working through this procedure establishes the nature of the informal network. It spotlights the important figures in the network, the members who belong to more than one network, and also figures who might provide links to other teams. The next step is to make use of that information. This requires a change of management style. Figure 6.4 demonstrates the nature of the informal network which can be uncovered, taking its starting point as the media services technician. The analysis is as follows.

Degree Centrality
This is reflected by the educational television producer and the learning support officer, who exchange with seven and eight people respectively. Prospective leadership qualities can be found here. These are also the key positions as far as communications are concerned.

Boundary Spanners
Both these players are also inevitably Boundary Spanners, working closely with academic staff who would in many cases be in positions of influence, as well as other staff who could provide information and distinctive viewpoints.

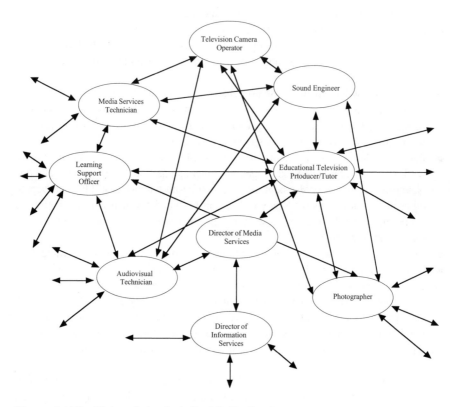

Figure 6.4 The Network Analysis for Media Services

Peripheral Players
The director of information services could be regarded in this light, and will be making a a connection with the director of media services only. While this reflects a potentially bureaucratic approach to management, and is hierarchical, this figure nevertheless is the classic Peripheral Player, interacting lightly with the group but with significant access to other networks.

Network Centralisation
This network is potentially very strong. It has a well-distributed pattern of communication, with two major players but with a number of strong players such as the audio visual technician and the photographer. These are also in important front-line positions where there is potentially valuable information available about user needs and their perceptions of the service. If the network had fewer strong players it would be centralised.

One weakness from a change management point of view is that nobody seems able to bypass the director of media services and speak to the director of information services without going through an intermediary. This could be seen as a barrier to the development of a more potent network. It is also evidence of the collision between informal networks and the formal organizational structure.

Extracting the Information

It is not necessary to make use of software for the kind of sophisticated network analysis which predominates in the literature. This level of activity is often applied to analysing networks linking organisations with other organizations. Examples can be found in all the counter-terrorism services operating today, which make use of enormously sophisticated techniques and equipment not currently required for the analysis of network operations in information services.

In contrast, what is set out here are some useful practical steps, most of which are common sense. They can assist a manager in understanding the hidden networks which reveal 'How work really gets done in organisations'.

Some of the information will already be available in the official records. There are also clues which can be picked up from personnel documentation. The rest of it depends on the willingness of the manager to adopt a new style of doing things: to observe, to engage in dialogue and to establish relationships which might not have occurred in the normal way of things in a formally-structured service. This could involve a seismic change in management thinking.

Small-Scale Research Techniques
These can play a valuable role in identifying the connections:

- Questionnaires
- Interviews
- Focus Groups.

The Social Element: Building Relationships
To understand the informal network it is necessary to build up a rounded view of relationships. This involves observing what happens in social exchanges as well as working situations. Analysing this will help increase understanding of how work relationships are developing, because people who talk to each other for work reasons will often talk to each other for other reasons, and vice-versa. Simple things like managers sharing coffee breaks and eating lunch in the same place as everyone else, and joining in the general conversation, will help build up the picture.

Using Parts of the Formal Structure
Enlisting the support of some of the usual suspects, the middle managers and the front-line supervisors, will also be of benefit. Leavitt (op cit) comments on the pivotal role of

middle managers, aware of the levers of power without having their hands on them, and in conventional organizations doomed to walk a tightrope between the 'humanising and systemising forces.' Front-line staff, by contrast, can be sufficiently removed from senior management as to embolden them. In a properly managed network there is much they can contribute. If both these groups – middle managers and front-line staff – are discharging their roles as they should, and if the proper relationship between them and senior management exists, they will be able to reveal much about the informal patterns which run beneath the surface. The middle managers also have a key role to play in change management, and are important figures in developing new approaches to managing.

Making Use of Experience
Long-serving staff probably know more about the below-the-surface operation of an organisation than most people. Any manager with a concern to use the informal networks, and that should mean all of them, cannot ignore this source of information. The same is true of the person who is often the critical element in this process – the boss's secretary. She, or perhaps even he, is a gatekeeper and a bridge. The secretary can be used as a conduit for information the staff would like the manager to know, and can also be used by the manager to convey a message to staff – often one that would not necessarily be better sent by formal channels. Good secretaries, acting with discretion, can also provide much information about who wields influence in the department, who the informal leaders are, and who exchanges information with whom.

Confidence-Building
As individuals are identified and informal leaders emerge, they must be wooed and cultivated by management. Confidence-building measures at this stage can involve asking individuals their opinions, giving them information, and gradually building up use of the informal communications system. This is in any case based on relationships: communication is far more effective if it is conducted between people who know each other on more than one level, and not simply on a professional or managerial level. Developing effective communication with individuals in positions which are strategically important for the informal group is a critical factor in harnessing the power of the group, or indeed in eliminating the possible negative effects of informal networks.

Getting Involved
This exercise should not be regarded as one in which managers adopt an information-gathering role in order to manipulate or even subvert the network. It is the beginning of a process of sharing the work of the organisation, and improving the contributions of all the staff. It is impossible for managers to succeed in making the best use of informal groups if they stand on the sidelines and observe, or even worse, meddle. Managers need to give something of themselves to the group, in the shape of a more direct intervention in the work, for example – advising, contributing expertise and skills where it is

appropriate, and generally moving towards what David Packard termed 'Managing by Walking Around'. This later came to be known as Managing by Walking Around and Listening'. It is the best way of obtaining information and building relationships and it should be practised on a regular basis, as an integral part of the manager's role at all levels, and as an essential part of the communication and relationship-building process.

As well as helping managers cement relationships with key players, network analysis has other advantages. It is immediate communication, and it can produce immediate feedback. It improves decision-making because managers find themselves in the possession of information they might not otherwise obtain in a timely manner. It also short-circuits the formal communication process by permitting staff to talk to managers one or two levels above their line managers, but it does this in an open way, with the line managers also involved.

The listening component is yet another vital part of managing the informal group. Without active listening, and processing and acting on the information provided, the walking around part is no more than physical exercise.

Getting involved must also lead to some positive results, so where possible appropriate information gleaned from this activity must be acted upon and the connection between the two must be obvious. If this is not so, the exercise is seen to be a sham and is not effective.

Changing Your Management Style
By definition, informal groups cannot be managed in conventional ways. The traditional command and control, rules-based approach has to be replaced by a consultative approach which breeds involvement. Taking the steps described in this section, in order not only to obtain information about the groups and the networks, but also to become part of them, usually requires a change of management style, as hinted at earlier. The willing sharing of responsibility and authority with a group of people who gradually assume the power to run their own working lives, and making a direct contribution to the work means adjusting the balance between managing and doing. By concentrating on understanding and becoming a part of the informal network, managers are taking the first steps in developing organic structures. The huge advantage of starting from this point is that as the network is used properly and becomes stronger, it will introduce many of the features of decentralised management, but in a perfectly natural and unthreatening way. It therefore lays the foundation for managers to move forward, and formalise new structures which are flatter and which empower and involve people in the shared control and operation of the service. While arguably leading to better management of change, the process can also be viewed as a first step in the adoption of teams.

Chapter 7

Teams in Change Management

One constant theme of Peter Drucker's work not referred to in the previous chapter was his view that once a manager came to rely on subordinates, rather than his or her own skills, for information on what was happening inside an organization, then the organization was in trouble. Organization development is naturally coloured by many motives, including a genuine belief in collaboration and the benefits of a flexible approach. The introduction of teams is often seen as a panacea for all the ills of an organization, including the manager's inability to see what is happening in other parts of the organization. Why this has not led to superbly healthy and vigorous library organizations everywhere is a mystery, given the number of managers who reportedly run team-based libraries (Pugh, 2004 op cit).

What are Teams?

The misunderstandings begin here. Work units do not become teams because they undergo a change of label. Neither does decentralisation, transparency, or the devolution of authority to middle managers and supervisors lead to a team-based organization. Power and decision-making can be moved down an organization without actually involving structural change or change in managerial attitudes, and therefore without any change in the basic way of running a bureaucracy. Many middle managers have their job titles changed to team leaders while remaining conventional line managers with no difference in behaviour or responsibility.

There are bewildering arrays of descriptions and labels attached to teams. A trawl of the literature reveals cross-functional core work teams, cross-functional management teams, executive management teams, management teams, self-contained teams, project teams, work teams, functional teams, knowledge-work teams, integrating teams, innovation teams, flat teams, hierarchical teams, structured teams, unstructured teams, action teams, leaderless teams, virtual teams, management teams and some other very unlikely-looking teams indeed.

It is not always easy to detect the difference between some of these teams in practice, and this is an illustration of the difficulty caused by the lack of standardised terminology and a clear definition when it comes to team organisations. In change management the secret is to keep the conception as simple as possible, and use three types of teams. This might also be a good idea for team-based organizations in general. This book will deal with the basics:

- Work teams concerning themselves with service delivery
- Management teams to set the course, monitor and support
- Special project teams to take care of specific change programmes.

It is possible to add functional or process teams to this list. However, I would argue that if this means teams based on the discharge of a routine service like inter-library loans or cataloguing, then functional teams, working in comparatively narrow areas, are barriers to the spread of expertise and have little to contribute to knowledge-based organisations.

There are brilliant examples of the correct and imaginative development of team-based organisations in information services, and there are organisations where there is confusion and superficiality surrounding the issue of teams. The term is sometimes applied indiscriminately to work groups whether or not they are actually teams, and can even be used shamelessly in a classic bureaucracy. Here it seems to be as much an attempt to convey the ethos an organization is trying to create than anything else. There are many other examples where managers are working to develop a team structure through cross-divisional or cross-functional project teams, while at the same time the organization retains the old fault lines between the thinkers and the doers, and managers cling tightly to exclusive control of strategy, policy and finance as executive prerogatives. This may be a moderately good start, but unempowered teams are an oxymoron, and will not change behaviour or culture, nor will they create organisational renewal. It is another case of tinkering with the hierarchy while still leaving the power structures, systems and behaviour untouched.

The meaning of teams is not negotiable. The still widely used, but wickedly overworked, definition of a number of people whose skills are complementary, who make common cause, who subscribe to agreed aims and a particular style of working while accepting accountability for their performance, will suffice as a starting point but there is more to it than this. Genuine teams exhibit:

- Ownership of their work and the space in which they operate, while acknowledging the claims of other teams, departments and sections
- Diversity, or heterogeneity, in their makeup
- Boundary-scanning ability
- Multiple leadership
- Multiple skills and talents alongside specialist knowledge
- Flexibility
- Creative friction
- A learning climate.

Another way of looking at this is to go back to Mintzberg's organisational types

(1979). Of these, the primitive organisation was the one most suited to innovation and change. Forgetting the downside of this structural type for now, on the positive side it was small and it could change direction quickly. Without a large establishment, communication between members was easy, and peer and team influence could develop unhindered in an environment of greater equality. Given the reduced size of the establishment, skills and roles became interchangeable to a great extent, and it was also easier to forge commitment to shared aims and objectives and a common vision.

This chapter began with Drucker's comments on the difficulties arising when managers are forced to rely on subordinates to tell them what was happening in the parts of an organization they could not see. One of the benefits of the small, rudimentary entities described by Mintzberg is that visibility is assured. This is because of the primitive structure and the role of the leader, who today would be called a player-manager. This is half of what is being aimed for in creating a team-based organisation. The other half is the equally difficult trick of doing this while creating a structure which also retains the advantages of the big organisation, and this depends on how well teams relate to each other.

Teams and Change Management

Organizational change in libraries is the result of the interaction of a number of phenomena. While there are numerous causes of change in library services, they are interrelated and cannot be viewed in isolation. Chapter 1 identified some of the characteristics of change in information services:

- Diversity and unpredictability
- Complexity
- Competition
- A mixed economy
- Cross-boundary working and collaboration
- New skills and increased specialisation.

The argument was put forward that while these forces were creating discontinuous change, for which we had no template in past experience, the responses to them tended to be mixed, with some genuinely innovative ideas emerging alongside a tendency to to rely on conventional and well-tried organizational responses. To meet these challenges, there is a general need for an approach based on:

- Dynamic organization development
- The strengthening of learning processes
- The facilitation of collaboration
- An acknowledgement of the relevance of human resources management in change management

- Innovative management skills, styles and leadership
- Novel views of motivation
- The ability to capitalise on new ideas about organizations: creativity, creative abrasion and the ability to make use of differences.

Buchanan and Huczynski (op cit) categorise change on a continuum running from shallow to deep. The deepest change in an organization involves changes in

> . . . how we think; how we solve problems; how boundaries are defined; the way we do business; frame-breaking, mould-breaking, fundamental strategic change. (2004)

These two writers consider structural change, of which implementing teams has to be considered an example, to be shallow change. I would dispute this assertion, and doubly so where teams are concerned. Structural change cannot occur in a vacuum, and it influences many other aspects of organizational life. As such it is the basis of organization development. The strengthening of an organization's ability to deal with this kind of change embraces all the issues described in this chapter and in Chapter 1. Our thinking about what libraries should do, and how they conduct their activities, clearly involves issues which are fundamental and strategic. The way we work is changing because of technology, but also because of other related factors such as changes in user habits, commercialisation and competition. Changes to address these issues are strategic and deep-seated, and structural change affects everything.

At the same time, collaboration is an increasingly important characteristic of library services, and boundaries are shifting and disappearing. Improving our ability to cope with this kind of change is also a strategic – and therefore a whole-organization – issue. As far back as 1961, Burns and Stalker's classic work identified the need for organizations to change their internal structures to cope with external change, and later, in 1969, Warren Bennis was but one of a number of writers who challenged the capacity of the bureaucracy to handle this kind of substantial change.

Before the emergence of the knowledge worker began to attract serious attention, most of the models of team organizations which had some currency were drawn from industry. Typically based on a production line, teams in industry usually embrace a limited number of separate skills so that roles are easily interchangeable. They are characterised by well-defined and very often repetitive tasks, and they have to be given sufficient responsibility to manage their own affairs. This allows them to take upon themselves what was previously a management responsibility for organising work. Their performance is measurable. Ultimately they are capable of becoming self-managing and discharging a range of responsibilities from recruitment through budgetary control and procurement to training, quality control and customer liaison.

Some of the general principles on which these teams work are applicable to libraries. Teams in manufacturing industries can be responsible for an entire area of work rather than a specialised part of it, and they can be empowered and self-managing. A lot of libraries began their experiments with teams by looking at the places where the closest analogy with these forms in other organisations could be found. This often led to cataloguing teams or acquisitions teams. Here the operational conditions most resembled the industrial production line which created such favourable team-building conditions. This is no longer true, not only because the essential nature of the work has changed, but also because acquisitions and processing can be cross-boundary integrating activities in an electronic world.

In other areas of information services, or any other knowledge-based activity, many of the characteristics described above do not apply. Technology and other changes are creating an increasingly complex environment in which user demands and expectations are changing. Service delivery will rely more and more on the interdependence of quite distinct specialisations, while concurrently divisions between professionals and non-professionals are in some respects becoming blurred. As the idea of the personalised 'just for you' information service gains ground, then the non-routine and unpredictable element of the work will become more obvious, while more and more of the routine aspects will be completely automated. In these conditions the kind of benefits sought and gained by industry and commerce will not always be available. There ought to be no doubt of the additional difficulty of organising people into genuine teams in information services where operations are non-standard, but equally there ought to be no doubt that there are a number of models around, which demonstrate the remarkable results of teamworking in complex and non-routine areas calling for combinations of skills.

There is also a cost, and a time lag before results really begin to be seen and might justify the effort. Behind this is another assumption which needs to be challenged, which is that effective teams can be created in a relatively short space of time and with limited managerial involvement after the teams have been set up. The variable but fairly long lead-in time for creating what is a truly team-based organisation makes it a long-term project. It also involves a massive investment of intellectual and emotional capital and as much financial investment as can be provided. The desired behavioural change is often seismic.

If this cameo of the nature of change in information services is right, then organizations need to develop certain characteristics in order to successfully cope with these changes. Aguirre et al (2005) offered the results of a world-wide survey conducted over a two-year period. This research examined the state of organizational health on a global basis, covering all the industrial and commercial sectors and government, corporate and not-for-profit sectors. There were responses from 30000 individuals backed up by the results of another 20000 separate surveys. The research assumed that effective change management can only be achieved in the context of a healthy organization. What emerged from the investigation was an interesting pattern, and one which sets out the basic principles of a team organization.

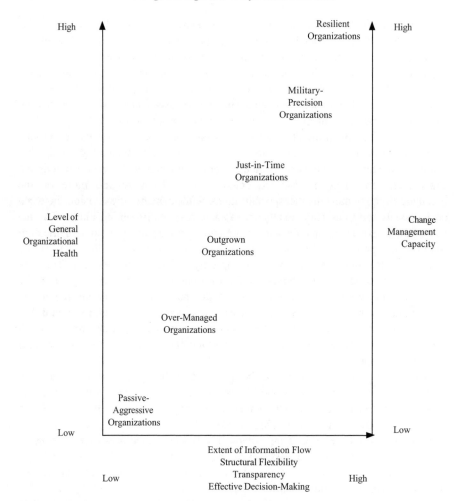

Figure 7.1 Change Management and Organizational Health

General Organizational Dysfunction

Less than 30 per cent of respondents considered that their organizations were healthy, citing various problems. Not unexpectedly, senior managers expressed a more positive view of organizational health than people lower down the organization. The major problems identified were:

● Lack of clarity in decision-making
● Confusion over responsibilities and authority
● Poor information flows

- Structural faults, particularly in organizations which had outgrown the structure they possessed – by implication suffering from a lack of effective delegation, and also from dislocated senior management
- Clear evidence that organizational health is related to the size of the organization.

Organizational Types

The research, which is ongoing, also identified typical healthy and unhealthy profiles. Figure 7.1 shows the relationship between these organizational types and organizational health. The observations in this section draw on the work of Aguirre et al (op cit).

The Passive-Aggressive Organization
This is the organization which on the surface is well-adjusted. It has a well-honed mechanism for producing consensus, but is poor on execution.

The Over-Managed Organization
There is a case for saying that many libraries inhabit this particular hinterland. Here, there are too many levels in the organization, it spends too much time analysing and forecasting, and it is bureaucratic and politicised. Where conventional bureaucracies are concerned, all these charges are difficult to refute.

The Outgrown Organization
Organizations with structures and management styles which have not changed over the years, and are still heavily centralised, can be said to fall within this group.

On the positive side, Aguirre et al identified some organizational types which, by virtue of their comparatively healthy state, might stand a better chance of coping with unpredictable change:

The Just-in-Time Organization
Inconsistency is the hallmark of this type. These organizations are not always well prepared for change, but when faced with a significant challenge they can change direction quickly. They do so 'without losing sight of the big picture' – in other words both their strategy formulation and execution are sound.

The Military-Precision Organization
Still centralised, this is the kind of organization which manages change through efficiency. Strategy execution is good, coordination is good, and the senior management team, which tends to be small, gets involved.

The Resilient Organization
This is the profile which has to be developed if organizations are to become good at

managing change. They demonstrate adaptability and an all-round competence in strategy formulation and execution. To develop adaptability means dealing with the issues of communication, decision-making and structural weaknesses. Without improving these aspects, it is difficult to build in the capacity to adapt quickly without reverting to a dictatorial, command-and-control approach. This brings its own problems. It is also possible to place these organizations on a continuum related to their capacity to manage change.

The Options for Creating a Healthy Organization Fit For Change

What this is leading to is the position that there are basically four options for organization development: taking power back, moving power down, implementing cross-functional teams, and developing real teams. All of these manoeuvres can lay the basis for managing change in certain circumstances. They are not all equally good for organizational health, and this has implications for the long-term management of change.

Taking Power Back

This has been known to work with spectacular results. In extremis, it can happen in the most organic structures, and has been employed with success by the most laid-back and enlightened managers. In dealing with a major emergency, where a change initiative has stalled, or where the process has hit difficulties which cannot be surmounted in any other way, this kind of intervention is realistic. To concentrate power in the hands of a few people at the top of the organization, and to devise procedures and systems for the micro-management of the organization from this dizzy vantage point, may work for well-defined change projects in stable and predictable environments. Allying this with charismatic leadership can create a dynamic organization, but one which has diminished long-term prospects.

Moving Power Down

Authority can be devolved in bureaucracies. Without structural change this simply creates mini-bureaucracies at various points in the organization. The danger of excessive control, the throttling of initiative, the denial of opportunities for growth and development, and the certainty of failing to utilise human resources to the full will be ever-present.

This is not the way of prosecuting organization development. It does not create the capacity for self-renewal and change driven from within the organization. The likelihood is that the organization will instead become reactive, and respond to external factors with piecemeal change projects.

Cross-Functional Teams

These are a partial solution for organizations which remain bureaucratic but which see the need for a developmental process which works across the whole organization. They can offer many of the advantages of a genuine team organization. Yet they can be cramped and restricted by the tension which occurs between functional management, hierarchy and conventional structures on the one hand, and the horizontal working process of a team pulled together to run a multidisciplinary project on the other hand. Maintaining the balance between these axes is a problem which might well be manageable if an organization has no more than one or two teams working in this way at any one time. This may well be particularly true if the change projects are temporary or short-term, and have clear objectives. These are some of the lessons of matrix management.

To use multidisciplinary teams to any significant degree within what remains a bureaucracy can create a significant managerial problem, and this has sometimes been demonstrated by the experience of matrix organizations. It is particularly difficult when the teams need to relate to each other as well as to the hierarchical structure. In these situations there is a tension-inducing balance to be maintained between opposing forces: team autonomy and managerial control. If they remain manageable, matrixes can undoubtedly stimulate new thinking and improve management across functions, but they are at best a half way house. In practice, it is obvious that cross-functional or multidisciplinary teams will continue to feed into a hierarchical structure, and this limits the degree of development which can take place.

Developing a Team-Based Organization

There are parts of a library where organization by function is appropriate and works. Where jobs are well-defined, repetitive, self-contained, precise, unchanging or routine, and reliant on an individual input, team dynamics do not apply to the same extent. This is not to say they are totally absent.

The acquisition of material is an example. The management of a journals collection is another. The organization of resources is a classic example, and by default proves the case. The knowledge of the cataloguer, or metadata expert, could have an enormously more powerful impact if it were to be located inside a team directly serving users, and in direct contact with users and other information services staff, rather than in an inappropriately-named cataloguing team which does no more than what is implied in its title; that is, it creates catalogues.

These observations lead us towards identifying where teams can be valuable in change management, and where they can actually facilitate change by improving the health of the organization and its capacity to accommodate change:

- In dealing with the unknown, because of the existence within the team of multiple

perspectives, talents, skills and knowledge
- Where a range of skills are required
- Where things are complex, in the sense of not being susceptible to conventional solutions or approaches, or where there is unpredictability and instability
- Where issues cut across traditional internal boundaries
- In forming the foundation stones of an adaptable organization, able to respond quickly to external change, generate ideas and innovate, motivate and support
- In creating a healthy organization. Teams are a solution to most of the problems identified by Aguirre et al (op cit).

It is worth developing these points in some detail. The major criticisms of organizations identified by Aguirre and her colleagues were that decision-making was unclear, there was confusion over responsibilities and authority, information exchange was not good, delegation was poor, and senior management was at arm's length at least. Poor execution, too much analysis, too many layers in the structure, inertia and inconsistency were also mentioned as problems.

A team-based organization offers a way of eliminating these problems. In doing so it strikes a massive blow for organizational health, and by extension for the capacity to manage change.

The Contribution of Teams to Change Management: Institutionalising Change

Sharing Management Responsibility

One of the huge advantages of teams in managing change is that management itself becomes a shared responsibility, and is part of the development of individuals in the organisation. In the management team, in operational or functional teams and in project teams, management skills and behaviour are distributed. Middle managers in particular, with a little luck and some learning and support, can emerge as leaders.

Changing managerial behaviour is a necessity in change management, and successful teams help to accomplish this. The team ethos itself, where responsibility and decision-making are shared, is one factor. The other factor is that teams strike a blow against deference, through the cut and thrust of team activities, the open culture promoted within teams and the sharing of responsibility on a non-hierarchical basis. Some managers, when they become managers, stop learning and insulate themselves. Hierarchies exaggerate this tendency, creating an impediment to an important kind of learning in the change management context – the learning of new behaviour. Group dynamics and the development of team roles are antidotes to this.

The two characteristics referred to above, the emergence of new forms of middle management and the development of a mature learning culture inside teams, are key indicators. They confirm that a real team exists.

Teams, Learning and Change

The learning capabilities ready to be unleashed by teams go much further than changing management behaviour. It is a truism to say that individuals put into a team context will learn from each other, influence each other and offer support. Stewart (2006) goes to some lengths to demonstrate what might be considered to be obvious – the fact that inter-dependent teams who rely on each other for information, support and other inputs, develop much closer sharing behaviours. This is especially true of the kinds of learning associated with change management. Team learning is a social activity and as teams, or at least groups, become more widespread features of library operations the strengths of this setting can be used to learn some skills relevant to practical change management:

- Team working, obviously
- Social interaction
- Problem-solving
- Conflict resolution.

Some adult learning techniques like learning from others and the sharing of experience are of course particularly appropriate for teams in knowledge-based organisations. As Casey (1993) pointed out, this is particularly apposite for the management team. This is also an aspect of teams which was explored in considerably more detail by Pearn et al (1995).

In some circumstances it should also be possible, and desirable, for team members to learn how to do each other's jobs. While this is a feature of teams in industry the trick is more difficult to achieve, but nonetheless still worthwhile, in some of the non-routine areas of information services, particularly where there is a high degree of diversity, as in teams which bring together librarians and information technology specialists.

Teams and Structures

Another thing to assert about managing change through teams is that teams do not entirely do away with structures. Team organisations are still multilayered, but the number of layers is reduced and the relationship between them alters. Instead of the hierarchical reporting system, there is a communication system which is multi-directional and which has far fewer filters built into it. The system is also as strong sideways as it is up and down. This derives from the overlapping and interlocking nature of the team structure. Allied to the information system, team structures help organisations to handle information more effectively. It has been known for a long time that complex internal and external organisational environments, uncertainty and sophisticated technological change, obviously create a massive increase in the sheer amount of information which an organisation has to process. Through sharing, team structures are a contribution to handling this.

Teams, Integration and Diversity

The diversity in the groups contributing their skills to modern information services is not confined to the integration of IT-based staff with more traditional groups. In many universities there is a strengthening link between computer services and media services (Mumford, 1998) which also adds to the need for integrationist structures, and the catholicity of public library management structures has been commented on elsewhere. Teams are the only structural option which can provide this vital multifaceted organisational framework effectively, and which can integrate at all organisational levels. This is an advantage compared to the more limited integrative power of matrix management, for example.

As the organisation becomes more sophisticated, the integrative function can develop through devices like locating parts of the same area of responsibility in more than one team. It can be strengthened by shared membership between teams, as well as the obvious cross-functional teams which will be set up.

The literature sometimes reflects uncertainty about the effects of heterogeneity in teams. The argument is put forward that heterogeneity leads to greater conflict, while homogeneity promotes unity. Underneath this there might lie a misunderstanding of the significance of conflict in teams, which are not organisms designed to thrive on unswerving unity. Teams are a safe place for harnessing the creative benefits of conflict and differences. The process of conflict in teams should be controlled, subject to rules, impersonal as far as possible, and considered as a mark of a healthy team. It can then produce startling results. High-performing teams thrive on heterogeneity as much as they thrive on autonomy, and maybe the two go together. Weiss and Hughes (2006), considering the importance of structure in circumstances calling for collaboration, emphasise the positive role the acceptance and proper management of conflict can play in strengthening collaboration.

Heterogeneity is also important in the development of creativity in organizations. The differences are the elements which encourage multiple perspectives, debate and the ability to bring forward a wide range of potential solutions to problems.

Teams and Empowerment

Empowerment cannot occur in the absence of an organic organisational structure. Out of all the examples of what might be called less artificial ways of structuring organisations, the team structure probably offers the best promise of developing true empowerment. Teams distribute power and decision-making centres and lead to the sharing of management responsibilities. Consequently it is easier to develop collaboration and the broad perspectives that go with taking in hand more of the responsibilities of the job and taking a wider view of the relationships between tasks within a work area. This flexibility is characteristic of good change management.

Teams and Efficiency

Finally, teams should improve efficiency. The team approach to managing change should increase the mutual support factor, improving morale and motivation and at least potentially removing some of the stress from the contemplation of change. There should be gains from the simple process of bringing more experience and a greater range of insights to bear on organisational problems. The removal of hierarchical barriers and role-based authority should allow individuals to maximise their contribution to the achievement of team and organisational objectives.

In sum, teams are a force for behavioural change in managers and managed. They can establish a powerful learning environment for the skills of managing change, they are integrative while supporting diversity, they have a motivational function and they can improve performance.

Team Structures, Leadership and Communication

Change in bureaucracies, or even matrix organizations using teams in some areas, will be confined to specific parts of the organization. The emergence of insulated pockets of innovation can be caused by:

- Organizational barriers to communication and the transfer of ideas
- Inappropriate leadership in areas where change is not a priority
- The wrong mix of staff
- The ingrained view of the ownership of processes, functions and projects by discrete areas of the organization.

Moving to a team-based structure is a way of embedding change management and making it an established feature of the culture.

Team Responsibilities and Authority

Teams only work well in areas where they are given all the responsibility and authority they need to achieve their objectives and discharge their duties. The area they work in has to be sufficiently wide and demanding to give them the scope to use that power and authority.

The area of influence for a team must break down traditional boundaries. The problems here are often seen in the development of digital information services. To give a team responsibility for meeting the information needs of a particular group of users, from resource selection and organization right through to exploitation, is appropriate. To then create a separate division of electronic information, which is sometimes the case, is to reduce the impact of that team, and underlines the need for a clear understanding of the link between strategy and structure. If teams are imbued with an awareness of their own power, and a realization of the breadth and comprehensiveness of their influence, there is less scope for uncertainty or frustration, and more scope for growth and the use of imagination and innovation.

Teams and Communication

The boundary-spanning nature of teams is critical. Communication develops more effectively when people are charged with learning to share things between themselves and with other teams. Even in teams, communication still depends on learning the habits and skills of listening, dialogue and information-sharing, and it also depends on some multiple membership of teams and the use of the available technology. Good communication comes much easier when the issues which usually bedevil cross-organizational communication, such as ownership and sharp demarcation of territory, are absent.

Communication depends on relationships. In a team-based organization there is a greater opportunity for the development of trust, reliance on each other, and simply getting to know each other. In a specific change project, and in the wider task of managing change at an organizational level, these valuable characteristics are easier to develop than they would be in an organization limited by conventional structures.

The Remoteness of Senior Management

Teams are self-managing. They learn to collaborate and to take decisions collectively. They have in their grasp the power to decide how they will work, and this gives them control. Senior management will need to respond by changing themselves in order to manage change better. As the organizational layers disappear during this process of creating teams with power and authority, managerial remoteness goes with it. Empowerment and control over one's own affairs is also an antidote to inertia, and is enhanced when execution of strategy is unambiguously in the hands of a team which also has a real and influential stake in strategy formulation.

These are not the only ways in which teams are an antidote. They are also an effective immunisation against some of the centralising forces unleashed as organizations get bigger and more complex. There is a natural tendency for organizations, as they grow, to add more levels and vertical divisions. The best contemporary examples of this tendency can be found in some of the structures which have been developed to deal with the convergence of academic support services in universities. Teams, because of their characteristics and functions as outlined here, work against the grain of this movement.

When it comes to embedding change in an organization, the effect of the internal boundaries found in bureaucracies is to make it harder for innovation to be disseminated. Teams also counteract this, through their boundary-spanning function and their links with other teams.

Motivation

In the context of facing change, motivation depends on challenging people to extend themselves and push themselves beyond the comfortable certainties of traditional working. Teams are a sound vehicle for presenting people with tough challenges which stretch them, and for giving them the support they need in facing these challenges. Teams create an environment in which it is safe to try new ideas, to take risks and to learn from failure, and they can do this partly because they broaden the range of motivational strategies a manager can make use of.

Teams also tap into people's need to belong in a way which other organizational forms cannot to the same extent. Glaser (2005) argues this point trenchantly, and this sense of well-being contributes to awareness of self-worth, another necessity for motivation.

An important outcome of all of this is that motivation and commitment increases. Ownership, the ability to set targets and to collectively extend the reach of the team are vital factors in improving organizational health and giving people a stake in their own development and growth. If this is repeated across an organization, it creates an organization fit to manage change.

Teams and Creativity

The issue of organizational creativity – the ability to develop new thinking and apply innovative solutions to problems – is central to change management. Amabile (1998, for example), during the course of a decade-long investigation of creativity in various arenas, has challenged a number of assumptions. In doing so, she established some key characteristics of a creative environment. Creativity flourishes when there is:

- No fear. The team environment is a safe one, where people can take risks without undue fear of failure, and where individual weaknesses can be compensated for by the strengths of others.
- Less pressure. One of the myths challenged by Amabile is that pressure stimulates creativity. The reverse was found to be true. The sharing of responsibility by teams reduces pressure in the workplace.
- Consequently, collaboration leads to more creativity, while competition is a factor which actually weakens the creative output. Team environments are places where collaboration is a key skill. They are places where competitiveness should be an internal force, as individuals strive to improve their performance as a personal issue rather than pitting themselves against others.

- Creativity is a product of intrinsic motivation. One of the problems sometimes raised when teams are considered is that reward systems in organizations are out of synchronisation with collaborative efforts, and this is a disadvantage in a team context. Amabile found that it is recognition which is a crucial factor, and not necessarily material rewards. In this respect, teams score in their ability to work in some ways as a community, to attend to the social aspects of work and to reward, praise and celebrate.

- Amabile's general conclusion was that people are more creative if they are involved in their work, if they like it, and if they have some control over what they do. Teams offer some freedom to work in a supportive and risk-free environment. They are places where committed individuals can find a challenge in their jobs which they might not find in a more prescriptive environment where the status quo prevails.

The Problems of Using Teams to Manage Change

Teams are not a universal panacea for all organizational problems. There are areas where they are not entirely suitable for organizational structures in general, and inevitably areas where they are less appropriate for change management. The disadvantages of teams can be magnified in the pressurised environment of organizational change. In the early stages of team development, members of the embryo team will bring the usual baggage with them:

- Territoriality
- Personal agendas
- The possible impact of a reward system which might not, in the view of the team members, be attuned to teamwork and shared responsibilities
- A comfortable reliance on the old structures and relationships.

McKenna and Maister (2002) gave their views on how to maximise the team contribution to change management, and what teams can bring to the process. Teams are good for:

- Setting a challenge.
- Sharing information.
- Striking a balance between the required level of support and allowing people to take risks and extend themselves. Psychological safety, as suggested earlier, is a key benefit of team working.
- Encouraging diversity and divergent thinking, while ensuring that unanimity comes out of the collaborative process once a decision has been taken. Fischer and Boynton (2005) refer to the problem of 'traditional' teams, almost invariably built around people who were in situ at the time the team was set up. They compare the

resulting group-think with the creative friction which emerges when a team is hand-picked and brings a range of perspectives – and egos – to the situation. But this has to be balanced by the older idea of Lewin (1958 op cit), that there has to be a clear understanding that team failure is also an individual failure, and that the fortunes of each member are bound up with the success of the team.

● Not taking things too seriously all the time – making work fun.

Teams, Change and Human Resource Management

I would add one significant element to what McKenna and Maister have said. There was an earlier reference to the importance of regarding human resource management as a strategic issue for change management. What is meant by this is that the personnel mix, the way people are selected, the criteria relevant to team membership and their continued development and acquisition of learning, are central issues. They are, however, issues which are too important, in a perfect, transparent and decentralised world, to be left to senior management. Once the principles are established, HRM should be a process which, if not exactly left entirely to the teams, will benefit from a major input from them.

Critical soft management skills are better delivered from within the teams. Motivation, support and general day-to-day welfare in a working situation are more effectively provided on the spot. This is also true of the vital learning and development component of teams. There is a plethora of evidence that most of the learning in work situations not unsurprisingly occurs from work itself, on the job, and from peers. The organization and delivery of this should be a team responsibility. None of this can be accomplished without a large input into the mechanisms of team membership, and without some control over the qualities a team seeks when there is a change of personnel.

An important issue in the effectiveness of a team is how it renews itself. Securing this means giving the team a significant input into the people and the job specifications used, and for the recruitment and appointment process. This is a part of empowerment, and the criteria they devise should attract:

● People who will not uncritically accept the status quo
● People who will display divergent thinking
● Communicators who will be unafraid of proposing new ways of doing things, and defending their proposals
● Risk-takers
● People with the mental hardness to accept temporary failures, learn from them and continue to think creatively and develop new ideas
● People who will integrate with the rest of the team and other teams
● Natural collaborators
● People who will be unafraid of the establishment.

These are issues to be tackled at ground level, with appropriate management support and advice.

The characteristics which teams should be looking for in their membership are themselves part of empowerment: the willingness to challenge accepted ideas is an aspect of the proper use of power. An openness to new thinking and a bias towards the creativity which comes from divergent thinking is a measure of organizational and team health. Sustaining this ability is a predictor of future health.

What About the Managers?

Much of this chapter has been about the workers. The question of where management fits into this scheme is important. Introducing teams into an organization is a sneaky way of creating a federal system. In a federal system, the centre – or the top – has two functions:

- To do what cannot be done by the decentralised teams working on the periphery.
- To maintain the links with the periphery which ensure that effective communication continues. This allows the centre to make the input of skills, knowledge and experience – particularly political – which the team cannot provide, and to take from the teams essential knowledge, experience and differing perspectives which will similarly inform the work done by senior management.

Teams are empowered to influence the work of other teams where this is relevant, and to influence the decisions and deliberations of management teams in whatever form they might exist. They are given managerial responsibility for the areas and issues they can manage as efficiently as managers; where they cannot do this, the responsibility remains with the managers. An active communication process within the team structure and between teams and the management team is a structural feature which holds everything together. If a management team is going to play an effective role it is not enough to simply empower teams. There has to be a change within the management team itself if proper communication is to ensue.

It is perhaps inevitable that when the shift towards a team structure begins, the management team is made up of individuals who previously enjoyed positions of hierarchical authority. What is not inevitable is that when the opportunity for a reorganisation of the team occurs, usually through the departure of an original member, the replacement is also made on the well-tested hierarchical basis, so the idea of non-hierarchical authority, central to this entire concept of change management, is undermined.

In a team-based organisation, management teams are there to manage overall performance and to set mutually agreed goals for other teams. They develop the big picture, put the work of other teams into a wider context, provide integration and fulfil cross-functional responsibilities. They establish behavioural norms for other parts of

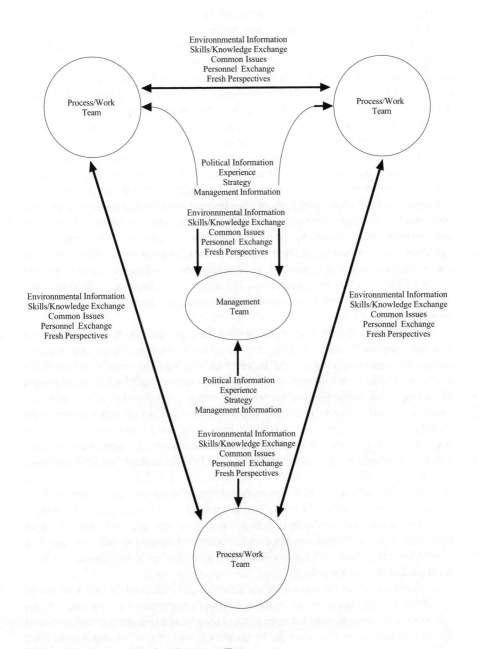

Figure 7.2 Communication Between Teams

the organisation, help design other teams and ensure the coordination of the work of all teams in line with agreed strategy. Admittedly, there has to be a degree of hierarchy in this, but management teams are no different in some respects from any other team: membership should be based on roles, skills and abilities and on the representation of all the interests of the information service, and not entirely on position. Properly constructed teams have a balance within them which is created by team-building and selection. There is no logic in not doing the same for management teams. What this means in practice is opening up the management team to people who would not automatically be within the traditional managerial orbit.

In the management team, in operational or functional teams and in project teams, management skills and behaviour are distributed. This is the only way in which team leaders can emerge as a new form of middle management. It is also a neat way of getting around one of the problems of management education in librarianship – the often sudden transition from being a front-line professional to management, without any serious developmental support. Gradually introducing less experienced members into a management team provides a learning exercise which again offers a safe way for potential managers to broaden their experience. This has been a notable feature in the development of communities of practice, where it is not uncommon for new and less experienced members to adopt what is close to an apprenticeship role.

The value of strong teamwork in creating the circumstances which help managers change themselves has been referred to earlier. The cultural shift towards sharing and openness, the increased rigour with which business can be conducted in a non-hierarchical enviornment and the development of questioning and dialogue are all key characteristics. We are also beginning to understand more about the dynamics of creativity in organizations, and teams are a key factor in this. The possibility of managers instinctively becoming more cautious – or even conservative – as they grow in their roles has also been commented on. The differences which should exist within teams, and the friction arising from exposure to different viewpoints, expressed in a less hierarchical and rules-bound arena, and reflecting different traditions, are important ways in which openness to learning and change can be inculcated in managers. Supported by the emergence of multiple leadership and other prospective changes such as a return to the idea of player managers, these developments can underpin the development of the new approach to middle management which has also been identified as a key characteristic in successful change management.

Without change in the makeup of the management team, and the development of an effective communication spine, these developments will not be possible. Figure 7.2 sets out the critical links between process teams and management, in the form of the flow of information between the teams and the way responsibilities are allocated and shared. It also underscores the need for a holistic approach to the design of organizations fit for the prosecution of change.

The case study which follows is based on work done over a number of years by Hilarie Owen, who has carried out a major study of elite teams in a military context. The lessons are applicable to all sectors of management, and, after all, what is change management if it does not involve learning from others?

Case Study 5: The Red Arrows

The Situation

The Red Arrows are a Royal Air Force aerobatics team trained to give flying displays using high-speed jet aircraft. Over the years, many management trainers have investigated the team processes used to achieve the high performance of the teams. The following is a description of how this process appears to work in the team, and is drawn from the work of Owen (1996).

The team is made up of nine members, with three new members replacing three experienced members each year. The training begins in October/November of each year when the three new members join the team. When new pilots are recruited, senior officers draw up a shortlist. The team together decide on the final list to be considered, and the three new team members are provisionally chosen by three senior officers. The existing team itself has the ultimate decision. All members of the team have to be experienced operational team leaders.

Initially, the new members work alone with the team leader to learn the necessary new skills and build confidence. Once they have achieved the necessary standard in the small group, the experienced pilots are gradually added to the formation.

The Training Sessions

Each session is made up of a combination of flying skills and social interaction in the form of meeting visitors, attending schools to speak to students, and other publicity activities. The practical training lasts for three months, and is broken down into three parts:

Briefing

The Team Leader outlines the manoeuvres to be practised, and reports the weather conditions.

Flying Activity

The manoeuvres are practical and are filmed while visitors watch. Initial training is carried out a higher altitude than would be expected for an actual flying display.

The Debriefing

The Team Leader examines each stage of the practice. Pilots criticise themselves and each other. When an individual is criticised, the Team Leader asks the rest of the team to comment, and agree or disagree. The Leader is also criticised.

Important learning points are highlighted by the Team Leader, and the rest of the team comment, agree or disagree as they see fit. The whole team finally decide what to do next. Following this, the video of the training is watched by everyone. The team again criticises and identifies learning points.

During the training, the pilots wear green flying suits. At the end of the training, they are formally presented with their red flying suits to be used in displays.

Within the team are two pilots who break off from the main formation and fly the most spectacular moves on their own. This is known as synchro flying.

At the end of the first year, one of the new pilots is chosen to fly this role in the second year with a more experienced pilot who will then be in his third and final year in the team. This means that in the second year, the pilot will be learning novel and technically harder routines with an experienced pilot. This second pilot therefore adopts a teaching role.

On one occasion, the team's progress was reviewed by an Air Vice Marshall. After watching the display, the debriefing proceeded as normal.The criticism was wide-ranging and detailed. The team suggested some changes, to which the leader agreed. He ended the session by referring to a number of good points and congratulating the team. The Air Vice Marshall then gave his views, and suggested some changes, which the team declined to introduce. The Air Vice Marshall ended by underlining the praise and congratulations of the Team Leader.

Some Comments from Team Members

The Senior Pilot in the synchro flying duo:

> This can't be learnt from a book. I have to teach it by explaining it and doing it. Confidence is also important. The other pilot has to trust me. The errors here can only be small ones.

The Team Leader:

> I had a good role model to help me. If I can match him with the team, I'll be O.K.

> I have a broad outline of what is to be achieved and by when. They get on and do it and let me know of the snags.

A new pilot:

> The approach of flying with the Team Leader first has worked. Mistakes can be put right in the next exercise when they are still fresh in your mind . . . I am better at talking to the public, better at debriefing and realising my errors, which leads to confidence.

Some general comments from team members:

> None of us want to be seen doing badly . . . . but I don't want to be seen doing better than the others . . . The will to succeed. We want to be the best team there has ever been.

> Ego and self-respect. Standing among your peers is important and you want the team to do well . . . Personal satisfaction . . . peer pressure . . . being a perfectionist

> I have no qualms about following him [the team leader]. He's cool, calm and professional and not gung-ho.

> Rank doesn't matter. He accepts criticism and suggestions . . . He looks at us, not obviously, not looking over your shoulder.

> If a pilot criticises another, the Leader asks if they all agree . . . they usually do . . . the Leader may say 'was that a little wide?', or 'you were low Jerry' or 'you were just a fraction out Barry'. . . he always prefaces his remarks with 'what do you think?' One of us usually nods and says 'I came out of it wrong' or whatever . . . Then we agree what to do next.

> These new guys have just left a command where they were team leaders, leading front line missions. Now their flying is being criticised every time they go up, and they have to take this in their stride . . . what you have are ordinary young men with a job to do, no primadonnas.

Analysis

Team Selection

The character of this team is in many ways a model of team behaviour and team dynamics. The composition of the team is decided in an exemplary way, and is based on a number of key principles. It also follows a set procedure:

- The necessary skills and experience – an operational flying record and team leader experience. One of the advantages of this is seen later in the development of multiple leaders.
- The selection process gives considerable responsibility to the team itself. This is an essential element if the team is to remain focussed on its key tasks, and if it is

to work together to achieve the very demanding standards and objectives it has been set.

- Membership also rotates, with a percentage being replaced each year. One of the major problems with teams is the development of complacency. This can come from increasing familiarity over a long period of time, when operating in a comfort zone can creep into the culture of the team. Stability in membership contributes to team development and effectiveness, but there are times when regeneration and the introduction of new blood has to be considered. Rotation of members is obviously a force for renewal, and it also leads to consolidation of ideas and analysis of where the team actually is on the part of the other members, because they are regularly involved in the kind of organizational appraisal which should accompany the introduction of new blood. One difficulty with change management is that it is a constant process, and without the introduction of new ideas into the team, and the mix of experienced and new members shown here, things can be taken for granted and without it stagnation will undoubtedly occur.

Team Learning

In this case study, the learning process is also of a high standard. New members work initially with the team leader, and benefit from sharing his experience and skills levels. Much of the learning is also carried out at a higher altitude than the actual flying displays – both of these features to some extent support learning in a comparatively safe environment where errors can be made and become part of the learning experience.

The learning is holistic. There are aspects of social interaction which are crucial to teams, and these are practised alongside the key skills.

The ritual of awarding the red flying suits to replace the green suits used in training is also important. This is a small signal of the celebration of success which contributes to the sense of well-being of all teams.

Analysis and criticism are parts of the learning, and of the general team process. There is a tendency to assume that teams are places where there is consistency and conformity, seen at its worst in the emergence of 'group-speak'. Teams are more profitably seen as arenas where there should be clear and relevant criticism in a depersonalised and constructive way. It is out of the differences between members, and again the ability to express these differences, that some strengths of teams come.

Empowerment

While the team is a self-managing unit overall, with little overt involvement of the wider organization, transparency and empowerment is also practised within the team. The team leader sets the objectives and there is agreement on what to do. The team itself decides how, and execution is in their hands. This arrangement is reinforced by constant feedback and communication.

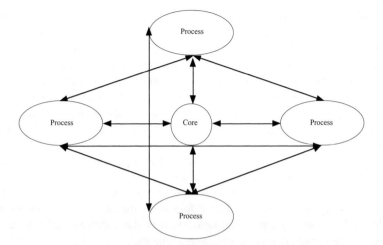

Figure 7.3 A Simple Team Model

A related point here is that there is no hierarchy within the team, and the larger RAF hierarchy is not a powerful factor. In one instance, the suggestions of an Air Vice Marshall were rejected by the team.

Team Culture

The culture is very powerful, as the general comments of the team indicate. There is more than a suggestion here of one of Lewin's basic principles (1951). This is the acceptance that although there is debate and criticism, the fate of the individual is enmeshed with the fate of the group. The statement that

> None of us want to be seen doing badly . . . but I don't want to be seen doing better than the others. . . . Standing among your peers is important and you want the team to do well.

indicates total willingness to accept the goals of the group while setting the highest personal standards. It recognises that the achievement of the group itself is the key measurement of satisfaction and success. The motivational effects of role models, setting targets which stretch the participants, and constantly striving for perfection are as expected in high-performance self-managing teams. This is a genuine team ethos.

The Value of Self-Renewal in Change Management

The value of this example is that change management is a process which needs to be constantly renewed, and achieving this renewal is one of the prime contributions of the team approach. The motivation, based on example and striving for excellence, the setting of consistently high standards in all aspects of the work, the rewarding of achievement, and the renewal which comes from team procedures like selection, analysis, debate and criticism, and the absence of a hierarchy and rigid systems, all contribute to this. It is clear that renewal is much more than the replacement of members, important though this is. It is also to do with performance evaluation, the constant exploration of new ideas, and the development of existing team members. Above all, there is the vital function of learning in a team environment, from peers and from the team as a whole, based on constant practice and providing the basis of continual development.

Figure 7.3 is a typical team model. Process teams possessing all the powers and responsibility to manage their own business can meet a range of information needs for a community of users. Built around the process of providing information rather than a functional configuration, they are linked to a small managerial core. The model is scalable and is based on a powerful network. It is also capable of relating to other clusters and can work across organizational boundaries.

One final point remains to be made. Organizations are made flatter partly to give people more responsibility and help them to play more dynamic and wider roles. They are also made flatter in order to improve the speed of their ability to respond, whether this is to user requirements or to meet the challenges of change. Kirkman et al (2004) assert that the empowerment which comes from teams makes processes better and provides greater satisfaction for clients or users. They also stress the critical nature of empowerment in organizations where people spend less time in face-to-face contact. Library service managers increasingly face the issue of managing distributed organizations, particularly in change initiatives. Teams are the best way to flatten organizations, the best way to empower people and the best way to manage people who cannot be seen so easily. As such they are a cornerstone of change management.

Chapter 8

Leadership for Change

Organizations face the need for change because their current operating procedures are in some way not adequate for emerging circumstances. Some would say that there is, in other words, a performance deficit. Managing the movement from the current position to the desired one, while maintaining the development of the organization, is one of the primary tasks of leadership.

Throughout a change process, particularly one which involves the sort of organization-wide change advocated in this book, circumstances will make significant demands on leaders. Change will involve:

- The possible jettisoning of long-established practices
- New professional and social relationships
- Psychological issues
- The need to simultaneously maintain an organization and take it through a significant change of direction – now known in the literature as 'ambidextrous leadership' (Byrnes, 2005)
- Role change
- Skills development
- For some individuals the possible loss of influence and prestige within the organization; for others, the challenge of significantly more responsibility
- Combating principled opposition to the change, based on professional disagreement
- Dealing with resistance fed by adherence to the status quo.

The Demands on Leadership

There is a delicate balance to be maintained by change leaders, stemming from the conditions under which change initiatives take place today. While the mix of skills and knowledge which makes for good leadership in contemporary organizations remains relevant, organizational circumstances mean that the significance of some leadership characteristics is heightened.

There are many obvious dichotomies in modern information services, and this book has undoubtedly rehearsed the full repertoire of these on more than one occasion. According to the literature, it is likely that Adam Smith, using a slightly different form of words, was the first to point out that specialisation would probably increase the need for communications which integrated different parts of organizations. This much is obvious, but our increasingly specialised and increasingly dislocated organizations make it a critical issue. The heady days of the 'seamless web of information' and the 'one-stop shop' can be contrasted with the technology-led growth of more specialisation. Integration, and that means strong cross-departmental communication, is a function of leadership, and a vital one in change management.

Commercialisation, presented as radical change and improvement, is another issue for leadership. Outsourcing, for example, whatever the benefits in terms of efficiency and cost-effectiveness, also leads to a loss of skills and competencies as vital aspects of the operation of a library pass into the hands of commercial organizations. This is true however well-crafted and tailored to service needs these operations might be. It can be plausibly argued that some characteristics of contemporary change might actually damage the capacity to manage future change, because of the loss of skills and knowledge. There are also added implications for morale and development:

> What is happening now – the contracting out of whole systems and the . . . outsourcing of parts of the library, and the deliberate deskilling being practised in several forms – will have devastating effects. . . The quality of the service will suffer as skills and experience are lost, opportunities for rounded personal and professional development will be diminished, motivation will become even more problematic as morale suffers, and more of the same will be recommended as a solution for the problems which will undoubtedly arise.
>
> It is also worth pointing out that what is often lost in 'reorganizations' is not just skills, experience, expertise and specialist knowledge, it is influence as well. (Pugh, 2005)

If organization health suffers, so will the ability to manage change. While these are all changes which provide special challenges for leadership, the context in which they are occurring is also changing in a negative way. The exercise of leadership inside an organization is a challenging task. Practising it in times of change, and when the organization itself is sometimes working outside its boundaries in partnerships and collaboration with other services and commercial organizations, is increasingly difficult and complex.

Cultural Change

Within the information services organization, the culture is changing. It is now based on diversity, in terms of the people working in it, and the novel roles they discharge. Before the digital revolution it was based on homogeneity, with uniformity of training and education, agreement on procedures and a common heritage. Cultural diversity – in the professional sense – in an information service is a health-giving feature, but one which has not made the task of exercising leadership any easier. Information services are staffed by people from different traditions who have come through education and training which might have priorities which differ from those of the librarian, but it is still necessary to fashion common values. The need for leaders who can bridge the gaps between the various specialisations now found in information services, create organizations which give them all the opportunity to work in their own ways, and still create unity, is a fairly obvious one.

The Dimensions of Change

The size of the change is also a problem. The staff of library services are being asked to work in different ways, with members of other professions, while at the same time they absorb some new principles which they might sometimes find ethically challenging. Asking people to work in a radically different way, and especially in the face of increasingly urgent commercial demands, imposes a strain on leadership. This is one of the differences between the tactical change reflected in many individual change projects and the whole-organization change championed by this book. When leaders are involved in a process which will effectively lay down a totally different set of premises on which the service will run, which is where technology and other forces will take us, then the extent of change can present a major obstacle.

For most of their history, libraries have worked on assumptions which have been widely accepted. These assumptions are being challenged by new ideas, and Kuhn, as early as 1962, unsurprisingly predicted that the new ideas would be resisted. They always are.

It is arguable that what is being faced by libraries represents a sea change. There are now overt attempts to replace human expertise with the computer, strident calls for the introduction of market or commercial principles, and the potential for an equally muscular and assertive self-sufficiency on the part of the information seekers. That our attempts to manage this change are as yet incoherent tends to support the view that there is a challenge in facing the nature of this change. In Kuhn's opinion, we see our present arrangements as normal, and it is therefore difficult to engineer a shift.

The Skills of Change Leadership

Leading change therefore calls for special skills: making sense of complexity and uncertainty; communicating; motivating a variety of people; clearly articulating a view of where the organization should go in uncertain times. It also still demands the technical skills of change management – the ability to achieve objectives and to make a difference; the ability to deal with personal fears and the psychology of change, including the skill of reassuring individuals and removing worries about roles and performance. In these circumstances the need to know the organisation and its people becomes exaggerated. It is even more important than it would be when managing in stable circumstances, or managing gradual, system-consistent change.

All this falls heavily on a leadership which therefore has to match the need for continuity with the imperatives of increasingly discontinuous change. Coping with this process means adopting the already-mentioned ambidextrous leadership – matching fundamental change with continuity and maintaining what is good in an organization. To aid this, there are a number of principles which leaders can take note of (see Figure 8.1).

The Development of Trust

Trust is generally a good thing, and I am almost certain that most leaders would be in favour of it. The need for it is also increased when people are being asked to face a degree of uncertainty which has rarely been a characteristic of librarianship until the last 10-to-15 years or so. This is particularly true of situations where libraries face the consequences of technological change, and where the political dimension of library management becomes more important as libraries face the type of pressures encountered by other public services. Difficult change processes are more easily accomplished on a basis of mutual trust. Bibb and Kouri (2004) define trust as:

- Honest communication, even if it is unpalatable
- Straightforward competence on the part of leaders
- Transparency, fairness and tolerance in the way the organization is run
- Freedom to experiment in a safe environment and a no-blame – but not responsibility-evading – culture
- Visibility of leaders – personal contact at a professional and social level
- Good intentions, on both sides
- Acceptance that trust is a two-way process – earned by all the parties involved.

The research carried out by Bibb and Kouri for their book also indicated that 90 per cent of employees felt that they did not work in an atmosphere of trust. This is a significant obstacle to good leadership in stable conditions: for leading in times of change it is a major challenge. It is also important for inter-organizational cooperation and for collaborative projects involving more than one organization. Madhok (1995) stated that trust can only be built up through repeated and successful interactions over time – one-off exercises are no good – and also made the vital point that where trust is established it will enable participants to make allowances for the inevitable conflict, inequity and occasional minor betrayal. Svejanova (2006) reviewed the arguments and expanded them. The elements of trust are telling the truth, demonstrating disinterest, sharing responsibility, ambidextrous leadership and confidence-building measures.

Trust is also important in the context of structural change and changes in managerial styles, both key elements in change management. Langfred (2004) identified the link between high levels of trust and low levels of monitoring. The more responsibility which is given away and shared with followers, the more likely people are to invest a measure of trust in the ability and character of their leaders.

Truth-Telling

The ethical stance of a leader, and the leader's probity, should be above question. The basis of trust is truth-telling, and where this is not possible for valid political, tactical, or sensitive personnel reasons for example, saying nothing is the best option. Hidden agendas may be unavoidable in change management sometimes, but where this is so they had better remain hidden. Transparency – honesty and clarity – is a key and sometimes elusive issue in change initiatives, and it is what truth-telling means in this context.

Disinterest

The motivation of leaders is a complex matter, but leaders need to demonstrate that organizational needs, staff needs and user needs, in no particular order here, will always take precedence over self-interest. This is a highly-sensitive issue because it touches on what drives a leader. Personal ambition is an important characteristic, but it has to be at least balanced by commitment to the organization and to followers. Being even-handed, transparently fair, decentralising authority and cultivating open decision-making will go some way towards creating this balance.

Sharing

The building of trust is made much harder if the traditional divisions between managers and managed are maintained, if the practice of multiple leadership is not encouraged, and if those outside formal leadership arrangements are not allowed to contribute to the task of steering not only the change process but also the organization in general. It could be expected that the sharing would also extend to problem-solving.

Establishing trust was a comparatively straightforward matter in culturally monolithic library services where attitudes to authority and power were more conformist. As an aside relating to the previous point, life was also easier for leaders when promotion depended on seniority and little else. Apparently 'Buggins's turn next' was coined in the early 20th century by a First Sea Lord.

Survey after survey of employee attitudes indicate a desire to take more responsibility along with a view that management operates in some ignorance of what actually happens in organizations, and lacks awareness of what it is like to be performing at lower levels. Even given the propensity towards conservatism with a small c in librarianship, it is a reasonable assumption that there is a willingness to take more responsibility, and leaders need to respond to this.

Information services based on culturally different components, and often with a history of shotgun marriages, present a challenge of an entirely different order. Sharing has to be based on understanding and celebrating differences, and allowing them to flourish within an integrative structure. This is another of the paradoxes of contemporary leadership in information services – how to encourage diversity while at the same time preserving unity.

Ambidextrous Leadership

In times of discontinuous change, leaders need to develop dual abilities (Byrnes, op cit). They need to inspire, and to do this partly by the truth-telling considered earlier.

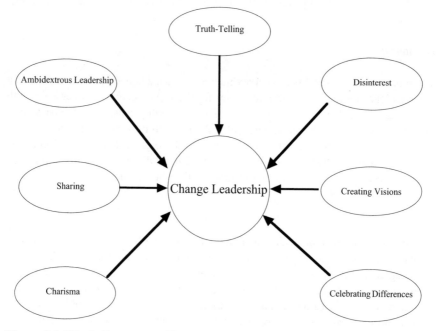

Figure 8.1 The Influences on Change Leadership

Allied to this is the ability to paint a picture of the nature of the organization they are trying to develop, so that it can capture the enthusiasm of followers. This has to be done while continuing to focus on the existing state of the organization, its sustained ability to function, and the state of health in its present circumstances.

Confidence-Building

Kanter (2004) suggested that confidence is an essential organizational foundation. It is based on open systems, and is supported by a culture which involves:

- Open communication
- Self-scrutiny

- Respect
- Teamwork
- Accountability
- Collaboration
- Initiative.

The Principles of Practical Change Leadership

In terms of the actions of leaders who wish to build confidence, this means:

- Sharing leadership.
- Working out a simple story which will tell everyone how the organization will work and where it is going.
- Identifying and encouraging talent.
- Building teams: this is the safe way to show confidence in individuals. It creates an environment in which people can learn, be supported, and make mistakes. Their weaknesses can be compensated for by the strengths of other team members, and their successes can be celebrated. Teams are also a vehicle for open communication, motivation, and sharing power and responsibility.
- Leaders attending to self-development. This has a behavioural consequence. It means leaders doing all of the things they would have done to them. It involves maintaining a realistic grasp of organizational reality and what is possible. It embraces sharing power and embarking on systematic learning. It needs the acknowledgment of personal weaknesses, and finding ways of compensating for them. It is about the ability of leaders to demonstrate a belief in their own vision. In short, it is modelling the kind of behaviour leaders expect from others.
- 'Going for quick wins' – setting up some projects which produce immediate results and so give people some impetus and prepare them psychologically for more testing and difficult developments.

This is all work in which leaders set the pace. They can build confidence by embarking on a range of change projects or initiatives, at least one of which must be designed to produce swift success. Kanter sees this as part of the task of creating winners. It is especially important when the organization is engaged upon long-term redesign. The small changes which work,and which produce obvious results and improvements, are vital to the success of the overall enterprise. Kanter also considers confidence as a multilayered characteristic. It is not simply a case of making an impact on individuals:

- Self-confidence is instilling the belief that individuals can make a difference and can achieve.
- Team confidence develops when a group of people have faith in each other, and understand that the fate of the individual is bound up with that of the group.

- System confidence is to do with the general capacity of the organization to support accountability, collaboration and the exercise of authority. It is a matter of creating the right organizational structures and routines.
- Confidence is more than an internal matter. It extends beyond the information service. Without the confidence of higher authority and users, there will be less inclination to provide funding and support.

Summary

We are looking for a set of leadership characteristics which include the ability to:

- Establish a climate of trust
- Create transparency and honesty throughout the organization, so that people know what is happening, how decisions are taken, and have an input into the process
- Build confidence
- Ensure continuity while managing change.

Leadership Theories

Developing leadership styles appropriate for times of change is a change project in itself. There is a conventional view of leadership in libraries, and this needs to be replaced by a leadership style, or styles, more fitting for managing in times of change. We now have organizations which are:

- Technologically driven and technically complicated
- Hybrid – a mix of the traditional and the novel
- Complex, in that there are many variables and unknowns surrounding the organizations
- Increasingly personalized from a user point of view
- Specialized, yet with a need for multiple skills
- Facing competition
- Unpredictable
- Reflecting a mix of traditions, training, ways of working, and priorities (Pugh, 2005).

They are also organizations which have a need to:

- Develop collaboration and learn to work across sectors
- Become entrepreneurial, in that there is a growing need for new ideas and innovative thinking
- Develop teams as an effective way of prosecuting change.

Traditional Theories

These, and their benefits for change management, can be very quickly summarised, if not quite disposed of. What has been described above are some desirable characteristics of good leaders in contemporary organizations. Classical theories of leadership are generally agreed to encompass the four main strands of trait theory, behaviourist theory, contingency theory and visionary leadership. Leaders also tend to be identified by their position in the organization, and by their use of legal power. Their behaviour is inclined to be directive, but can involve the ability to create a vision others subscribe to, and perhaps the exercise of charisma, which is generally seen as the creation of a self-image so powerful that it will persuade others to follow a particular course of action or subscribe to a particular idea. What all this amounts to is the view that leaders are people set apart by their position in the organization, the way they exercise power and the personal characteristics they demonstrate. This is one reason why structural modification is so important in change management. Structures are not only the means of getting work done. They are also symbols of position. Leadership is assumed through individuals working their way up the organization, and therefore exercising power in a certain way. Reshaping this tangible symbol of leadership is part of changing the nature of leadership itself, and emphasising that leading change in contemporary organizations, while it will be based on classical theory, will require a more sophisticated and refined approach.

Trait Theory

The bedrock of early leadership theory, trait theory has a certain attraction to those of us who remain convinced that the single most important factor in the practical exercise of leadership is the personality of the manager – this author included, with some important qualifications.

Most experts who have researched and written about trait theory all agree that some important leadership characteristics are shared by most leaders. The willingness, indeed the desire to lead, must obviously be present, for example. The fact is that some of the skills which trait theory normally attributes to leaders are arguably those which contemporary organizations most need, and which would probably be required by all change projects. It may be unfashionable to press this point, but these are desirable professional characteristics as much as they are desirable leadership characteristics. If a professional librarian fails to exhibit the necessary characteristics of motivation, durability, energy, example-setting, cognitive skills and integrity, then it could be considered to be a poor show.

A substantial problem with the trait approach is that modern change theory, and some of the more exciting models of the change process, as well as some key ideas like teams, presuppose multiple leadership. Trait theory, assuming that leaders are set apart by a number of things, not least their personal characteristics, tends to rule this out. Given the complexity of information services, this position may need some adjustment.

The trait approach also fails to take into account the contingencies imposed by organizational circumstances and the attitudes of followers. The latter are of critical importance in organizations based on collaboration, teamwork and sharing. So the best that can be said about trait theory in the context of managing change is that it will provide a reasonable description of what might be expected of leaders. This is correct not only in change management but in a general sense. It also provides a guide to what might be expected of the other half of the leadership equation, the behaviour of the followers. On their own, neither of these contributions are sufficient.

Behaviourism

The Ohio State University Leadership Studies Program set out to analyse the exercise of leadership, and identified two general behaviours considered to be significant:

- Consideration: key skills are those of communication and support for subordinates
- Initiating Structure: in group or team situations, controlling and directing the work.

The importance of communication has already been emphasised. Leaders also need the skills of creating a framework within which other people in information services can exercise all their talents. This as true of a team-based organization as it is of a bureaucracy. The conditions in which change is taking place require an ability in organization design and development, with the objective of establishing a structure in which creativity can flourish.

Contingency Approaches

As indicated above, neither of the basic approaches to leadership provide sufficient flexibility. Organizational circumstances demand something else. Trait theory and the behaviourist approach may work well in stable conditions, but in uncertain and complex situations a different response is needed.

The key factors in establishing desirable leadership styles in times of change will be found in the emerging characteristics of contemporary information services. This means leadership which, while it still relies to an extent on a combination of expert and legitimate power, also recognises, for example, that transparency is a valid organizational characteristic.

Leading organizations where there is a greater degree of self-assurance coupled with increasing expertise, depends as much on influence as it does on the use of conventional power. With the emphasis on teamwork, partnership and collaboration, the result is a demand for a much more malleable form of leadership than that which is allowed for by conventional theories.

The most appropriate models for contemporary organizations reflect an understanding that leadership should be practised at all levels, and by different individuals under different circumstances. This means that the basis of leadership in change management will be found in a combination of ideas.

To summarise, we can take ideas from some conventional leadership theories, and add to the list some characteristics which derive from particular organizational needs. We are left with the need for leaders who reflect the following characteristics:

- Strong communication skills
- Motivational skills
- Trustworthiness
- Honesty
- Disinterest
- The ability to develop power-sharing
- A talent for confidence-building
- Organization development skills
- Sympathetic character traits
- An ability to take a contingency view of leadership skills.

These characteristics amount to a mix of charismatic leadership and transformational leadership. The picture can be added to by some acknowledgement of Drucker's view (2004). In the context of decision-making, Drucker makes the point that some great leaders demonstrated the antithesis of charisma, and so he counselled against the danger of stereotyping leadership. This is particularly germane to our consideration of leadership in times of instability and discontinuous change. In his view, good leadership also depended on decision-making, communication, action and a sense of the collective effort in delivering objectives and leading an organization. The emphasis was on acquiring knowledge and converting this into effective action. These actions took place in a context of accountability and responsibility, which the leader was also involved in developing. Drucker related his views specifically to knowledge-based organizations. In doing so, he set out an effective change template:

- What is to be done?
- How will it be done?
- Who will do it?
- By when?
- Who will take the decisions?
- Who will be affected by the decisions and actions?
- How will those affected be informed and consulted?
- Who else should be told about the actions?

The implications of these steps are enormous, touching on objective-setting, decision-making, organizational structures, communication, sharing and responsibility. These are concerns which, while they may be transactional, are also transformational:

> Systematic decision review also shows executives their own weaknesses, particularly the areas in which they are simply incompetent. In these areas, smart executives don't make decisions or take actions. They delegate. Everyone has such areas; there's no such thing as a universal executive genius.

> Most discussions of decision making assume that only senior executives make decisions or that only senior executives' decisions matter. This is a dangerous mistake. Decisions are made at every level of the organization, beginning with individual professional contributors and frontline supervisors. These apparently low-level decisions are extremely important in a knowledge-based organization. (Drucker, 2004)

The argument so far is for a mix of leadership skills, including the ability to attend to structure, method and implementation. It also takes note of other key skills such as identification with the human resource implications of change as manifested in decision-making, consultation, responsibility, empowerment and communication. Some authorities would see this as unnecessarily restrictive, because change management also requires an element of inspiration. Even here, Drucker's list of key tangible characteristics is not purely transactional. It is also a description of how transformational leaders behave. Drucker describes actions which help build good relationships, improve communication, identify talent and encourage people to take responsibility and execute decisions.

Leadership in change management requires one more component. This is the ability to inspire.

Visionary Leadership

Sashkin and Rosenbach (2000) focus their comments on the issue of appropriate leadership for today's organizations, and for those of tomorrow. Leadership characteristics are behaviours which are obviously influenced by attitudes, and Sashkin's visionary leadership is relevant. Visionary leaders:

- Present key ideas clearly, and in a way which engages the enthusiasm of followers. They use the talent of lending clear-sightedness to the abstract complexities that exist in modern organizations.
- Practise active listening – a dialogue in which personal emotions and opinions are suspended, and which creates constructive feedback.
- Develop mutual trust and confidence based on a match between what a leader says and what a leader does.
- Act as if they care about the people they work with.

- Encourage followers to extend themselves by tackling tasks which stretch them, as a form of motivation.
- Provide the necessary support to ensure the best chance of success, while creating an environment in which it is safe to try things and to experiment with a minimal fear of failure.
- Demonstrate self-confidence and a belief in the ability to achieve results.
- Persuade followers to share the same belief in the ability of the leader.
- Want power as a means of coordinating activities throughout the organization.
- Paradoxically give power away by decentralising authority and responsibility, but follow this through by providing the necessary support.
- Can create a picture of what the organization should be like: a picture which is not their own exclusive vision, but one which followers will be able to contribute to, believe in and support. This picture should be clear and simple, and will explain what the organization is for, what it should look like in the future, and how this ideal vision will be realised.
- Take the picture a stage further, and persuade people to identify with the vision and commit themselves to the future of the organization. This is done by giving them more control over their own work and setting them challenging tasks, so it involves organization design, job design, and organizational learning.
- Build a broad appeal. This is part of the transparency issue. Making it clear how things are done, and the reasoning behind developments and arguments, is a way of extending the reach of the leader. If management processes are more open, leaders become more visible. This can be supported by developing professional relationships with staff across the organization, rather than with a few senior staff or the occupiers of key posts. In other words, hierarchy is anathema to modern leadership.
- Learn from their own mistakes. This is the best way of using experience.
- Model the desired behaviour – a key leadership characteristic for visionary leaders.

Conclusions

Leadership for change in contemporary organizations calls for a mix of conventional leadership skills, transactional and transformational leadership, visionary and charismatic leadership. As such, there is little which is revolutionary in it. It is a matter of applying basic principles with a little shift in emphasis. It is important to stress that while good leaders will share certain characteristics, there is much about transformational leadership, charismatic and visionary leadership which is nothing to do with traits. If this is so, it is an optimistic view because if leadership characteristics are not reduced to traits, then good leadership can be learned. It is therefore appropriate to end with a reaffirmation of the significance of modelling the right behaviour. This behaviour embraces not only the less tangible aspects of transformational leadership, but also concentrates on the more 'managerial' aspects of leadership. It is not necessary to enter into the sterile 'Can managers be leaders?' debate, but it is necessary to recognise that:

- Planning
- The ability to work with detail
- Practical involvement

are vital, and will provide the necessary balance. Leadership is a practical, in other words an obvious, activity. Invisible leaders are weak leaders:

> In my experience, the best leaders are also great managers, and the best managers have strong leadership capabilities. To be successful, you must have both a passion for improving your organization and the capability to drive your efforts through to completion. (Byrnes, op cit)

At the other end of the scale, in a situation which is complex and uncertain, aspects of visionary leadership play their part. By using a mix of method and inspiration, leaders can control the uncertainty to some extent, and this is a source of real power in modern organizations. Parks (2005) is another writer who insists that leadership can be taught. He uses the metaphor of the artist to convey the essence of modern leadership:

> Acts of leadership require the ability to walk the razor's edge without getting your feet too cut up – working that edge place between known problems and unknown solutions, between popularity and anxious hostility . . . to remain curious and creative in the complexity and chaos of swamp issues, often against the odds . . . awareness of working within a dynamic field of relationships in which the effect of any single action is not entirely controllable because in a systemic, interdependent reality, every action affects the whole. On the other hand, if one learns to understand the nature of the system that needs to be mobilized (the underlying structure and patterns of motion), he or she can become artfully adept at intervening in ways that are more rather than less likely to have a positive affect in helping the group to move to a new place, creating a new reality . . . More even than a captain of a team or the conductor of an orchestra, in a theater production at some point the director has to let go and know that the cast will make critical decisions . . . Effective leadership in change management is acting to 'maintain the equilibrium in the system, while creating a new reality'.

Chapter 9

The Psychology of Change

The standard approach to change management inevitably tends to reflect a concentration on process. Implementation is after all the biggest single cause of problems. The provision of information, the consultation process, the research, questions concerning who will be involved and the skills and experience required, all receive attention. The psychology of change, including motivation, is relevant to all of these features. As perhaps the aspect of change management which is on a par with implementation as the most crucial aspect, this is yet another issue which should be treated as a strategic concern, planned for and incorporated into the process from the outset.

The psychological problems of change management stem from several sources:

- The predominant characteristics of the organization
- The feelings of the staff involved in the change
- The attitudes of managers and others involved in change initiatives
- The process of change itself.

The Organization

Freedom of Expression

All organizations require compliance with the prevailing culture, and conformity to the norms is a major characteristic of behaviour. Traditional organizations are programmed to work around differences, usually by stifling them. This book refers elsewhere to the view, at the time of the major wave of convergence in academic support services in UK universities, that differences between the various parties involved in the reorganization presented problems. This is still a commonly-held position (Hanson, 2005), but one which is called into question by some of the emerging ideas about organizational creativity, which challenge homogeneity.

Managers, if they are keen to create homogenous organizations, can run into consequences when a change programme is conceived. A concern with the need to manage differences so that they are reduced or eliminated actually weakens the creativity needed for effective change programmes. Development which is likely to equip an organization to manage change better is stifled. Of equal importance, the pressure to conform found in most organizations can have undesirable psychological effects on some personnel. Perlow (2003) and Perlow and Williams (2003) reported on extensive research across a large number of organizations. These ranged from small businesses to government bureaucracies. They confirm that the pressure to conform, and to stifle contrary views, is powerful, leading to a weakening of the creative impulse and then to a drop in productivity. Paradoxically, it may be that conformity also brings familiarity and that in turn acts, for some people, as a psychological barrier to engagement with change.

For other individuals, this pressure can have significant negative psychological effects in another way. On the part of staff who are attuned to change, and welcome the challenges it brings, the pressure to conform to the status quo can create:

- Resentment
- Anger
- Reduced self-worth
- Loss of respect all round

which will result in additional difficulties when it is necessary for employees to embrace change. This is particularly so if the change is seen as management-sponsored. Martin (in Hanson, op cit) is clear on the psychological problems encountered in a major change initiative:

> LIS staff reactions were varied ranging from apparent denial that the change was taking place and the reinforcement of old job and territorial boundaries, through to excitement and impatience to get on with the new . . . Some staff were confident and proud of their skills until the first day in their new jobs, when they suddenly felt vulnerable . . . Computer Centre staff saw themselves 'taken over' by the larger Library department, whereas some Library staff saw themselves 'taken over' by IT. Staff uncertainty, fear of change, lack of confidence, and the effect of losing the familiar was variously expressed and often in criticism of others. Those who were pleased with their appointments and promotions tended to remain quiet, so staff morale was not necessarily boosted by these positive outcomes.

Encouraging Differences

At the root of the difficulties described here is the need for an organization to confront the differences between people, and use them productively and positively. There is an impulse to conform within even the most plural, structurally and procedurally relaxed organization, and as a matter of organizational health this has to be dealt with. Neither consensus nor unanimity is necessarily and always a good thing, but the consistent encouragement of freedom of expression in all directions is a critical psychological support. It is also an important source of energy which can be tapped in managing change. Embracing dissent is vital.

A Culture of Widespread Ownership

Hierarchies reinforce exclusivity. Lack of power over what is happening, or more realistically, a feeling that there is no way of exercising influence during a time of change – or indeed at any other time – is another negative psychological force. The retention of information, influence and authority in parts of the organization makes it harder for people to identify with change and give their energies to it.

Specialisation inside organizations also encourages exclusive ownership. This is linked with the comments in the previous chapter about the kind of leadership which breaks down hierarchies, and reduces the sense of impotence often felt in conventional organizations.

The easiest way of creating a culture of broad ownership, where people will feel able to contribute in areas outside their own specialisations, and which will bolster an individual's sense of well-being – a key factor in the acceptance of change – is simply to share information. The more radical this process is, then the better the results will be. Information-sharing is the first step towards ownership.

Whatever the extent of information-sharing, it is vital that the entire organization sees as much of the important data as possible. This is the information on which decisions will be based, and is much more than the customary reports, often covering what has already been done, which appear in organizational newsletters. Sharing this kind of information, crucial to decision-making, does much to neutralise the feelings of lack of control, powerlessness and the resultant feeling of reduced self-worth. It might also minimise the fear of new routines and processes, as well as the trepidation aroused by possible involvement in new personnel groupings which disrupt long-standing relationships. The key information to be shared is:

- What is wrong with the current situation, and why it is wrong
- What the objective of the change will be
- How it is proposed to get to the final destination
- Of vital importance, what the change means for individuals.

In practice it is unusual to encounter fear of change as such. The other issues described here, such as feelings of powerlessness and uncertainty, are the things which actually cause the fear. Injecting transparency removes that fear, because it makes the implications as clear as possible.

The next step is of course the obvious one. It is illogical to provide key information on strategy, policy and process, and the reasoning behind actions, and then fail to give the new owners of that information some involvement in the way the information is used. In other words, giving information must be accompanied by opportunities to use that information in decision-making. The decision-making process itself must become broad-based. That is, it must be widely owned, and this will have a positive psychological effect. Any major decision, which will perhaps alter the whole modus operandi of an organization, is one which has to be shared. Allied to this involvement in decision-making are the impact of organizational learning processes, and staff development. Conventional wisdom, but not, as someone has pointed out, 'conventional practice' therefore dictates a range of techniques for broadening involvement in management – flatter organizations, groups and teams – which actually institutionalise involvement. By doing so, they lift the psychological pressure, and particularly the fear, of change.

Creating Trust

This section should be read in conjunction with the comments on trust in Chapter 8 on leadership. For a balanced view of trust in organizations see Dietz (2004).

Openness, comprehensive communication, the kind of ethical leadership advocated in Chapter 8, and involvement are vital in the creation of trust. Trust depends to a great extent on the track record of the organization, and on its health in general. When people are faced with a change, it is not enough to explain things clearly and involve them in the change. Nor is it sufficient to address their current emotional states. Their view of how the organization has behaved in the past also plays a part in how people face change proposals, and accounts for the equanimity, or lack of it, with which they contemplate new ideas. An organization with a record of badly-managed change, a lack of fairness and probity in the way it handles its business, and a history of failed project management, for example, will need to deal with some fundamental issues if it is to break down negative feelings about change.

Managers themselves will need to take on the task of changing perceptions and altering the organizational memory in order to create a positive attitude to change. Part of this will involve managers acknowledging organizational weaknesses and past errors. This is the first step towards convincing everyone of the need to change, and helping people to articulate their own dissatisfaction with the status quo. It has to be followed by the opening of a dialogue ranging over the current problems, the implications if things do not change, and the benefits of embracing change. There must also be an honest and realistic assessment of the difficulties ahead. Once this is in place, it is possible to inculcate trust through open communication, participation and motivation.

The Feelings of the Staff

For the individual, there may be psychological implications stemming from attitudes, skills issues, location, responsibilities and roles. Providing at best some reassurance in these areas, and at least clarity and honesty about what is likely to happen, will further reduce uncertainty and worry. If the change is complex, then arrangements for support during the implementation period must also be communicated to staff.

If this support is going to make a difference to how people feel about change, it has to make use of all the existing organizational systems. It requires the sensitive management of the personnel, and it calls for a range of learning support techniques. There is a school of thought which draws attention to the roles of coaches and mentors in change management, but this seems to me to be an abstruse and rarified point. There is evidence that coaching and mentoring schemes in information services tend to be unstructured and underdeveloped. Where they do exist they should be inculcating skills, attitudes, methods and values which are the basis of good management and good organizational learning as such. To home in on these techniques in the specific context of change management has always seemed unnecessary. However, Metz (2002) is very practical and focused on the information services sector, and correctly identifies the problem to be faced:

> For some libraries, competition and defensiveness, rather than collaboration and resourcefulness, characterize their state of readiness [for change]. In some libraries, relationships are often based on competition and conflict rather than collaborative efforts.

She goes on to advocate coaching transition, clarifying the nature of the change, establishing new roles, responsibilities, and relationship as the business of the coach in change management. Communication is emphasised, as is dealing with resistance and conflict, the use of models and at bottom supporting learning. This rather makes the point. If coaching and mentoring schemes are not already operating inside a powerful organizational learning system, and are not regarded as a natural part of organization development, wheeling them out to specifically to deal with change may not be the best way to deal with change-related problems. The time for putting these features in place comes much earlier, when organization design and development is considered. What is clearly important is that all the available support for learning is harnessed to the change effort, that any new skills and knowledge requirements are identified and that resources are provided (see Figure 9.1).

Self-Efficacy

Bandura (1995, 1997 and a number of later papers) wrote about self-efficacy. By this he means 'the belief in one's capabilities to organize and execute the courses of action required to manage prospective situations' (1995). Bandura argued that motivation, and the capacity to achieve, depends on people's willingness to believe in themselves and their abilities. It is this belief which eventually dictates how they apply the skills and knowledge they possess. Conversely, it is self-doubt which causes underperformance. For the manager considering the psychological issues to do with change, it is therefore not simply the individual's view of the organization which is relevant, but also the state of their belief in themselves. Individuals will come to a judgement on what they can aim to achieve, based partly on what they think is within their capabilities, and partly on what they think the organization will be able to deliver for them. These judgements will be based on views formed over time. Both of these factors can be manipulated by good leaders, and it is this self-belief which a manager needs to nurture if doubt and uncertainty are to be removed from the change process.

Self-efficacy is obviously affected by the individual's perception of his or her own ability. It is also affected by past performance, in that previous successes breed confidence. This is why creating the circumstances in which people can perform to their optimum, by removing negative organizational factors, is an important managerial task. Here I would obviously concur that the coach has a role to play in performance improvement. Broady Preston and Pugh (2006 in press) review this area.

A further influence to consider is that of fellow workers and superiors. Watching how other people perform can be both inspirational and deflating, as it can induce fear of failure or belief in success, depending on how well the behaviour is modelled or the task is accomplished. On the positive side, modelling is a motivational technique which can be deployed to good effect by managers, and is considered later in this chapter.

Self-belief is seen as something which affects emotional states. Poor self-belief can

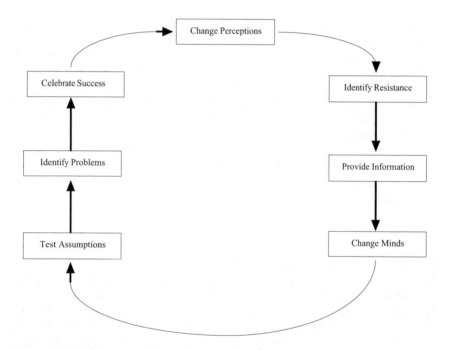

Figure 9.1 The Process of Dealing with Psychological Issues

exacerbate the negative feelings stirred up by change, because individuals involved may feel that they are incapable of accomplishing the tasks they have been set. These reactions can bring on feelings of inadequacy, anxiety and anger, and can also lead to a negative approach to problem-solving, which is one of the key change skills. The job of the manager, and of peers, is to strengthen people's positive feelings and help them develop a view of their own self-efficacy. Realistic and justified approval of performance, and sober encouragement to aim for achievable objectives, can do much to remove negative moods and feelings which otherwise create barriers.

The Psychology of Resistance

People will not resist change as an automatic reaction. They will resist the way in which change is handled, because it is sometimes seen as destabilising at an organizational level, and threatening at a personal level. They will resist imposed change, or top-down change.

It is helpful at this point, when considering potential resistance, if managers put themselves in the position of other staff. If the business of the management team is conducted in a transparent and participative manner, it should nurture an understanding of the reaction to forced change on the part of others. If something is imposed on management by institutional management, they would themselves probably feel resentment amongst a host of other emotions. Why should this very same reaction be considered unreasonable on the part of others who may face unilateral change? It should be obvious that there is a need to extend throughout the service the collaborative and consensual mode of conducting business.

The question of rewards can also be part of the mindset of the resister. For some, one of the outcomes of a change project will be material reward. For others, this will not be so, and there will sometimes be all-round losers. The task of management, in planning how to deal with resistance based on a suspicious view of the personal outcome, is to present the change, as far as possible, as a rewarding professional and personal development. For the losers, it is also vital to create the opportunity of a way out which allows for the retention of some dignity.

Principled opposition to change for professional, strategic or tactical reasons requires a different response. This is not a problem, but an asset to be fostered. Staff adopting this position can be amenable to discussion and collaborative problem-solving. Even from an opposing position, they can make a valid and positive contribution which will often lead to a considerable improvement in a change project. In this case, the psychological difficulties usually lie within the manager's reaction to criticism, and it is worth noting that managers also can have problems with self-worth, trust, feeling a lack of knowledge and lack of confidence.

The other main reasons for resistance to change call for a more subtle approach because they are less tangible. They are based on fear, uncertainty, again feeling a lack of knowledge, suspicion and even complacency – stemming from the fact that the organization may be operating smoothly and the staff may be happily coasting in the comfort zone. Reactions can be based on:

● Uncertainty or misunderstanding about the reasons for the change

- Fear of role change, or changes in working environments
- Anticipation of possible skills inadequacies in new situations, or lack of appropriate experience
- Satisfaction with things as they are
- Suspicion of managerial motives — such as cost-cutting or political machinations.

Dealing With the Resistor – The Process

Figure 9.1 sets out the separate stages involved in dealing with the psychological issues in change management. The steps in creating psychological well-being throughout the organization are discussed in the following section. The process of information-sharing, involvement, the creation of trust, the psychological support and the inspirational role managers can play all go some way towards alleviating psychological concerns and worries. There is also a way of actively dealing with resistance during the change process. This does not mean the sometimes unavoidable necessity of reacting to unforeseen trouble, but planning to identify resistance, dealing with its causes, and using resistance positively where possible in order to improve the process. This is part of the strategy of change management, and it is an early consideration in the process.

If we go back to earlier chapters where Lewin's work was discussed, the first stage in the process of change in Chapter 4 was the unfreezing. This is the stage when the organization is prepared for the change. It is where the current situation is questioned, so it is the first opportunity to deal with resistance, by setting out to change the mindset.

This first stage is where any information deficit is also likely to make itself felt as it exacerbates the uncertainty and insecurity. Attention to this deficit is the beginning of the process of changing minds. Gardner (op cit, 2004) set out a template for changing people's minds, which included the use of reason, the deployment of comprehensive research, the use of change agents to alter behaviour, multiple channels of communication to persuade people, the skill of helping people to identify with the aims of the change, and the ways of achieving resonance – hitting on the things that will strike a chord with the people who need to be persuaded. Mind change is feasible 'if . . . leadership approaches the problem in a number of different ways' (ibid).

Lewin's second stage in the process (op cit, 1951) is when the change is introduced. By now the original emotional reaction should have been modified, but there is still a great deal of uncertainty. Here unpredictable resistance can occur, so the process of mind change Gardner set out should be continued. A key point in his approach is that mind change is long-term: a single battle won does not ensure success. In this second stage, the information process and the openness of the approach is even more important if resistance is to be handled constructively. This is also the stage where the resistor can be at his or her most valuable, as a force for testing assumptions, identifying problem areas and improving the project.

The third of Lewin's stages, when the change becomes systemic, and is an accepted feature of the organization, is not the end of dealing with resistance and the psychological aspects of change. Once the process reaches this stage it is a time for metaphorically celebrating its success. Objectives have been achieved and the process of information-sharing, debate and involvement in problem-solving has improved organizational health. It has created a positive experience which has the potential to change perceptions of the organization. Now is the time to build on this and continue the momentum, because everyone involved will be psychologically better prepared to work in a changing environment. In Gardner's terms (op cit 2004, 1993) there has been:

- A successful demonstration of things being done in a different way, of ideas being properly developed and explored from multiple viewpoints
- There has been a rational and reasoned approach to a change project.
- People have become comfortable with a new idea, and it feels right – this is Gardner's 'resonance'.
- Rewards have been earned.

In other words, the essential mind change that must be a part of change management has taken place. Fisher and Shapiro (2005) suggest that it is essential to work with the underlying concerns everyone has. These are:

- A need to have one's point of view understood
- A need to feel a part of things
- A desire to protect or enhance status
- A desire for autonomy as far as possible
- A need for clarity, particularly where role change is involved.

Managing these concerns will lead to the successful management of the psychological aspects of change.

Motivation in Change Management

It should be obvious from the foregoing that some of the theories of motivation are more appropriate to change management than others, particularly so in information services and other public sector or non-profit organizations. Here it is likely that standard theories – motivation by numbers – might not fit.

A second problem is the danger that in practice motivation will attract little attention from managers. There can be a fatalistic air about the approach to what is a key topic, with a tendency to assume that it is an inner concern for staff, but not a concern which managers will automatically engage with. Motivation is yet another area of management which is often felt to be a naturally-occurring phenomenon, needing no thought or planning. During a change process attention will be paid to communication, consultation and information-sharing, but there will usually be little overt consideration of the underlying feelings of staff. Some resistors may be identified, and there is undoubtedly a view that motivation ought to be an inherent feature, depending on the inner strength of individuals. Therefore managers will not automatically follow the necessary overt action plan to identify the factors which drive people, and then create the circumstances in which these forces will flourish. In reality, motivation requires as much thought as any technical aspect of management.

The Challenge of Motivating in Times of Change

A change programme is an acute challenge to even the best motivated individuals. For those involved, it means moving out of the comfort zone. It can encompass:

- A reappraisal of working practices which have been developed over a period of time
- A reconfiguration of working groups and relationships, with implications for professional, personal and social frameworks
- The mastery of new skills, knowledge and working routines
- A reappraisal of professional ethics
- A reassessment of basic professional principles
- Moving outside a conventional, safe and predictable working situation
- A questioning of how and why things are done instead of an acceptance of conventional wisdom
- A change in culture.

The change process itself can sometimes involve fundamental alterations to the way in which organizations are managed. These also present motivational challenges to people embracing a tradition of working which is overwhelmingly based on effective but unadventurous operational procedures which are arguably not the answer to the organizational challenges of the 21st century. There are some interesting examples of the kind of change discussed here. In the late 1980s, NASA's Lewis Research Centre at Cleveland, Ohio was heavily committed to the space shuttle project. When the shuttle at last became operational the centre was faced with a problem of re-focussing its energies on the development of the orbiting space station. A multi-disciplinary team of highly skilled specialists which had devoted itself to the former project now had to re-direct its efforts. This was set in the context of poor morale and the threat of closure. Burke et al (1985) reported on a series of measures designed to solve these related problems: the replacement of autocratic management styles by participation; a new mission and new objectives; the fostering of a creative environment; a broader involvement in strategy formulation with new structure; quality circles; new roles for middle managers; a holistic approach to the running of the centre; new technology; reinvigorated leadership. At about the same time, Wheaton and Smith in an interview with Noel Tichy (1984) detailed the process of cultural change at Honeywell Inc: a new statement of objectives; an all-embracing and all-inclusive policy for the running of the organisation; the diffusion of knowledge and skills widely amongst the units inside the organisation, all of which operated with a high degree of independence; leadership; team-building; and new roles for middle management.

As new organisational forms emerge, the way in which power is exercised changes, and where the use of power becomes implicit rather than explicit there is a difficult adjustment to be made by people who are used to working according to a set of rules and regulations. The situation is further complicated by the nascent relationship with users emerging in the wake of the electronic library and educational changes. Organizations which are management-driven and based on past practice will be replaced by a culture which supports a capacity to adapt to external forces and create conditions which foster innovation. Brunnson (1982) argued that clear ideologies inhibit the ability to handle change, and even, in a never-to-be-repeated argument as far as I have discovered, that irrationality was a necessary characteristic of organisations which would be good at change management. It is a shame that this thesis will probably never be deliberately put to the test in libraries. It certainly directs the debate away from rigid hierarchies and sterile bureaucracies, and towards organic management. This idea is also in tune with the organizational need, assessed in Chapter 2, to foster learning and creativity through the dynamic forces unleashed by heterogeneity and the exploitation of differences in organizational life.

The point is that culture is one of the most important forces acting upon motivation. If it reflects a true learning environment which reverberates with people's inner views of themselves, presents a positive view of the organisation now and in the future, and if it promises to match their expectations then it will motivate. The cultural changes described above changed people's attitudes, and improved their sense of well-being. Laying down this change culture is a matter of:

- Structural change
- Teams
- Management styles
- Empowerment
- New behaviour
- New leadership
- Learning
- Sharing information, experience and knowledge.

The implications of this for motivation are profound.

Basic Motivational Needs: Security

Among the contributions culture makes to motivation, it should be a source of security. Most of the novel organic forms are very good on the things that matter in change management, like flexibility. Flexibility can be assessed from the ability of the organisation to deal with change in the external environment, through the permissive nature of the structure, the speed of decisions and the loci of the decision-making processes, in the way skills are deployed, in the expansiveness of the learning experience and the comprehensiveness of the information system. All this comes at the price of some loss of structural or overt control, and consequently can create feelings of insecurity. Many people feel uncomfortable without these systems of control. Taken with the more covert supervision exercised in organic management systems, the culture offers a set of norms to guide behaviour and assist management. By presenting a framework of control it contributes to organisational stability and so begins to address the well-being of the staff through providing some sure reference points in a changing environment.

Some of the needs, for security and reassurance in times of significant change, can also be met by due attention to the change process, as described earlier. The creation of trust through comprehensive and open communication, and the involvement which can come from an acceptance of the need for transparency, can replace some of the certainty and security which comes from operating in stable environments with accepted and standardised ways of doing things to meet predictable user needs. Managers can also remove some of the uncertainty by taking an incremental approach to change, rather than the big bang approach seen in a number of contemporary change programmes. This kind of all-or-nothing approach will work in an organization with a strong culture of change. In an organization without this cushion, beginning with a series of small projects involving small gains will boost confidence and begin to take the edge off the uncertainty of change, as well as act as a springboard for more ambitious and challenging projects.

Security can also come from a knowledge of how failure will be received. The capacity to make an effort in a risk-free environment is important if people are to be innovative. If they are to do this in an environment without the safety which comes from rigid structures, clear demarcations, and prescribed roles and responsibilities, then the consequences of failure must not involve personal penalties. Rather, they must involve constructive analysis and learning which can be applied to future challenges. Anything else will increase the insecurity and self-doubt. Failure can be caused by lack of knowledge, skills or experience, and it can be caused by managerial inadequacy in the shape of poor resources or support. It can be rectified through providing learning opportunities, better resources or through working with others who can compensate for weaknesses and bring their own strengths to a project. This is another argument for the team structure. Teams are a way of providing the security which people seek in the workplace, by offering an environment in which people can use their strengths while the strengths of others can compensate for their weaknesses.

Motivation starts before change programmes are planned, and is best seen as a continuous element in the flow of organisational life and the exercise of leadership. The roots of motivation are in the seed bed of cultural change and organisation development. It is the character of the organisation itself which influences the constructs people create, and dictates the basic degree of receptiveness to change. In brief, laying down the right culture is an important prerequisite for motivation. It can eliminate some of the problems with hygiene factors. The effects of the extrinsic issues which Herzberg felt were demotivators will be diminished if certain other characteristics are present. These characteristics must embrace supportive management and also set down guidelines which offer some degree of certainty in times of turbulence. Through team building the culture should provide some of the elements of support and comfort. It should also be capable of supporting an appeal to the higher motivators.

Higher Order Needs

Personal achievement, recognition, professionalism and personal advancement in a general sense are the features in organisational life which drive people on, according to Maslow (1943, 1968) and Herzberg (1959, 1974). They are therefore impulses which can be harnessed to engender a positive response. The open culture described in this chapter depends on empowerment. It depends on job enrichment through giving people more control and responsibility over the areas they work in, and it can include job enlargement through widening the area of responsibility. It involves learning. These characteristics are built on the elimination of lower order difficulties to increase the sense of well-being. They go further, and support an appeal to stronger motivators like professionalism and a sense of achievement.

An aim of organisation development is to set up structures and to design jobs so that teamwork, self-direction, learning and new behaviour will flourish. Another objective is that of achieving a fit between the individual's view of himself or herself and the organisational view, so it satisfies personal construct theory. The right culture is the foundation of motivation in the management of change. It is an organisational feature which encourages commitment.

In change management, the significance of some of the satisfiers and the dissatisfiers is heightened. Changing a system, or part of a system, or developing a new service, naturally puts a premium on the higher level motivators and appealing to these offers incentives for everyone involved. The kind of organizational structures proposed in this book, the changes in managerial styles, and the attention to participative change processes will remove many of the motivational difficulties caused by Herzberg's dissatisfiers – those organizational features which act as obstacles and demotivators. They are also positive motivational factors, and appeal to the higher order needs. Change projects are a fecund seed bed for development, once the basic issues to do with the need for security have been dealt with. We have already touched upon this area with the consideration of Bandura's ideas about self-efficacy (1997).

The very least that can be said about flexible structures, teamwork, learning, devolved management and the other desirable features of innovative organizations is that they have a fair chance of making work interesting. They will create challenges for people. Individuals will sometimes find themselves in positions where the challenge may be slightly beyond their capabilities, bringing with it the risk of failure, but providing a testing learning experience. Expectancy theory (McInerney and McInerney 1999) suggests that managers need to identify those of their colleagues who have a high need for achievement. They are the people who will make a dynamic contribution, because of the value they attach to success achieved by using their capabilities to the utmost. Conversely, staff with a lower need for success and achievement will be concerned first to avoid failure. Knowing the staff involved, and identifying the key motivational forces, is an important task of management. Framing a project so that it presents the right degree of challenge, and using it as a learning and developmental opportunity, is important. Objectives and targets need to be set with the capabilities and psychological makeup of staff clearly in mind. Setting the challenge inappropriately high or low will act as a demotivator.

Managers have already at hand the tools to do this, in addition to their skills in understanding the psychology of the people they work with. Job enrichment and job enlargement, and team structures, are the key motivational weapons in this respect.

One of Maslow's higher order needs (op cit) was self-esteem, and this comes from a belief in one's own ability and also in one's value to the organization. Self-belief involves self-analysis and achieving a realistic and honest view of one's capabilities. It means encouraging people to set their own targets, and providing the necessary support to help them achieve these targets. It also involves that most difficult of things, particularly for managers, that of seeking and accepting feedback from others.

Learning and development also plays a part in increasing self-belief (Cox, 2001). Self-esteem is important for the long-term, in that it is an essential pre-requisite for sustaining motivation. Once it is weakened, high-achievers become risk-avoiders.

Managers can create the circumstances which underpin motivation. They can also model the behaviour they wish to see others adopt. Beyond this, motivation in times of change is an internal matter for each individual, because some of the organizational features which support people are inevitably modified or removed in times of change. McInerney and McInerney (op cit) assess what might be termed theories of self-motivation, which they call intrinsic motivation. These are forces which come from within the individual, and the characteristics can be summed up as:

- Curiosity – manifested in a willingness to explore new ideas and try new ways of working, and to understand why things are done the way they are and why they need to change, rather than simply be concerned with how things are done
- A desire to improve performance
- Problem-solving ability
- An interest in work for its own sake.

This takes the argument full circle, to underline the view that this extremely powerful internal desire to take part and achieve things is the crucial factor in motivating people in times of change. It sums up a number of points made throughout this book, but particularly that organizations must be made interesting places to work in. This can only be done through Organization Development (see Chapter 2):

- Making work challenging
- Giving people the responsibility for organizing themselves, and let them choose how they work
- Giving them power
- Helping them to learn
- Using every channel of communication possible, and tell people everything you can
- Sharing leadership.

There are a number of specific managerial actions which will lay the basis for a well-motivated workforce. Managers need to:

- Convince people they can achieve in the new environment
- Design jobs to permit development and learning
- Engage in real and ongoing structural change
- Foster cultural change
- Develop and sell a vision
- Give people responsibility
- Communicate
- Change themselves
- Dispense with bureaucratic behaviour. (Pugh, 2005)

Steers et al (2004) review the major theories of motivation. They trace the development of ideas back to the hedonism of the Greek philosophers, which ties neatly in with the suggestion that making work fun is an important motivator. They refer to the social influences on motivation which were prominent in the literature of the 1930s. They also deal with the view that there is really no hierarchy of needs, but a complex mix which has a subtle influence. Approaching motivation on the basis of organization development and the actions managers can take to alter the organizational culture is a way of acknowledging this complexity.

Chapter 10

The Skills of Change Management

It is possible to take a strict textbook view of the skills of managing change, and identify a whole range of artifices like planning, budgeting, leadership, team-building, communication and so on, which will provide a snapshot of the desirable skills base for managing change. It cannot be disputed that change management requires the technical skills of management, and it is a simple matter to list these attributes. Considering the skills issue solely from this standpoint runs the risk of espousing the mechanistic approach to managing a process. To do so is to misunderstand the nature of change today.

General management skills are of course important, but in the context of change management there are some skills which need to be emphasised above others. Whether change and its treatment is regarded as a series of separate actions, or more imaginatively as a permanent and most significant influence on the way organizations are run, there are critical points in the process where certain managerial skills carry even more weight than usual, and where some less observable or definable skills become much more relevant. These are the concerns of this chapter.

Leadership Skills

In an examination of prevailing political cultures, Bentley (2005) refers to the belief that strong leadership can be the most important factor in envisioning and creating change. He goes on to argue for the contrary view: that there is little evidence that significant renewal comes from the conventional way in which leaders are seen to wield power, that is in a formal way. Success instead can come from:

- Accepting the need for new thinking, and searching for novel solutions which, if handled properly, will come from a variety of sources
- Giving power to people who have the knowledge, information and skills to solve problems – those close to the seat of the issue
- Supporting learning
- Creating the overall capacity for change.

Encouraging these characteristics is a problem for managers, because they represent much of the intangible face of an organization, and this cannot be so easily analysed or described. In a crucial way these characteristics also depend on relationships, because sharing power in particular, which is the fundamental issue, depends on trust.

Creating Trust

The critical issue of trust was given a fuller treatment in Chapters 8 and 9, so this section should be read in the context set out there. If there is one single skill which a manager needs to develop in order to manage change effectively, it is the skill of establishing trust. The justification for this has already been put forward: creating the right kind of organization for supporting innovation and change depends substantially on the intangible characteristics, and trust is the wellspring of these. Paradoxically, when we reach this point we are not only considering skills, but traits and character (see Chapter 8 in particular). In some practical situations there is no way of disentangling skills, traits, character, trust and leadership. The capital residing in relationships, and the capital which managers can create if they can inculcate trust and belief on the part of others, represents a key resource in change management. At its simplest level this is an easily-stated matter. It is first to do with telling the truth, or what is truth in an organizational context. This caveat is important, not in a cynical way, but simply because differing organizational perspectives create many different realities, most of which are equally valid. Consistently delivering objectives is the other important way of creating trust, but it is also much more than these two characteristics.

The relationships upon which trust is built are linked to the organization's intellectual capital – knowledge, skills and experience, and are therefore supported by the actions and beliefs of managers in promulgating learning and encouraging development. Trust can also be founded on the functions and characteristics of the networks which exist inside the organization, whether formal or informal. This underlying structure plays a part in supporting individuals, increasing understanding, and bolstering mutual confidence. Working with the networks is also a way in which leadership can be exercised, character and values can be demonstrated, and the belief in leaders can be fostered. The skills of leadership in understanding and working with the organizational networks are important in developing mutual support and the willingness to share objectives and follow; in other words trust. Here this book is admittedly straying into troubled waters to do with the assertion above that it is impossible to separate traits, character, trust and leadership, but leadership always requires the demonstration of personal and professional values, a set of principles, and an ethical stance. There is no better way of putting this than returning to Gardner (op cit, 2004):

> . . . the central component in the moral realm or domain is a sense of personal agency and personal stake, a realization that one has an irreducible role with respect to other people and that one's behaviour towards others must reflect the results of contextualized analysis and the exercise of one's will . . . The fulfilment of key roles certainly requires a range of human intelligences – including personal, linguistic, logical and perhaps existential – but it is

fundamentally a statement about the kind of person that has developed to be. It is not, in itself, an intelligence. 'Morality' is then properly a statement about personality, individuality, will, character – and, in the happiest cases, about the highest realization of human nature.

Gardner was led by these considerations to add moral intelligence to his list of different forms of intelligence. It is only fair for us to note that his standpoint is not without controversy and has its critics. It may be also that here lies the weakest part of this argument, but in general what he says above can be taken as the summation of important leadership and management skills in change management: a considered approach to dealing with other people, high principles and something to be found in the character of the manager. To act in this way, managers need first to understand themselves, and feel confident in what they do and how they do it.

The Skill of Self-Awareness

A manager's self-awareness does not stop at honest assessment of personal strengths and weaknesses, and the ability to see oneself from the perspective of others. It should also be developed to help a manager understand the limits of other people. An awareness, for example, of the causes of stress, or the danger points where some control can be lost, are pointers which should help a manager refine the understanding of how other people are feeling during a change initiative. It can help indicate where an intervention is necessary, and where a change of managerial style will be advantageous. In a conflict situation, or where a manager is dealing with a problem of resistance, it can also act as a very necessary calming influence on the manager him or herself, and avoid a precipitative reaction which will exacerbate what is already an uncomfortable situation.

Openness

Trust depends on openness. Managers can put this in place by giving people a say in their own affairs. Creating a culture in which people feel in control, and in which they can share things with management, is the first step. Moving authority down the organization is a part of this, as is changing the organizational structure.

Specifically, where change projects are concerned, the process invariably has to be open, participative and with genuine sharing. The need for the change, the development of a range of ideas on how to deal with it, the thinking process, the listening and the dialogue, the dissemination, the implementation and the adoption are all phases where openness begets trust, and helps a manager build up the intellectual and emotional capital referred to earlier. In all these activities, the demonstration of a willingness not only to share, but also to hand over significant ownership, is a tangible example of the creation of trust.

To sum up, using participative management is a people-skill which is the foundation of creating the relationships on which much of change management depends.

Empathy

The skill of putting oneself in the position of others, and not simply understanding their point of view but also understanding why they think as they do, and what emotions lie behind their views, is a skill all managers need to develop. It is based on the ability to consider other perspectives in a neutral way, and it leads to the growth of the capacity to at least give some weight to the interests and concerns of others.

In the introduction to this chapter, the point was made that change management skills should not be reduced to a purely mechanical oversight of a process. The need to manage relationships should be an inbuilt characteristic of managers: in change projects, it is doubly important. Empathy ensures that issues are dealt with in a non-judgemental way and that personalities are not considered, except where they are clearly an influence on the course of a project.

Goleman (1996) argues that the insights which come from empathy can strengthen relationships, so its relevance to change management is clear, particularly in the approach to teams. For the manager involved in change, it is an important source of balance because it gives some space to the views and feelings of others without in any way reducing the validity of the manager's position.

It also helps to create a non-adversarial culture. In teams, empathy helps people to accept differences in points of view and positions. It assists debate and discussion and supports the safe and neutral environment teams need to exploit differences and develop creative abrasion. Because an empathic manager can increase the sense of well-being of others, encourage them and increase their self-belief, it is a motivational tool as well.

On a practical level, the ability to empathise almost guarantees the acquisition of information about where people see the problems in change. It helps them articulate their worries, and offers a reasonable prediction of where some resistance is likely to be encountered.

The fact that empathy assumes the absence of judgement is another precursor of the development of trust. It is also good for morale, being an important psychological support, and it strengthens commitment.

One of the key issues in a devolved management system where ownership is shared, and where decision-making is shifted to the lowest appropriate point in the organization, is the level of support individuals and teams need. This is also relevant to the concept of the player-manager, and the general idea of changes in management styles. Any assessment of the skills and competencies of a group or an individual cannot be made wholly on concrete premises. There must be some understanding of the psychological makeup of those involved, and vitally, of their capacity to be stretched in a way which sets them challenging but achieveable targets and helps them develop. Too little control risks failure, too much stifles initiative and is counter-productive. Without the understanding empathy brings, the ability to make this judgement is hampered. It should also be used to illuminate the degree of involvement in a change project from the moment of inception throughout the entire operation.

Emotional Intelligence

Goleman's basis for advocating empathy as a managerial skill (op cit 1996, and 1998, and Emmerling and Goleman, 2003) is that of emotional intelligence (EI). Emotional intelligence has been widely and variously defined, but its major components are generally agreed to include:

● Self-awareness: this means understanding one's current emotion at the time it is being felt.
● Self-control or self-management – being able to contain negative feelings and make use of positive ones, and in a professional setting not allowing the emotions to influence the way relationships and incidents are handled, or lead to misunderstanding. This also involves anticipating situations and preparing for them emotionally as well as intellectually. In addition, it means that the ideas of emotional intelligence and empathy should be part of organizational learning and development.
● Using emotion as a motivational tool.
● Appreciating that other people in personal, professional or social networks will be prey to the same emotions.
● Looking for what other people need out of a situation or a discussion.
● Removing power from the equation: most exchanges take place against the background of an imbalance of power, which has to be eliminated by both sides if empathy is to be created. At the same time, it is not necessary to agree with the other party in the exchange in order to create empathy.
● A willingness to provide feedback, to reward and praise, and to contribute to the development of others in the organisation.

Managers are struggling to deal with discontinuous change which brings with it the need to understand increasingly large volumes of information and work collaboratively in ways which are relatively new to them. Emotional intelligence is essential in this process (Cherniss, 2001). Deegan (2002), investigating emotional intelligence and leadership in physicians, summed up the position:

> There is a body of evidence suggesting leaders and managers with a well developed complement of emotional intelligence competencies are more effective than peers (with similar education and experience) who lack a highly refined set of these qualities . . . Firms led by chief executive officers who exhibited outstanding emotional intelligence competency levels had better financial performance . . . senior health care executives were more adept at integrating key emotional intelligence competencies such as organizational awareness, and relationship skills such as influence, into their professional activities . . . senior partners with

emotional intelligence competency profiles reflecting high levels of self regulatory, self management and social skills consistently contributed higher levels of profitability when compared with their 'typical' colleagues. The contribution of emotional intelligence to effective job performance increases as an individual assumes greater responsibility . . . outstanding leaders complement these abilities with maturity, self awareness, empathy, active listening skills and other characteristics that make a meaningful difference in their performance and contribution to the success of the organizations where they work.

If we look at the skills of leadership from the point of view of the kinds of intelligence needed, there would be little argument about the skills of analysis and problem-solving, logical thinking and an attention to the power of reasoning and systematic analysis. Gardner (1993) identified the ability to understand what other people wish to do, what their motivation is, and what they want. These are the interpersonal skills which support collaboration and cooperation, and generally working with other people. The other side of this kind of skill and intelligence is that it depends on self-understanding, or self-knowledge.

Listening Skills

The conscious effort to develop empathy and strengthen emotional intelligence begins with the consolidation of some skills which do not come naturally to most people. The skill of listening, and the associated skill of developing dialogue, are notable additions to a manager's change management capability. Because both of them are used naturally and instinctively, they are often also used ineffectively. Hargie and Dickson (2004) provide a good place to begin, with an overview of interpersonal communications. In a change situation, the ability to use effective listening skills is doubly important. Hilberry (2004) in a contribution on leading innovation as part of the Banff Center Leadership Development Program, drew analogies between leadership in times of change and artistic endeavours, and emphasised the 'artistic competencies of reflection, insight, and intentional listening.'

Overcoming the inbuilt process which is a conditioned response while listening to other people is the first step. The recipients of a verbal message tend to concentrate on rehearsing how they will respond, or even allow their attention to wander to extraneous matters. The first action in developing strong listening skills is to consciously focus on what is actually being said, rather than the response to the message. The emphasis is on the act of listening, analysing what is said, and identifying the key issues. Only when the speaker stops should the response be prepared, and then following a certain procedure.

This process requires complete detachment. The other people involved in the exchange will doubtless inspire a range of emotions in the listener, and these should be discarded in favour of total objectivity. This is the first step towards understanding the emotions and attitudes which lie behind the message. Detachment allows the listener to avoid overt personal criticism of the speaker, and psychologically the parties are better placed to understand each other's feelings and motivation if this neutrality can be created. It can then be reinforced by an expression of interest, some prompting and questioning and some physical signs of receptivity and understanding. Paraphrasing the key points as the first stage in the response confirms the listener has been focussed on what is being said, reinforces objectivity, and is the beginning of the essential dialogue.

Listening is an activity with several stages. The stage described above is that of attending. It provides reassurance and confirms attention. Working through this stage correctly also involves a willingness to be comfortable with silence. This is not always negative, and does not inevitably signal that a participant has finished speaking. It can indicate time being taken to think, and understanding this is another part of empathy.

Attending is therefore the opening stage, and it overlaps with the listening stage itself. Once the recipient of the communication has clearly engaged with the sender, then listening, in the sense of concentrating totally on what is being said, and on understanding the message, is the second stage. This is where it is necessary to avoid the temptation to think ahead of what the speaker is saying, indulge in internal conversations which might or might not be relevant, plan an answer or even allow attention to wander.

These two sub-processes represent clearing the ground. The key issue of creating empathy then takes centre stage, as the listener seeks out the emotional content of what is being passed on. By the use of more questions, and body language, the listener can indicate concern over the feelings behind the message, before moving into the final stage of responding.

Dialogue and discussion form the basis of this stage. The positive elements in what has been said, those points which are most relevant, or those which are generally agreed to be correct, can be reaffirmed, while amplification or clarification can be sought on other less certain or contentious issues. The implications of key statements can be teased out through discussion, and the mutual understanding of the emotional aspects of the message can grow.

Dialogue

Peter Senge remains the major contributor to the use of dialogue in organizations. In a parallel train of thought to that developed by Gardner and by Goleman, Senge (1990) interpreted dialogue as understanding the meaning of what other people say. It involves the probing of views and stances, in an attempt to reach understanding and identify points of agreement and mutual interests. It is non-confrontational and its purpose is to develop and share insights into what others think. It is also a means of teasing out the weaknesses in ideas and standpoints, and therefore strengthening them. Central to Senge's position is that this process of dialogue cannot operate properly where there is formal authority, the use of position, deference or power imbalances. Dialogue is meant to examine issues and proposals, so there has to be open discussion without restriction.

The Context

Listening and dialogue are not practised as part of a set-piece situation where the processes can be switched on and off as requires. They are permanent organizational features, and have to run in the background through everything an organization does. They have to be assiduously practised until their performance improves and becomes second nature. This means they are part of an organizational subsystem. The organizational networks explored in Chapter 6 are an essential support for this subsystem. Apart from the information-sharing aspect, networks are creative – they support the sharing of ideas, they aid in the growth of understanding, and they increase the exposure of managers in what is to be a culture of openness. They also allow leaders to model the kind of behaviour which inculcates trust. As far as change is concerned, networks can tell managers much more about how people are likely to react to change, and about where resistance and bottlenecks lie, than most other techniques. Networks can not only be used to build relationships, but through the kind of dialogue and general exchange which occurs, they also help to maintain relationships in a healthy condition. They are essential to the communication subsystem, and so support some of the essential skills of change management.

Building an Organization Fit For Change

Because library organizations traditionally follow a basic design blueprint intent on creating a structure which favours certainties and stability, the skills of organization design will make a difference to change management. Here, I would not begin the process of organization design from the conventional starting place. This position can be tested by asking any manager to draw an organizational chart. Most library managers, and indeed most managers of any stripe, would begin with a box at the top containing the word 'Director'. Below this, the various levels and responsibilities will be etched in and made fast. Chapters 6, 7 and 8 considered the implications of this approach, and suggested some alternative designs.

Starting the process in a different place, and considering the structure and the relationship of the parts from the point of view of the user, could produce a different shape. Asking what it is that the users want from a library service, considering how these needs relate to each other, and considering how the services can be delivered in an integrated way, will produce a different kind of organization. Apart from being flatter, it will be a closer match with the characteristics needed for the optimum management of change, identified ad infinitum and itemised clearly in Chapter 2. The skills of looking at the organization from the user perspective, visualising something different, and building it, offer the prospects of an organization which can sustain long- term change, through:

● Improved communication

- Better knowledge-sharing
- Better learning
- Dynamic staff development
- The application of relevant skills and knowledge without hindrance by artificial internal boundaries.

It is worth repeating here the principles laid down by Neilsen (2004). Organizations should be based on:

- Openness – not only in the full disclosure of most information held by an organization, but also on the free flow of communication unhindered by rank, hierarchy, or other internal obstacles
- Transparency – a level of participation in the decision-making process which participants are comfortable with
- Competence – continuous learning open to all as of right, and including decision-making, problem-solving, strategic thinking and active listening – all of which are crucial to full participation in the operation of the organization
- Alignment – freedom from conflict; the complications of ownership; the understanding that self-interest is best served within the larger interests of the organization; the acceptance of common and unifying interests as the best guarantee of a healthy organization.

To this I would add process-based rather than functionally-based service delivery, partnership in all aspects of management. These are the principles which will produce a design for the future.

This chapter has considered the skills of change management which are concerned with dealing with people. They emphasise emotional engagement with the concerns of individuals involved in change. There are techniques of budgeting, project management and planning which are also relevant. It is in keeping with the general tenor of the kind of change management consistently advocated in this book to suggest that although these are significant, they involve more tangible skills and are therefore easier to grasp and to use than the skills of people management which are covered in this chapter. In adopting this approach, it is hoped that the book will demonstrate a consistency which is itself a virtue in managing change.

The final passages of this book have departed from what might be considered to be the textbook view of the skills of change management, while acknowledging the significance of the technical aspects of management. Curzon (2006) for example, has produced an impeccable manual concentrating on the process of change and emphasising the practical skills which form the essential foundation stones. This is a totally defensible and valuable approach, not least because the causes of failure rooted in poor execution are well known. However, there is an important balance to be struck. Much attention is now being paid to the idea of 'corporate DNA' – the characteristics which make it more likely that an organization will enjoy a long life. This is a developing idea, and the literature indicates it is to do with the intangible features considered in this chapter, and which significantly influence the success of an

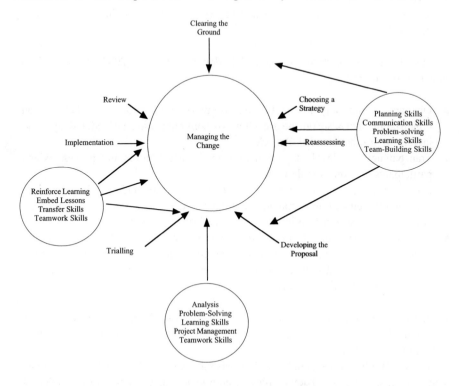

Figure 10.1 The Application of Skills to the Change Process

organization. Bargatze (1999) provides an introduction. Corporate DNA means attributes such as ethics, values, the organizational vision, trust, and human resource policies including recruitment. Some authorities consider that the corporate DNA can be identified by looking at the networks, and particularly the intranet, and one of the key factors, unsurprisingly, is the ability to innovate. More precisely, writers allude to the capacity of the organization to create a vision, to experiment and take risks, to encourage ideas, and to reinvent itself. This ideal state also requires a talent for anticipating changes in the environment, and it is based on an ethical stance involving trust, honesty and integrity. These are the features which managers need to develop in order to create the circumstances in which the tools of change presented by Curzon (op cit) can be used to steer information services through the turbulence and unpredictability of contemporary change.

The Broad Applicability of the Skills of Managing Change

Trust, empathy, self-awareness, openness, listening and dialogue skills, are universal requirements in change management. Change initiatives work at their most efficient if these skills and the values underlying them are found throughout the organization. Once again, these are matters for organizational learning and the system for developing these talents should already be in place, because they are not only the skills and attitudes needed to cope with change, they are essential for organizational and personal development. The skills considered here in fact describe the kind of individual organizations need for change management.

This point can be extended, and considered from the point of view of the kind of organization that efforts at creating generic change are likely to produce. There will also be a requirement for:

- People-handling skills
- Project management skills
- Transferable skills as organizations introduce job enlargement and job enrichment
- The skills of self-management
- Decision-making and problem-solving skills
- Learning skills, in particular self-learning and learning from work.

This list covers the entire change process, and the emphasis at various points in the change process will change, as Figure 10.1 demonstrates.

The Theoretical Basis for Skills Acquisition in Change Management

The organizations featuring throughout this book can be variously described as systems-based, flexible, transparent and devolved. How the skills are developed is as important as identifying the actual skills needs. It would be incongruous if permissive management styles were to be perpetuated by prescriptive learning methods based on a narrow definition of training rather than learning. Organizational learning in contemporary organizations should look to theories which fit with their organizational characteristics. This means an emphasis on self-learning, learning from peers, team learning and learning from work in general, and the approach is based on those learning theories relevant to contexts where there is less bureaucracy and particularly less hierarchy. This is a context where opportunities for appropriate learning should occur at all organizational levels, irrespective of the position or responsibilities of the learners. Pugh (2001) sets out an approach to learning in information services which is based on theories taken from Andragogy, problem-solving, learning based on equality between the learner and the facilitator, team learning and self-managed learning. Much of this has its roots in the consideration of gestalt theory earlier in this book. Knowles (1984) described the key characteristics of a form of learning which is relevant to change management. It is based on:

- Problem-solving
- Participative methods
- Developing the whole individual and leading to attitude change
- Learners who can take control of their own learning.

Choosing the Techniques

To make an impact, the techniques will have to be selected with reference to those modern theories which best underpin the organisational characteristics we are striving to create and sustain. They are the methods at the developmental end of the spectrum, and those methods which make the most of the way staff learn. In the change process this gives a strategic, active role to the trainer as a learning facilitator, a provider of training, a consultant and a change agent.

The general aim is to work on the development of learning throughout the organisation as one of the key conditions for change. This requires a network of learning activities including team and group learning, coaching, mentoring and self-directed learning.

Team Learning

The trainer's input emphasises (Pearn et al, 1995):

- Improving learning skills
- Demonstrating that shared, team learning can be beneficial
- Inculcating the skills of team-based learning:
    - Listening
    - Understanding
    - Dialogue
- Learning about the other specialisations represented in the team
- Developing multiple viewpoints about the work of the team
- Creating an atmosphere in which learning can occur
- Learning to take more responsibility
- Learning to use and resolve conflict
- Learning the dynamics of team activities
- Learning new leadership skills.

Senge (1990) indicates that when this process is in full flower it contributes considerably enhanced insights and improved problem-solving, particularly about complex issues. It obviously creates the capacity for united action in pursuing innovation or change, and it is a seed bed for the growth of learning. This is partly because of the ways in which new knowledge can be spread through the information system of the organisation, and partly because of the cross-fertilisation that occurs through overlapping and multiple team membership.

Coaching

Although the discussion of coaching earlier in this book included some structures and reservations about the way the technique can be applied to change management, it is still a vital support to team and individual learning. To reinforce the general point, Metz (2002) sets out the principles and applications of learning in the same context.

Coaching is a way of building a degree of independence, if not complete self-sufficiency, into team operations. It can be used to improve the skills and knowledge bases and broaden understanding so that teams work effectively with a much modified and less overt degree of managerial control. As a technique it has the essential links with reduced bureaucracy, flexible structures, empowerment, communication and establishing more equal relationships between manager and managed.

The impact is to be seen at best in improved team performance, individual development and much better work in a particular job or role. Because good coaching identifies individual needs and passes on responsibility while still retaining involvement it permits development to take place in a secure environment where errors will be corrected before damage occurs. It is therefore a good way into individual learning and self-development. It also involves work-based learning.

A good coach has the style of a facilitator rather than a manager and will extend skills, increase responsibility, hand over power and add to job satisfaction through exploiting and nourishing the learning climate. This is done by a process of observation, analysis, criticism, support, sharing, trust and motivation.

Mentoring

In the literature of library management there is an increasing tendency to combine or confuse the characteristics of coaching and mentoring. They are not the same thing: they are related but different. Coaching is an activity in which, in today's organisations, all managers must involve themselves, and it should be applied wherever it is relevant to meeting an identified need. Mentoring is something which senior managers should only involve themselves in as a matter of choice, and very often it will only be applied to selected potential high-fliers. On that basis alone, some trainers would say that mentoring, being a very selective form of development, is a poor technique. For once, this is a traditional view. Mentoring is now often seen as a very wide-ranging activity that embraces various staff in all parts of the organisation and in widely differing circumstances. It is even applied to familiarisation programmes for new entrants, and many practitioners would consider the view of mentoring expressed in this book to be unnecessarily restrictive.

Mentoring should not be job-specific. It is longer-term and it is primarily concerned with individual developmental needs, and as such it has a legitimate contribution to make to the general training effort in change management. It can be seen as an aid to organisation development and as a way of perpetuating a culture. Coaching on the other hand should embrace all staff and is job-orientated, both for groups and individuals. Development through coaching is therefore within the boundaries of the individual or team role and is more specifically task- or skills-based.

A coach's interest in a group or an individual is operational: it is to do with maximising the ability to carry out a function, task or group of tasks. A mentor's interest in an individual is personal. Having cleared this up, it is important to repeat that mentoring is a relevant training technique for change management, with one other caveat. In change management, the mentor needs to be chosen with extra care.

One of the clear functions of mentoring is to develop managerial skills. Provided the mentor can demonstrate the management attitudes described in this book, there is a role to be played. The activity is then buttressed by:

- Assessment to identify areas where development is needed
- An agreed learning plan
- Feedback
- The provision of some of the learning experiences
- Agreement on specific strategies and actions.

Mentoring is suitable for a flexible organisation, and, as in coaching, some of the outcomes are accelerated learning, the quick transfer of valuable knowledge from the mentor to the subject and a strengthening of organisational culture through contact with influential and more experienced individuals.

Self-Development

The various emphases on individuals taking responsibility and on work-based learning in change management make self-development a feasible and attractive option for training inputs. Self-development obviously places the individual in the position of taking responsibility for learning, and it clearly goes on all the time while the job is being carried out. It can be linked to related coaching and mentoring programmes, and requires some investment in the essential skills of how to learn. In addition it teaches responsibility through giving to the individual a say in what to learn, what not to learn and how to apply the learning to the workplace, with all the consequences of this freedom. It can also be tied to team development through the establishment of learning groups, because it need not be a solitary or individual activity. It fits well with the concern of change management with making most use of the true potential of everyone in the organisation. Perhaps the key point about self-development and the role it can play in change management is that if it is organized and structured it is at the heart of learning and development. It meets all of the requirements set out in this chapter. It is:

- Self-managed
- Embedded in the day-to-day life of the organization:

It develops a sense of self-worth. It teaches setting priorities, problem-solving and decision-making. It requires clear objective-setting, discipline and organization which aids the development of project management skills, and it makes a large contribution to self-knowledge and self-esteem. As such, it prepares the ground for the attitude change that is one of the bases of successful organizational change:

> We need to accept that we have massively significant learning processes that are outside our formal approaches to development: these we need to systematize and bring within the structure. Only when we do these two things can we control, and own, our own development. (Pugh, op cit 2001)

When we do this, we learn to manage ourselves, and then we manage change.

Bibliography

Adner, R. 'When Are Technologies Disruptive?: A Demand-Based View of the Emergence of Competition'. *Strategic Management Journal* vol 23 no 8, 2003.

Aguirre, D.M., Howell, L.W., Kletter, D.B., and Neilson, G.L. *A Global Checkup: Diagnosing the Health of Today's Organization.* New York, Booz Allen Hamilton, 2005.

Amabile, T. 'How to Kill Creativity'. *Harvard Business Review* (September-October), 1998.

Andrews, J., and Law, D. *Digital Libraries: Policy, Planning and Practice.* Aldershot, Ashgate, 2004.

Argyris, C. *Integrating the Individual and the Organisation.* New York, Wiley, 1964.

Ashcroft, L. 'Developing Competencies, Critical Analysis and Personal Transferable Skills in Future Information Professionals'. *Library Review*, vol 53 no 2 2004.

Bandura, A. *Self-efficacy: The Exercise of Control.* New York, Freeman, 1997.

———. (ed). *Self-efficacy in Changing Societies.* Cambridge, Cambridge University Press, 1995.

Bargatze, G.F. *Exploring Corporate DNA in the Age of People: a Business Handbook for the New Millenium.* Irvine CA, Griffin Publishing Group, 1999.

Bateson, G. *Steps to an Ecology of Mind: Collected Essays in Anthropology, Psychiatry, Evolution, and Epistemology.* University of Chicago Press. New Ed., 1999.

Baxter, A. 'Getting Smart is All About Using Your Intelligence'. *Financial Times IT Review*, 23rd March 2005.

Bennis, W. *Organization Development: Its Nature, Origins and Prospects.* Reading MA, Addison-Wesley, 1969.

Bennis, W., Benne, K. D., amd Chin, R. (eds). *The Planning of Change.* 2nd ed., New York: Holt, Rinehart and Winston, 1985.

Bentley, T. *Everyday Democracy: Why We Get the Politicians We Deserve.* London, Demos, 2005.

Bevan, E.R. *The House of Ptolemy.* London, Methuen Publishing, 1927.

Bibb, S., and Kouri, J. *Trust Matters: For Organizational and Personal Success.* London, Palgrave Macmillan, 2004.

Bradford, D. L., and A. R. Cohen. *Managing For Excellence: the Guide to Developing High Performance in Contemporary Organizations.* New York, Wiley, 1984.

Brass, D.J., Galaskiesicz, J., Greve, H.R., and Tsai, W. 'Taking Stock of Networks and

Organizations: a Multilevel Perspective'. *Academy of Management Journal*, vol 47 no 6, 2004.

Brody, W.R., 'Comment on the Value of Librarians'. *Johns Hopkins Gazette* 6th December 2004. http://www.jhu.edu/gazette/2004/06dec04/06brody.html

Brophy, P., Fisher, S., and Clarke, Z. (eds) *Libraries Without Walls 4: the Delivery of Library Services to Distant Users*. London, Facet Publishing, 2002.

Brophy, P., Fisher, S., and Craven, J., *Libraries Without Walls 5: the Distributed Delivery of Library and Information Services*. London, Facet Publishing, 2004.

Brunnson, N. 'The Irrationality of Action and Action Rationality: Decisions, Ideology and Organizational Actions. Journal of Management Studies 19 (1) 1982.

Bryan, L.L., and Joyce, C. 'The 21st-Century Organization: Big Corporations Must Make Sweeping organizational Changes to Get the Best From Their Professionals'. *The McKinsey Quarterly*, August 16, 2005.

Bryson, J.M., and Alston, F.K. *Creating and Implementing Your Strategic Plan : A Workbook for Public and Nonprofit Organizations*. 2nd ed., San Francisco, Jossey Bass, 2004.

Buchanan, D. A., and Huczynski, A. *Organizational Behaviour: an Introductory Text*. 5th ed., Harlow, FT/Prentice Hall, 2004.

Bucknall, T., 'Techno Teamwork: Involving all Staff in Library Automation', *North Carolina Libraries* vol 54 no4 1996.

Burke, W.W., Richey, E.A., and De Angelis, L. 'Changing Leadership and Planning Processes at the Lewis Research Centre NASA'. *Human Resource Management vol* 24 no 1 Spring 1985.

Burnes, B. *Managing Change: a Strategic Approach to Organisational Development and Renewal*. 2nd ed., London, Pitman, 2004.

Burns, T., and Stalker, D. M. *The Management of Innovation*. 3rd ed. Oxford, OUP, 1994.

Buttrick, R. *The Project Workout*. London, Pitman, 1997.

Byrnes, J. 'The Essence of Leadership'. *Harvard Business School Working Knowledge Newsletter*, September 2005.

Cage, B. 'Continuous Change Officially Becomes the Mother of Invention'. *Strategy Knowhow: a BNET Service*.
www.strategyknowhow.bnet.com/continuous_corporate_change.html January 2005.

Carr, D.K., Hard, K.J., and Trahant, W.J. *Managing the Change Process: A Field Book for Change Agents, Team Leaders and Reengineering Managers*. New York, McGraw Hill, 1996.

Casey, D. *Managing Learning in Organizations*. Buckingham, Open University Press, 1993.

Cherniss, C. 'Emotional Intelligence & Organizational Effectiveness'. in C. Cherniss & D. Goleman (eds) *The Emotionally Intelligent Workplace*. San Francisco, Jossey-Bass, 2001.

Child, J. *Organization: Contemporary Principles and Practice*. Oxford, Blackwell, 2004.

Collinson, C., and Parcell, G. *Learning to Fly: Practical Knowledge Management From Leading and Learning Organizations.* Oxford, Capstone, 2001.

Cox, R.H. *Sports Psychology: Concepts and Applications.* 5th ed., New York, McGraw-Hill, 2001.

Cross, R., and Parker, A. *The Hidden Power of Social Networks: Understanding How Work Really Gets Done in Organizations.* Boston, MA, Harvard Business School Publishing Corporation, 2004.

Curzon, S.C. *Managing Change: a How-to-do-it Manual for Librarians.* Rev. ed., London, Facet, 2006.

Cummings, T. G. and Huse, E. *Organisation Development and Change.* 4th ed., New York, West. 1989.

Davila, T., Epstein, M.J. and Shelton, R. *Making Innovation Work: How to Manage it, Measure it, and Profit From it.* New York, Wharton, 2005.

Davis, M. 'Building Innovative Bureaucracies: How Change is Compelling Structural Development'. *The Public Manager*, Winter 2003.

Dearnley, J., and Feather, J., *The Wired World: an Introduction to the Theory and Practice of the Information Society.* London, LAPL, 2001.

Deegan, M.J. *Emotional Intelligence Competencies in Physician Leaders: an Exploratory Study.* Cleveland, OH, Case Western Reserve University, 2002.

Demone, H.W., and Harshberger, D. *A Handbook of Human Service Organisations.* New York, Behavioral Press, 1974.

Dietz, G. 'Partnership and Development of Trust in British Workplaces'. *Human Resource Management Journal* vol 14 no 1 2004.

Drucker, P. F. 'What Makes an Effective Executive?' *Harvard Business Review* vol 82 no 6, June 2004.

——. *Managing in the Next Society.* New York, St. Martin's Press, 2002.

——. 'The Next Society'. *Economist Economic Survey*, Nov 1st 2001.

Edmondson, A. 'Free to Learn: Lessons in Successful Technology Implementation'. *California Management Review*, vol 45 no 2 Winter 2003.

Ellis, W.D.(ed.) *A Source Book of Gestalt Psychology.* London, Routledge and Keegan Paul, 1938.

Emmerling, R.J. & Goleman, D. 'Emotional Intelligence: Issues and Common Misunderstandings'. *Issues in Emotional Intelligence.* (On-line serial) vol 1 no 1. Available http://www.eiconsortium.org.

Goleman, D. *Emotional Intelligence: Why it can Matter More than IQ.* London, Bloomsbury, 1996.

Fayol, H. *Industrial and General Management.* London, Pitman, 1948.

Fischer, W., and Boynton, A. ' Virtuoso Teams'. *Harvard Business Review*, vol. 83 No. 7, July-August 2005.

Fisher, R., and Shapiro, D. *Beyond Reason: Using Emotions as You Negotiate.* Harmondsworth, Penguin, 2005.

Florida, R., and Goodright, J. 'Managing for Creativity'. *Harvard Business Review*,

August 2005.

Foster, R., and Kaplan, S. *Creative Destruction: Why Companies That Are Built to Last Underperform the Market – and How to Successfully Transform Them*. 2nd ed., New York, Doubleday, 2006.

Gardner, H. *Changing Minds: The Art and Science of Changing Our Own and Other People's Minds*. Cambridge MA, Harvard Business School Press, 2004.

——. *Frames of Mind: The Theory of Multiple Intelligences*. London, Fontana Press, 1993.

'Genysys Creates Opportunities for Virtual Learning'. *Multimedia Information & Technology* vol 32 no 2 May 2006.

Gillespie, R. *Manufacturing Knowledge: a History of the Hawthorne Experiments*. Campbridge, Cambridge University Press, 1991.

Gladwell, M. *The Tipping Point: How Little Things Make a Big Difference*. New York, New York Times, 2000.

Glaser, J. *Creating We: Change I-Thinking Into We-Thinking and Build a Healthy, Thriving Organization*. Cincinnatti OH, Platinum Press, 2005.

Glass, N. *Management Masterclass: A Practical Guide to the New Realities of Business*. London, Nicholas Brealey, 1998.

Goleman, D. *Emotional Intelligence: Why it Can Matter More than IQ*. London, Bloomsbury Publishing, 1996.

——. *Working With Emotional Intelligence*. London, Bloomsbury Publishing, 1998.

Gorman, G.E. (ed.) *International Yearbook of Library and Information Management*. London, Facet Publishing, 2002.

Gorman, M. 'On doing away with technical services departments', *American Libraries*, 10 July-August, 1979.

Gruber, H. E. *Darwin on Man*. Chicago, University of Chicago Press, 1981.

Gulati, R., and Kletter, D. 'Shrinking Core-Expanding Periphery: The Relational Architecture of High Performing Organizations.' *California Management Review*, vol 47, no 3, 2005.

Gupta, R., and Wendler, J. 'Leading Change: an Interview With the CEO of Proctor & Gamble'. *McKinsey Quarterly Web Exclusive*, July 2005. www.mckinseyquarterly.com/article_page.aspx?ar=1648&L2=18&L3=27&srid= 17&gp=0

Habermas, J. *Post-metaphysical Thinking*. Cambridge, Polity Press, 1992.

Hales, C. 'Bureaucracy-lite' and Continuities in Managerial Work'. *British Journal of Management* vol 13, 2002.

Hammer, M. 'Making Operational Innovation Work'. *Harvard Management Update*, Vol. 10 No 4, April 2005.

Handy, C. *Understanding Organizations*. Harmondsworth, Penguin Books, 1981.

Hanson, T. (ed) *Managing Academic Support Services in Universities: the Convergence Experience*. London, Facet Publishing, 2005.

Hargie, O., and Dickson, D. *Skilled Interpersonal Communication: Research, Theory and*

Practice. Hove, Routledge and Keegan Paul, 2004.

Hargreaves, D.H. 'From Improvement to Transformation'. Keynote lecture, *International Congress for School Effectiveness and Improvement – Schooling the Knowledge Society.* Sydney, Australia, 5 January 2003.

Havelock, R. G., Guskin, A., Forhman, M., Havelock, M., Hill, M., and Huber, J. *Planning for Innovation Through the Dissemination and Utilization of Knowledge.* Ann Arbor, ME Center for Research on Utilization of Scientific Knowledge, University of Michigan, 1969.

Heenan, D. A., and Keegan, W. J. 'Emerging Phenomena of Multimational Companies in the 3rd World: Characteristics and Implications'. *Havard Business Review*, Jan-Feb 1979.

Herzberg, F. *Work and the Nature of Man*. London, Granada, 1974.

Herzberg, F., Mausner, B., and Snyderman, B. *The Motivation to Work*. Cleveland OH, World Publishing, 1959.

Hilberry, J. *The Artistry of Inspired Leadership: Creating Meaningful Connections.* Banff Centre Reprint 019594, Banff, nd.

Hodgkin, A. Libraries on the Web: collections or services? Library + Information Update vol 2 no 7 July 2003.

Jones, O. 'The Persistence of Autocratic Management in Small Firms: TCS and Organisational Change'. *International Journal of Entrepreneurial Behaviour and Research*, vol 9 no 6 2003.

Kanter, R. M. *Frontiers of Management*. Boston MA, Harvard University Press, 1997.

———. *The Enduring Skills of Change Leaders*. New York, Leader to Leader Institute, 1999.

———. *Confidence: How Winning Streaks and Losing Streaks Begin and End*. New York, Crown, 2004.

Kaplan, R., and Norton, D.P. *The Strategy-Focused Organization*. Boston, MA, Harvard Business School Publishing Corporation, 2001.

Kellerman, B. *Bad Leadership: What It Is, How It Happens, Why It Matters*. Boston, MA, Harvard Business School Press, 2004.

Kibble, R., and Kissel, N.H. *Structure Is Strategy: Gaining Strategic Advantage Through Organizational Design*. New York/London, Marakon Associates, 2005.

Kinzes, J.M., and Mico, P.R. 'Domain Theory: An Introduction to Organisational Behaviour in Human Service Organisations'. *Journal of Applied Behavioural Science*, vol 19, 1979.

Kirkman, B.L., Rosen, B., Tesluk, P.E., and Gibson, C.B. 'The Impact of Team Empowerment on Virtual Team Performance: the Moderating Role of Face-to-Face Interaction'. *Academy of Management Journal*, vol 42 no 2, 2004.

Kirkpatrick, G. *Critical Technology: a Social Theory of Personal Computing*. Aldershot, Ashgate, 2004.

Klein, J.A. *True Change: How Outsiders on the Inside Get Things Done in*

Organizations. New York, Jossey-Bass, 2004.

Knowles, M.S. *The Adult Learner: A Neglected Species*. 3rd ed., Houston TX, Gulf, 1984.

Kuhn, T.S. *The Structure of Scientific Revolutions*. Pittsburgh, University of Chicago Press, 1962.

Lancaster, F. W. *Indexing and Abstracting in Theory and Practice*. 3rd ed., London, Facet Publishing, 2003.

Langfred, C.W. 'Too Much of a Good Thing? Negative Effects of High Trust and Individual Autonomy in Self-Managing Teams'. *Academy of Management Journal* vol 47 no 3, 2004.

Lankes, D.R., McClure, C.R., Gross, M., and Pomerantz, G., (eds) *Implementing Digital Reference Services: Setting Standards and Making it Real*. London, Facet Publishing, 2003.

Leavitt, H.J. *Top Down: Why Hierarchies are Here to Stay and How to Manage Them More Effectively*. Boston, MA, Harvard Business School Press,   2005.

Leonard, D., and Sensiper, S. 'The Role of Tacit Knowledge in Group Innovation', *California Management Review*, vol. 40 no. 3, 1998.

Leonard-Barton, D., and Swap, D.C. 'When Sparks Fly: Igniting Creativity in Groups'. Boston, MA., Harvard Business School Press, 1999.

Lewin, K. 'Group Decisions and Social Change'. *Readings in Social Psychology, Society for the Psychiatric Study of Social Issues*. New York, Holt, Rinehardt and Winston, 1958.

_____. *Field Theory in Social Sciences: Selected Theoretical Papers*. London, Tavistock, 1951.

Likert, R. *New Patterns of Management*. London, McGraw Hill, 1961.

_____. *Patterns of Management*. New York, American Management Association, 1955.

Linares, J. 'Leading Change: an Interview With Julio Linares', by J. Isern and J. Shearn. *McKinsey Quarterly Web Exclusive,* August 2005.

Mackinnon, D.W. *In Search of Human Effectiveness*. New York, Creative Education Foundation, 1978.

Madhok, A. 'Revisiting Multinational Firms' Tolerance for Joint Ventures: A Trust-Based Approach'. *Journal of International Business Studies* vol 26 no 1, January 1995.

Mankins, M.C., and Steele, R. *Closing the Strategy-to-Performance Gap: Techniques for Turning Great Strategy into Great Performance*. New York, Marakon Associates, 2005a.

_____. 'Turning Great Strategy into Great Performance'. *Harvard Business Review*, July/August 2005b.

Martell, C.R. *The Client-Centered Academic Library*. Westwood CT, Greenwood Press, 1983.

Maslow, A. *Motivation and Personality.* 3rd ed., New York, Harper & Row, 1987.

_____. 'A Theory of Human Motivation.' *Psychological Review* 50, July 1943.

____. *Towards a Psychology of Being*. 3rd ed., New York, John Wiley 1968.

Mayo, G.E. *The Social Problems of an Industrialized Civilization*. London, Routledge, 1949.

McGregor, D. *The Human Side of Enterprise*. London, McGraw Hill, 1960.

McInerney, D. M., and McInerney, V. Educational Psyschology: Constructing Learning. 2nd ed., Sydney, Prentice Hall, 1998.

McKenna, P., and Maister, D. *First Among Equals: How to Manage a Group of Professionals*. New York, The Free Press, 2002.

Metz, R.F. *Coaching in the Library: a Management Strategy for Achieving Excellence*. London, American Library Association, 2002.

Mintzberg, H. *The Rise and Fall of Strategic Planning*. New York, The Free Press, 1994.

——. *Structure in Fives: Designing Effective Organizations*. Englewood Cliffs, NJ, Prentice-Hall, 1983.

——. *The Structure of Organizations*. London, Prentice Hall, 1979.

Morgan, G. *Images of Organization*. London, Sage, 1997.

Morgan, S. Review of Brophy, P. 'The Academic Library'. *Update*, July/August 2005.

Mumford, A. 'View From the Hill'. *Ariadne*, issue 15, 1998.

Nielsen, J.S. *The Myth of Leadership: Creating Leaderless Organizations*. Mountain View CA, Davies-Black, 2004.

Neilson, G.L., Pasternak, B.A., and Van Muys, K.E. 'The Passive-Agressive Organization'. *Harvard Business Review*, October 2005.

Oh, H., Chung, M-H., and Labianca, G. 'Social Capital'. *Academy of Management Journal* 47, 2004.

Oliver, J.E. 'An Instrument for Classifying Organisations'. *Academy of Management Journal*, vol 25 no 4, 1982.

O'Reilly, C. A., and Tushman, M. L. *Winning Through Innovation: a Practical Guide to Leading Organizational Change and Renewal*. Boston, MA, Harvard Business School Publishing, 2002.

Ouchi, W.G. *Theory Z: How American Business Can Meet the Japanese Challenge*. Reading MA, Addison Wesley, 1981.

Ouchi, W.G., and Price, R.L. 'Hierarchies, Clans and Theory Z: A New Perspective on Organisational Development'. *Organizational Dynamics* vol 7 part 2, Autumn 1978.

Owen, H. *Creating Top Flight Teams: Unique Team Building Skills for the RAF Red Arrows*. London, Kogan Page, 1996.

Parks, S.D. *Leadership Can Be Taught*. New York, McGraw-Hill, 2005.

Pearn, M., Roderick, C., and Mulrooney, C. *Learning Organizations in Practice*. London, McGraw Hill, 1995.

Perlow, L. *When You Say Yes But Mean No: How Silencing Conflict Wrecks Relationships and Companies*. New York: Crown Business, 2003.

Perlow, L., and Williams, S. 'Is Silence Killing Your Company?' *Harvard Business*

Review vol 81 no 5, 2003.

Pinfield, S. *Beyond eLib: Lessons from Phase 3 of the Electronic Libraries Programme*. Bristol, JISC, 2001.

——. 'eLib in Retrospect: a National Strategy for Digital Library Development in the 1990s' in Andrews, J., and Law, D. (eds). *Digital Libraries: Policy, Planning and Practice*. Aldershot, Ashgate, 2004.

Powell, M. 'Designing Library Space to Facilitate Learning: a Review of the UK Higher Education Sector'. *Libri* vol 52 no 2, 2002.

Project Management Institute. *Guide to the Project Management Body of Knowledge*. 3rd ed. Newtown, PA, Project Management Institute, 2001.

Prytherch, R. *The Literature Review: State of the Sector Project*. Library and Information Commission Research Report 126, 2002.

Pugh, L.C. 'No Way Now But Down.' *Multimedia Information & Technology*, vol 31 no 4, November 2005.

——. *Academic Library Structures*. Unpublished small scale survey, 2002a.

——. *Change Management in Information Services*. Aldershot, Gower, 2000.

——. *The Convergence of Academic Support Services*. British Library Research and Development Report. London, British Library, 1997a.

——. 'Designing Library Organisations for the e-Future.' *The Nordic Journal of Documentation* vol 58 no 1, 2003.

——. *Leadership and Learning: Helping Libraries and Librarians Reach Their Potential*. Lanham, MD, Scarecrow Press, 2001.

——. *The Management of Hybrid Library Services*. London, Library Information & Research Group, Cilip, 2004.

——. *The Management of Innovation in Public Sector Learning Resources Provision*. M. Phil thesis, Leeds Metropolitan University, 1990.

——. 'Managing Multimedia in Troubled Times'. *Multimedia Information & Technology*, vol 28 no 3 August 2002b.

——. Review of Raitt, D. (ed). *Libraries for the New Millenium* in *Ariadne*, issue 12 November 1997b.

Raitt, D. (ed). *Libraries for the New Millenium*. London, Library Association Publishing, 1997.

Rittel, H.W.J., and Webber, M.M. 'Dilemmas in a General Theory of Planning'. *Policy Sciences* 4, 1973.

Rogers, E. M. *Diffusion of Innovations*. New York, The Free Press, 1962.

Rogers, E.M., and Shoemaker, F.F. *Communication of Innovations: a Cross Cultural Approach*. New York, The Free Press, 1971.

Rogers, E.M. and Adhikarya, R. 'Diffusion of Innovations: An Up-to-date Review'. In D. Nimmo (ed). *Communication Yearbook 3*. New Brunswick NJ, Transaction Press, 1979.

Roitberg, N. 'The Influence of the Electronic Library on Library Management: a Technological University Library Experience. *IFLA Journal* vol 27 no 1, 2001.

Rose, S. *The 21st Century Brain: Explaining, Mending and Manipulating the Mind.* London, Jonathan Cape, 2005.

Rulke, D., and Galaskiewicz, D. 'Distribution of Knowledge Group Network Structure and Group Performance'. *Management Science* vol 46 no 5 2000.

Sashkin, M., and Rosenbach, W.E. 'A New Vision of Leadership.' In Taylor, R. L., and Rosenbach, W. E. (eds.) *Military Leadership: In Pursuit of Excellence.* Boulder CO, Westview, 2000.

Senge, P. *The Fifth Discipline: The Art and Practice of the Learning Organization.* New York, Doubleday, 1990.

Sirkin, H.L., Keenan, P., and Jackson, A. 'The Hard Side of Change Management.' *Harvard Business Review*, October 2005.

Skinner, D. 'Evaluation and Change Management: Rhetoric and Reality'. *Human Resource Management Journal*, vol 14 no 3, 2004.

Steers, R.M., Mowday, R.T., and Shapiro, D.L. 'The Future of Work Motivation Theory'. *Academy of Management Review*, vol 29 no 3, 2004.

Stueart, R.D., and Moran, B., *Library and Information Center Management.* Greenwood Village, CO, Libraries Unlimited, 2002.

Stewart, G.L. 'A Meta-Analytical Review of Relationships Beween Team Design Features and Team Performance'. *Journal of Management*, vol 32 no 1, February 2006.

Svejanova, S. 'Revisiting Multinational Firms' Tolerance for Joint Ventures: A Trust-Based Approach Reconsidered'. *Journal of International Business Studies* vol 37 no 1, January 2006.

Tebbutt, D. 'Playing a New Service Game'. *Information World Review*, March 2006.

Terris, O. Review of Rafferty, P., and Hidderley, R. Indexing Multimedia Works and Creative Works: The Problems of Meaning and Interpretation.Aldershot, Ashgate Publishing, 2005. in Multimedia Information & Technology vol 31 no 2 May 2005.

Tichy, N. M. 'Interview with W. Wheaton and L. Smith'. *Human Resource Management* vol 23 no 2, Summer 1984.

Tidd, J., Bessant, J., and Pavitt, K. *Managing Technological, Market and Organizational Change.* New York, Wiley, 1999.

Tijdens, K., and Steijn, B. 'The determinants of ICT Competencies Among Employees'. *New Technology, Work and Employment*, vol 20 no 1, 2005.

Tucker, E., Kao, T., and Verma, N. *Next Generation Talent Management: Insights on How Workforce Trends are Changing the Face of Talent Management.* New Jersey, Hewitt Associates, 2005.

Tushman, M., and Anderson, P. *Managing Strategic Innovation and Change.* 2nd ed., Oxford, Oxford University Press, 2004.

Walton, G., and Edwards, C. Flexibility in higher education hybrid libraries: exploring the implications and producing a model of practice. Journal of Librarianship and Information Science vol 3 no 4 2001.

Watson, L., 'Coffee, Computers and Cooperative Learning'. *Multimedia Information and Technology*, vol 29 no 1, February 2003.

Weber, M., tr Parsons, T. *The Theory of Social and Economic Organizations*. New York, The Free Press of Glencoe, 1947.

Weiss, J., and Hughes, J. 'Want Collaboration? Accept – and Actively Manage – Conflict'. *Harvard Business Review*, February 2006.

Wertheimer, M. *Productive Thinking*. New York, Harper Torchbooks, 1959.

Wilson, H.J., and Harris, J.G. 'Executives: How do you Plan on Boosting Performance?' *Research Note: Information Worker Productivity* Issue 1, Accenture May 3 2004.

Index

transformational leadership 173-4, 175-6
transparency 45, 116, 126, 161, 179
    and leadership 167, 172, 175
    see also openness; sharing
trust 203
    developing 150, 166-7, 180, 188, 194-5
truth-telling 167, 168, 194
Tsai, W. 31
Tucker, E. 11
Tushman, M. 54, 100

uncertainty 5, 11, 46, 105
unfreezing 71-6, Fig 4.1
unpredictability 4-5
users
    characteristics of 4, 13, 28
    and information 10, 14
    involvement 4, 13, 14, 15, 35, 81, 90
    and strategy 52, 53, 54

and testing 91
values, shared 35, 165
Van Muys, K.E. 32
Verma, N. 12
visionary leadership 174-5

Walton, G. 16
Web 2.0 1, 2, 4
Webber, M.M. 31
Weber, M. 59
Weiss, J. 148
Wertheimer, M. 37, 38, 41
Wheaton, W. 186
whole-organization change 10, 32, 54, 57, 114, 165
'wicked problems' 31
Williams, S. 178
Wilson, H.J. 50
work teams 138, 155
work-based learning 6, 41, 44, 205, 206